Two week loan

J pythefnos

due date to avoid over...

Japan in Trade Isolation, 1926–37 and 1948–85

ii

LTCB International Library Selection No. 9

Japan in 1926–37 & 1948–85
Trade Isolation

Michiko Ikeda
Ph.D., Economics, Harvard University

WITH A FOREWORD Dwight H. Perkins

Research Professor of Economics,
Harvard University

 House
Press

Transcription of names

The Hepburn system of romanization is used for Japanese terms, including the names of persons and places. Long vowels are not indicated. Chinese terms are romanized using the pinyin system. The Wade-Giles system is used, however, for certain place-names outside mainland China. The romanization of Korean terms follows the McCune-Reischauer system. Russian terms are transliterated using the system of the U.S. Board on Geographic Names.

With regard to Chinese and Korean personal names, we have followed the local custom of placing the family name first.

Japanese names, however, are presented in Western order, with family name last.

First English edition published December 2008
by I-House Press
c/o The International House of Japan, Inc.
5-11-16, Roppongi, Minato-ku, Tokyo 106-0032, Japan
Tel: +81-3-3470-3211 or 9059   Fax: +81-3-3470-3170
E-mail: press@i-house.or.jp

Printed in Japan
ISBN 978-4-903452-07-4

Contents

PART I: THE PREWAR PERIOD, 1926–37

PART II: THE POSTWAR PERIOD, 1948–85

APPENDICES

TABLES

Tables

Figure

Tables in Notes

Statistical Tables in appendix I

FOREWORD

Dwight H. Perkins
Research Professor of Economics,
Harvard University

Much has been written over the past century about the perceived advantages and disadvantages of an open trading system with relatively few barriers to imports. Today the controversy over these issues focuses largely on whether globalization is a good or bad thing for particular countries or for certain economic groups within countries. Much of this debate is driven by local politics and by philosophical differences between the contending parties.

It is in this context that this book by Dr. Michiko Ikeda is both useful and timely. Dr. Ikeda takes us back to a time that most have forgotten if they ever knew about it. It is the period between World Wars I and II when a newly rising national economy, that of Japan, pioneered what today has come to be called export led growth but did so in the often hostile trade environment of the late 1920s and the Great Depression that began in 1929. By gaining access to archives previously unavailable ranging from League of Nations Reports to Ministry of Foreign Affairs archives in Tokyo, the Record Office in Great Britain, and the National Archives of the United States, this book tells the story of Japan's struggle to promote its international trade. It is a story of efforts to place special tariffs on Japanese exports on the part of the United States, boycotts by China, trade conflict with the entire British

Commonwealth of Nations, and others. Some of these efforts, the Chinese boycotts for example, were the result of Japan's aggressive military actions at the time, but the overall impact of this trade discrimination went beyond simply restricting Japanese exports. It also created a sense of vulnerability in Japan that played an important role in the nation's decision to try to solve its problems by military means.

This book, however, does not conclude with its analysis of the interwar period. It carries the story forward to the immediate post World War II era when Japan struggled to become a normal member of the international trading system by gaining membership in the General Agreement on Tariffs and Trade (GATT) that later became the World Trade Organization (WTO). As the book describes in detail, it took Japan five years longer than West Germany to become a member of GATT, and, when it did become a member, many existing members applied article XXXV to Japan, an article that in effect says that the member would opt out of applying the free trade rules of the GATT to a particular country, in this case Japan.

The great advantage of this careful historical study is that it puts in perspective what trade discrimination around the world often entails. Many of the arguments that one hears today about the problems created by the rise of the Chinese economy have a familiar ring to anyone knowledgeable about this earlier Japanese story. By looking at this historical Japanese experience, we can see these issues stripped of the emotions and politics of the present.

ACKNOWLEDGMENTS

I'm grateful to the following people in the writing of this book: Professor Alexander Gerschenkron and Professor Dwight Perkins at Harvard University, advisers for my dissertation, which forms the basis of this book. Also, without Professor Gottfried Haberler's one word on GATT Article XXXV, I would not have been inspired to start my research into its application to Japan and the limits of the GATT system.

I thank GATT (WTO) for providing me with a quiet atmosphere and facilitating my access to GATT documents; Jan Tumlir, former GATT Director of the economic and statistics section, who said that neither he nor anybody else could comprehend how Japan had endured the harsh trade discrimination in the 1930s; Mr. Aike Linden, former GATT vice president and WTO advisor, who kept GATT XXXV clause data relevant to my research in his files, and other colleagues of my GATT days.

The late Professor Dorothy Douglas of Smith College and Mr. Paul Douglas encouraged me to continue the research when my son was still a baby. I also thank the former LTCB International Library Foundation and Mr. Yasuo Saji for patiently turning into reality the publication of this book.

Lastly, I thank to my family: Fuku and Inosuke Nemoto, and Yuji and Masahisa Ikeda.

PART I

THE PREWAR PERIOD, 1926–37

Chapter 1

RESEARCH OBJECTIVES

THE BIG FIGHT OPENS.

A British poster (early 1900s) showing the fight over tariff reform led by the British Colonial Secretary Joseph Chamberlain. He wanted to move away from free trade toward preferential trade with the British empire, for example Australia, represented by the kangaroo behind him. In the background, America watches while the rising sun symbolizes the rise of Japan.

1. Introduction

Living in an age of increasing trade conflicts among advanced and developing nations—a great many of these conflicts involve Japan—and facing the present surge of protectionism, we worry about the direction of the world economy. Protectionist trends have increased worldwide despite recent warnings by economists. On the other hand, governments of advanced and developing nations have responded with much lip service to halting protectionist practices. The protectionist trend, nevertheless, seems to continue even though it has already been more than a decade since experts first warned of its potential dangers.[1]

Today the world economy is becoming increasingly segmented: "Blocs" of nations have formed to represent motivations that are not only economic, but also political and social. Under this trend, we economists wonder how the world economic course should be oriented for humankind to achieve a higher level of prosperity and happiness. In this sense, we would like to know how, and to what extent, we can brake progressing protectionism. We do not know how much burden today's protectionism imposes on the world economy. Nor do we know whether the development of protectionism inevitably parallels the development of the world economy as described in Alexander Gerschenkron's *Economic Backwardness in Historical Perspective*. His notion seems especially applicable when the world economy turns from an upward secular trend to a downward direction or to a plateau stage of growth, as it did in the 1930s and at present.[2]

The current intensifying trend of protectionism in many aspects involves the foreign trade of Japan. In reflection, we must ask how this parallels the trade friction of the 1930s and why that friction so intensely focused on Japan.

RESEARCH OBJECTIVES

During the 1930s, Japan experienced severely restricted trade in major overseas markets. This was a well-known fact among most economists. Nevertheless, exactly when it happened is unclear. Also unanswered: why it happened; which countries were involved; how it was practiced; how Japan reacted. Furthermore, what were the results of the restrictions? No research on this subject has yet been undertaken. It is almost completely unknown in the histories of Japanese and world economics.

In this study I will attempt to clarify the following subjects:

1. *The truth of the matter.* How valid is our common knowledge about the truth of unwritten Japanese and world trade history concerning the restriction of and discrimination toward Japan's foreign trade in the 1930s—when Japan was not a leading world power, but only one of the developing countries trying to catch up with the Western powers? These questions are relevant here:

    a. Exactly when and where and in which international markets among Japan's main trading partners were these restrictions imposed?

    b. What kinds of Japanese products received the greatest restrictions or discrimination, or both?

    c. What were the nature, methods, and extent of protectionist and discriminatory policies?

    d. What were the effect and long-term outcome of these policies on the levels, composition, and geographic patterns of Japanese trade?

2. *The facts.* What were the economic causal factors that generated the severe protectionism and discrimination against Japanese foreign trade?

Quantitative analyses of important items in the leading overseas markets will reveal the answers to this question and others of the same kind, along with some results of protective trade measures and the causal factors of trade conflicts—items usually hidden in aggregate trade statistics.

3. *Influence on the Japanese economy.* Discriminatory and protectionist measures imposed on Japan's trade not only brought on a curtailment in the volume of trade, but also inevitably distorted production, income distribution, resource allocation, and the whole path or development process of the Japanese economy.

4. *Japan's response.* Japan responded with retaliatory measures that evoked other repercussions. Therefore I wish to analyze the outcomes of Japanese trade friction in the 1930s in its interdependency in the dynamic world political economy.

Changes in trade patterns and commodity compositions accruing as a result of foreign trade restrictions required adjustments in the Japanese economy. Besides the retaliatory measures, a restructuring of the commodities traded and of overall trade networks was required. Japan's trading partners imposed further countervailing measures against Japan's retaliations, and the Japanese economy consequently was distorted. This brought on a need for further changes in trade policies to overcome the difficulties confronted in the markets.

5. *The real pattern of events.* I have also clarified to some extent the patterns of trade friction in case studies that reveal what really happened. Also discussed is how and why trade friction could easily occur in certain stages of catching up with relatively advanced countries.

If any of these points is confirmed, I may be able to refer to the trade friction of the 1930s as an unplanned experiment carried out in the framework of the world economy during the interwar period. I may also be able to add new findings to our knowledge of and present concern about today's intensifying world trend of protectionism. For example, on the one hand I may get some idea about the extent to which a country's economy can survive amid severe trade friction.

On the other, it may be possible to compare similarities and differences between the world economy in the 1930s and the world economy today in enhanced protectionist trends. The world economy has already experienced, often by involving Japan, a strong protectionist period in the 1930s—contrary to the allegations of some economists that world trade was relatively "free" in the interwar period. Different from experiments in the natural sciences, this world historical experiment of protectionism and discrimination and a compartmentalization of economies could not possibly be purposely repeated because of its exorbitant and incredible human costs.

THE ANGLE OF APPROACH

Japan's trade friction in the 1930s had two aspects described in Gerschenkron's "Relative" theory:[3] a backward country against advanced Western countries (such as Japan versus Great Britain or the United States), and a newly industrializing nation against even more backward countries (such as Japan versus China or British India). One theme of this investigation is addressing a belief that trade friction will inevitably occur as long as backward countries attempt to catch up with advanced countries. This belief exists because, first, the development of the world economy essentially embraces the industrialization of developing countries. Second, when a backward country once succeeds in its industrial upsurge, the growth rate of its economy is high, surpassing the growth rates of advanced economies, and continues to rise even amid a depression of the world economy. This research will cast light on one aspect of world economic development with some possible implications concerning today's trade friction evident in advanced and developing nations.

THE PERIOD OF SURVEY

In the first part of this book, the period of this study is the first 12 years of the Showa era in Japan, 1926–1937, ending when Japan entered its preparations for the war economy. The reasons why this period was chosen are described in section four of this chapter.

THE MATERIALS

To conduct this project, I relied heavily on declassified documents from the Archives of the Ministry of Foreign Affairs in Tokyo, Japan; the Public Record Office in Richmond, U.K.; and the National Archives in Washington, D.C. Materials from the League of Nations and publications of the Japanese government and other governments also were principal sources. Details are in the appendix and the bibliography. No work has been done previously on this aspect of trade restrictions through a use of the original data and documents, which were declassified by my request on a large scale in March 1988.[4]

The original documentation relevant to trade conflicts is available in Tokyo, London, and Washington. Its voluminous contents are random and disorganized. But when one reads of the chaotic voices crying out in consistently occurring events—garrulous condemnations, denunciations, and criticisms of Japan's trade—a stochastic logic may be found in the dynamism of the interactions of trade, economies, and politics in backward and advanced countries alike. On the other hand, the reader may be forced to a finale characterized by random phenomena. In this investigation, I am trying neither to apply nor to superimpose any stochastic equations to test the chaotic phenomena of trade friction. Instead, a reader must observe random events and listen to the chaotic voices in the hope of perceiving something logical that fits with the appearing patterns, for protectionism and discrimination, in some respects, are rooted deeply in human nature. They constitute one aspect of economic activities, and economic activities sometimes reveal stochastic phenomena from chaos, just as nature reveals stochastic natural laws. This general principle of all research made a lasting impression on me every time I faced the voluminous original materials from nineteen countries and regions, as well as from several international institutions, on which this study is based.

Finally, the GATT (General Agreement on Tariffs and Trade) rules referred to in this book have been superseded by the WTO (World Trade Organization) since chapters one to six were written in 1988. However the historical facts, analysis and conclusions are still valid and should be useful today.

2. Definitions of Protectionism and Discrimination

Protecting a domestic economy through trade restrictions has three objectives: (1) safeguarding a country's external financial position, (2) safeguarding its balance-of-payments position, and (3) shielding its domestic industries (either infant or declining) from foreign competition. A government can also protect its domestic economy by prohibiting exports of indigenous natural resources or manufactured products, especially for strategic purposes.

Protection is enforced by the use of several visible methods and means, which can be classified by where they are practiced. Restrictive measures, for example, can be imposed at the country's territorial borders, and the following typical measures are among many of these practical devices: tariffs, quotas, customs valuation systems, orderly import arrangements, voluntary export restraints, foreign exchange controls, and import licensing systems. They can be applied in different ways and at different rates, and they can directly and effectively curb trade in general, depending on their strengths.

Restrictive measures can protect domestic industries not only at the borders but also within the country. They can take the form of subsidies, grants, tax incentives such as allowances or refunds, favorable terms for industrial financing (at lower rates of interest and longer maturity periods), or favorable allocation of industrial resources.

Protective measures can also be defined as grants or aids that help the establishment of a training school attached to a factory, since individuals trained there can be used as skilled labor in the company to increase productivity. Whether this can be classified as an educational grant or as an indirect protection on a long-term basis, however, is not clear. Understandably, numerous practices could be classified almost endlessly as protection because

9

they will ultimately influence the quality and efficiency of economic performance in domestic industries.

Although the measures detailed above are the primary prerogatives of the government sector or local authorities, the private sector also participates in protective practices: for example, voluntary export restraints that are often the result of private agreements or are disguised under them. Frequently, however, these "private" arrangements are due to covert government "guidance" to private industries among competing countries.

So far, the term "protect" has been considered, but "protectionism" per se has a much wider meaning than "protect" does. If many countries "protect" their trade and these practices and ideas spread, thus inspiring other nations to follow similar measures, "protectionism" will result. When a protectionist measure is applied to the imports of some specific country's or countries' commodities on an nonegalitarian basis, it favors commodities from other countries and thus is discriminatory.

Another simple discrimination is when one country imposes restrictive measures on commodities of a specific country (or countries) while the protecting country itself is not producing these commodities. Today, discriminatory practices in trade are against the rules of the General Agreement on Tariffs and Trade (GATT) unless specifically recognized under GATT articles VI, XVI, XVIII, XXIV, XXXVI, and XXXVIII. GATT functions on a nondiscriminatory principle.

In our research, analysis is usually confined to protectionist and discriminatory measures practiced at territorial borders.

APPLICATION TO JAPAN

The methodology of our approach to clarify research objectives is as follows:

The Chinese boycotts that targeted Japan and then spread to Japan's main overseas markets will be analyzed as trade barriers.

After 1932, Western countries and their colonies imposed restrictive measures on Japanese goods, including prohibitive, antidumping, and compound tariffs; quotas; customs valuation systems; voluntary restraints of exports; and import licensing systems. They were justified, it was said, because of Japan's expanding exports in the face of declining world trade. These circumscribing moves were initiated because Japan was said to be dumping products via foreign exchange and, above all, practicing "unfair" competition.

These nations reproached Japan for dumping because the Japanese offered goods at "ridiculously" low prices. But falling prices can be based on two factors besides dumping: (1) a lower cost of production, and (2) a devaluation of the currency. Therefore lower prices offered to foreign markets have the three following causal factors:

i. Lowering the cost of production in exporting countries.

ii. The sale abroad of a product at a price lower than its domestic production cost, that is, product dumping, or, in other words, selling a product abroad at a price lower than the domestic sales price (ignoring such considerations as domestic consumption taxes which cannot be applied to goods shipped abroad, and transfer costs). This definition entails the sale of a product abroad at a price lower than the domestic (marginal) production cost.

The preceding sentence is important because at least two points should be considered: First, how one can reasonably measure the cost of production in the exporting country with a yardstick that depends on the value system of the importing country. Do you measure it in the exporting country depending on, finally, the purchasing power parity, because you cannot rely on a conversion of costs in an importing country at prevailing exchange rates in an interwar monetary disturbance period? This is true even today. Any yardstick that measures the cost of production in foreign countries would involve many index number problems.

Second, this cost-of-production argument ignores an industry exploiting scale merits, which was what happened in the Japanese textile industry in the 1920s and 1930s. A crucial point to this issue is that if the exporting companies are selling abroad at prices lower than the costs of production then time works against them. They could not long continue selling at prices lower than the marginal cost and would be forced to close, unless they were making profits at home.[1]

iii. The devaluation of the exporters' currency. In the period under study, Japan devalued the yen vis-à-vis other currencies, which is called foreign exchange dumping. Possibly, the foreign price of a product becomes cheaper via depreciation of the currency of the exporting country. Any combination of the above (i), (ii), and (iii) is a possibility. For example, compound price and foreign exchange dumping duties took place on Japan's products.

Today if (ii) is proven, the importing country applies product-dumping duties. In (i), the importing country can protect its domestic industry from further injuries by resorting (after an injury is proven) to GATT antidumping duties, as mentioned earlier, in the GATT rules. In (iii), either because of devaluation or even an appreciation of the currency of the exporting country, foreign exchange dumping tariffs are imposed.[2]

Historically, during the survey period many of Japan's trading partners imposed import surcharges for alleged dumping. For example, in 1932 Canada exercised a customs valuation system for Japanese products. The Canadian customs officially decided 49.85 Canadian dollars for 100 yen, when it was valued as 28.12 Canadian dollars as the year's average. This artificial application of the yen immediately created an additional foreign exchange dumping duty of 21.73 Canadian dollars (49.85 − 28.12 = 21.73). Furthermore, this inevitably led to Japanese products being levied with a product undervaluation duty, an application of a product dumping tariff. Therefore this system always resulted in compound dumping tariff practices: a foreign exchange dumping tariff plus a product dumping tariff.[3]

In many reports, records, and other writings in the documents relevant to our investigation, the contents of the term "dumping" are not clear on the above three causal factors of price reductions for Japanese products. Though condemning Japan for so-called dumping practices, most writings deliberately or unknowingly confuse the differences between dumping products and dumping foreign exchange and, above all, between dumping products and the first factor, a fall in production cost. The word dumping was often used as a covert refusal to recognize a decline in the price of Japanese products due to productivity gains and cost reduction on the Japanese side. Instead, foreign documents relevant to the subject often mentioned that the Japanese were offering products at "ridiculously" low dumping prices. This term, Japanese dumping, used by the import-competing industrialists and their supporters seemed often to disguise facts; the most important had been a shift of the domestic supply curve as described by Professor Henry Rosovsky.[4] He also pointed out that the charges of much talk on Japanese social dumping in the 1920s and 1930s simply reflected the growing power of Japan's modern industries to stand on two sturdy legs: cheap labor and a great inflow of technology.[5]

It is true that Japan's trade had expanded before world trade recovered in the 1930s. After a shrinkage, Japanese trade was recovering in 1934 when world trade reached bottom, as noted in table 1.1 in the following section. But were the nature and extent of protectionist measures justified by postulating the above causes of (ii) and (iii) ?

3. Export Trends of Japan's Main Overseas Markets

Why was it that Japan was subject to protectionism in the 1930s, given that it was a developing country vis-à-vis the advanced Western countries? Table 1.1 indicates both world and Japanese international trade in the deterioration and recovery stages of the period under our survey. Japan was the last country to readopt the gold standard in the interwar period. Japanese exports in dollar terms fell in 1929 from the 1926 level because of domestic deflationary policies to restore the gold standard. During the process of reestablishment of the gold standard system at prewar parity (¥100 = about US$49.50), the Japanese economy was undergoing a strong deflationary pressure. The combined effect of the yen's high appreciation and the Great Depression was seriously felt in Tokyo on almost the first day of Japan's readoption of the gold standard in January 1930.

The compound effect was a fall in Japanese trade in 1932 much greater than the decline in world trade that year: Japanese exports touched bottom at 41 percent of the 1926 level, but world exports fell to 54 percent, as shown in table 1.1. In 1934, when Japanese trade started to recover to 66 percent, the world export index was hitting bottom at 32 percent of the 1926 level.

This point needs to be emphasized. Statistics of the League of Nations used 1929 as the base year to compare rates of devaluation of the major trading countries, ignoring the yen's sizable appreciation that year as shown in the table N-1 in the Notes.[1] The use of 1929 figures to form the base year for comparisons became the focal point of those accusing Japan of highly undervaluing the yen, and this resulted in many countries applying prohibitive discriminatory measures to Japanese products.

Japan's trade in 1937 did not recover to the predepression level of 1926–29, as table 1.1 shows. Its rate of recovery, however, was

Table 1.1 Japan and world trade (in U.S. gold-dollar terms)

	World		Japan	
	Exports	Imports	Exports	Imports
1926	100	100	100	100
1929	94	94	103	91
1930	75	76	76	68
1932	54	54	41	36
1934	32	31	66	60
1936	35	34	81	71
1937	44	43	95	97

Sources: Statistical Table 1, Appendix I, of this book; *Statistical Year-Book, 1930/31* (Geneva: League of Nations, 1931), 162, and *1939/40* (1940), 182; *Memorandum on International Trade and Balance of Payments, 1926–28* (Geneva: League of Nations, 1929), I:16; *1927–29* (1930), 22; *1932–34* (1935); and *1936–38* (1939).

Note: The figures for world trade exclude Spain from 1934 onward.

higher than in all other nations. When in 1937 Japan's exports regained 95 percent of the 1926 level, world exports recovered to only 44 percent.

Japan's exports to specific countries and regions—notably China proper, the United States, Canada, Australia, and France—fell during the 1926–37 period, as shown in table 1.2. They sharply deteriorated to a low of 26 percent 1926 levels by 1937 in both China proper and the United States. In comparison with these declines, Japan's exports to the world market as a whole (top line in the table) fell to only 95 percent in the same period.

For our research, we classified China under two different groups: (i) China proper, which includes only north China, central China, and south China, and (ii) Kwantung leased territory and Manchuria/Manchukuo, which are independently treated. As a country, though, China includes Kwantung and Manchukuo.[2] Exports to China proper in 1937 registered a severe fall to only 26 percent of the 1926 level, as table 1.2 shows. But exports to Kwantung and to Manchuria/Manchukuo increased to approximately make up for this fall in China proper, as will be discussed later (table 2.1).

Shipments to the United States also dropped to 26 percent of the 1926 level by 1937. In 1932, Canada fell to 20 percent, Australia

Table 1.2 Indices of Japan's exports to selected countries

(U.S. dollars)

	1926	1929	1932	1934	1937
World	100	103	41	66	95
China proper	100	80	18	17	26
United States	100	104	31	28	26
Canada	100	106	20	21	49
Australia	100	83	42	78	85
France	100	148	30	56	68
British India	100	125	74	97	118

Sources: Statistical Table 1, Appendix I, of this book. *Financial and Economic Annual of Japan*, 1925–28 (Tokyo: Ministry of Finance, 1929), and 1935–38 (1939); *Japan Statistical Year Book 1950* (Tokyo: Statistical Bureau of the Prime Minister's Office, 1951); *International Trade Statistics 1931* (Geneva: League of Nations, 1932), 338, and *1938* (1939), 331.

to 42 percent, and France to 30 percent. Exports to British India had increased by 25 percent in 1929, but declined from that level in 1932.

Next, table 1.3 indicates the rising or falling relative importance of Japan's exports to its main trading partners during the 1926–37 period. Countries and colonies in the table are classified by trend of share of Japan's exports to each area, by whether they declined and stagnated or expanded and flourished over our survey.

Group A in the table denotes the shares of countries that declined and stagnated. The share of China proper fell to only 5 percent, from 20 percent, in the 12-year period from 1926 to 1937, and that of the United States decreased to only 20 percent, from 42 percent. Others in group A were Western countries and their colonies. As noted in the table, group A-I's subtotal share declined to only 34 percent of the total, from 74 percent, during the same period. Japan's exports to countries and territories in group A-II declined in 1937 after posting an aggregate increase in 1932 (1934 in the case of Latin America).

Japan had virtually no opportunity in 1937 to expand its exports in European industrialized countries and in some of their colonies and possessions, as presented in Group A in this table and in statistical table 1 in the appendix.

Table 1.3 Share of primary trading partners of Japanese exports

(percent)

	1926	1929	1932	1934	1937
Group A-I					
United States	42	42	31	18	20
China proper [a]	20	16	9	5	5
Hong Kong	2	2	1	1	1
France	2	2	2	1	1
Canada	1	1	0.5	0.4	0.5
French Indochina	0.3	0.1	0.1	0.1	0.2
Australia	2	2	3	2	2
British Malaya [b]	2	1	-	2	2
Egypt	1	1	-	3	1
Germany	1.4	0.6	0.5	0.9	1
Subtotal I	73.7	67.7	47.1	33.4	33.7
Group A-II					
British India [c]	7	9	13.6	11	9.4
The Netherlands East Indies	3	4	7	7	6
Latin America [d]	0.5	0.9	0.7	2	1.5
Subtotal II	10.5	13.9	21.3	20	16.9
Group B					
Kwantung	4	5	8.5	13	12
Manchukuo	n.a.	n.a.	1.8	4	7
Great Britain	2	2	4	5	5
The Philippines	1.3	1.4	1.5	1.6	1.8
Africa [e]	n.a.	n.a.	n.a.	4.1	6.4
Subtotal	7.3	8.4	15.8	27.7	32.2
The rest of the world	8.5	10.0	15.8	18.9	17.2

Sources: The same as for table 1.2.

Notes: a. The trade figures for China in this table are different from those in the League of Nations, *International Trade Statistics, 1938*, Geneva, 311.

b. Straits Settlements only.

c. Excluding Ceylon after 1935.

d. Argentina, Brazil, Mexico, Peru, Chile, Uruguay, and Ecuador.

e. Union of South Africa, Kenya, Uganda, Tanganyika, French Morocco, Belgian Congo, Anglo-Egyptian Sudan, Mozambique, and Nigeria.

Group B denotes countries where Japan's exports expanded, in contrast to group A-I. Exports to Kwantung and Manchukuo registered the largest increase. This explains why China was subdivided in our analyses: first, China proper (north China, central China, and south China); second, Kwantung and Manchukuo. To treat these two areas as simply "China," as the League of Nations and Japanese official statistics did, obscures the declines in China proper and the counterbalancing large increases in Kwantung and Manchukuo.

The table clearly indicates a significant shift in Japan's exports from group A-I to group B during the period under consideration. In the three years from 1926 to 1929, A-I absorbed some 74 percent of Japan's total exports, but by 1932 this had diminished to 33.4 percent and subsequently failed to recover. This decline is in contrast to the increases of total exports in group B: to 32.2 percent in the later period between 1934 and 1937, from 7.3 percent in 1926.

No less important was the expansion of Japan's manufactured exports: this rapid growth was the subject of loud reproach by its trading partners over the second half of the period under study, a development illustrated in table 1.4. By 1937, Japan's share increase in manufactured exports in this period was 3.4 percent over the 1926–29 level (i.e., 7 – 3.6 = 3.4). This appeared to have deprived manufacturers in the world's advanced countries of a 3.4 percent slice of their market. As Japan's share expanded, the shares of other countries in the table declined or stagnated after 1930.

Britain and France sizably declined. British India and Burma, possessions of the British Empire, either declined or stagnated. The U.S. position was stagnant too. Excluding Japan, the collective share of the advanced countries fell by 7.6 percent, to 46.5 percent, in 1936–38, from 54.1 percent in 1926–29. The decline in British and French share over the 12-year period implies that these countries were losing competitiveness in manufactured exports. Even without Japan, world manufactured exports became increasingly diversified to several other developing countries, such as Australia, by slicing the shares held by Great Britain and its colonies and by France.

The table of manufactured exports suggests that the underlying industrial output of Great Britain, of the United States, and of France was declining, but for Japan and the rest of world (with more developing countries), it was rising. Finally, Japan's share of world industrial output actually increased to 3.5 percent (1936–38), from 2.5 percent (1926–29).[3]

Table 1.4 Shares of world manufactured exports of seven selected countries

				(percent)
	1926–29	1930	1931–35	1936–38
Great Britain	21.6	18.8	18.4	18.6
United States	16.3	15.7	12.3	16.3
France	10.9	10.4	10.3	6.0
Canada	2.7	2.3	2.4	2.8
Australia	0.2	0.2	0.2	0.6
British India and Burma	2.4	2.0	1.9	2.2
Japan	3.6	3.5	5.2	7.0
Subtotal	57.7	52.9	50.7	53.5

Source: League of Nations, *Industrialization and Foreign Trade* (Geneva: League of Nations, 1945), 157–159, statistical table X.

Note: The original data include no figures for China.

4. THE JAPANESE ECONOMY IN THE SURVEY PERIOD

The period of this study is the first 12 years of the Showa era in Japan, from 1926 to 1937. Why was 1926 chosen as the base year? The Japanese economy did not recover from the Great Earthquake of 1923 in the Tokyo area until the end of the Taisho era (1926), which preceded the Showa era. At the beginning of Showa, the Japanese encouraged themselves with great expectations to enter a new phase in the history of Japan. They intended to recover well economically from still-dwindling economic activities as a result of prolonged stagnation from the 1921 postwar crisis and the aftermath of the earthquake. During the second half of the survey period, Japan was the subject of trade discrimination. In the final year of the period, 1937, the implementation of strict foreign exchange control symbolized the Japanese economy's departure from free trade; and Japan then plunged into an economy that would prepare it for war.

One important agenda item in Japan's Diet during the initial years of the Showa era was to reestablish the gold standard. Prime Minister Osachi Hamaguchi proclaimed that the country must be ready to lift the gold embargo so that "Japan could become a full member of the world economy."[1]

A latecomer in the world market, Japan had high hopes in the new era, hopes of being equally treated with the Western nations. The reestablishment of the gold standard at the old parity expressed the Japanese government's policy stance, which was to catch up with the West. Could that hope have been realized if one of the following had occurred? (1) Had the world economy not been plunged into the Great Depression within a couple of years; (2) Had the socioeconomic attitudes of the world powers been much closer, as they are today; (3) Had Japan not struggled so vigorously to improve its competitiveness in the world market.

In the first period of our survey, until 1931, Japan's economy experienced stagnation, deflation, and the Great Depression. An agrarian crisis spread over the countryside in the late 1920s due primarily to two factors: stagnant agricultural productivity and a collapse of silk exports to the U.S. market, which occurred much earlier than the influence of the Great Depression on Japan.

The bankruptcies of the Fifteenth Bank (a privately held bank) and the government-owned Taiwan Bank in 1927 started a series of bank collapses; they also caused several small- and medium-sized enterprises to fail. In 1928, when this financial crisis was over, Japan embarked on a deflationary policy to reestablish the gold standard at the prewar parity. This move deepened the wide-spread agrarian crisis.

With expectations of the gold standard being restored, which would generate a stronger yen, large companies in leading indus-tries had started serious efforts to increase production efficiency in preparation for impending international competition. The cotton textile industry especially made full efforts to achieve efficiency; its members purchased the most advanced technology of the time, cut wages, and reduced the number of factory workers. Other industries in the manufacturing sector followed suit. Many amal-gamations, mergers, and cartels formed in banking and industry during that period; the rates of market share concentration in big enterprises, especially in the five large *zaibatsu* (industrial-financial conglomerates), were the highest in the history of Japan's prewar economy.

The price index for all commodities fell to 83 percent in 1929 and to 61.3 percent in 1930 from the 1925 level because of this deflationary policy.[2] The foreign exchange rate appreciated 21 per-cent over the same period as a result of the government's overseas purchases of yen.[3]

In January 1930 Japan reestablished the gold standard, but the effect of the Great Depression soon began to be felt, and this fur-ther aggravated the hardship that the Japanese had been experienc-ing under the deflationary policy. The compound effects of that deflation and the Great Depression pushed the Japanese economy into a depressionary spiral in 1930 and 1931. Complaints and out-cries filled the cities and countryside. Jun'nosuke Inoue, the for-mer minister of finance who had initiated the deflationary policy in preparation for lifting the gold ban, and Takuma Dan, the direc-tor of Mitsui Bussan (the leading company of the Mitsui *zaibatsu*), were assassinated in early 1931. Japan broke with the gold stan-dard at the end of 1931, less than two years after its introduction. Great Britain had broken earlier, in September.

The second half of this survey, from 1932 to 1937, started with an expansionary economic policy launched by Finance Minister Korekiyo Takahashi; he lowered the interest rate and increased public expenditures to save millions of poverty-stricken peas-ants. Subsidies to the agricultural sector (especially for sericul-ture) and to the military for enhanced expenditures related to the Manchurian Incident (see chapter 2) were made possible by expanding the budget for 1932 by 33.6 percent over 1931.[4]

On May 15, 1932, the prime minister of Japan, Takeshi Inukai, was assassinated by members of an extreme right-wing and junior military officers' coalition. This serious event and the Manchurian Incident in 1931 promoted a significant turn in the Japanese polit-ico-economy. The balance of power in Japanese society, which had so far favored the doves working for international cooperation and the improvement of Sino-Japanese relations—especially the Kensei Party, the Minsei Party, and the mainstream of the navy—shifted to the hawks that aggressively encouraged expansion in China: the Seiyu Party and the major factions of the army, which were strong proponents of militarization.

The Takahashi expansionary monetary and fiscal policies real-ized their desired effect, to increase industrial output, in the sec-ond half of 1932.[5] This was a sign that the Japanese economy was about to rally. It then entered a fourth and new stage of indus-trial upsurge while the economies of other nations were still in the throes of the depression.[6] New products and new industries appeared and grew, with "light" industries gradually being sup-planted by "heavy" ones. Industrial output reached a prewar peak in the 1936–37 period, the ending years of our survey.

Exports too picked up in the latter half of 1932 because of a devaluation of the yen and greater efficiency in some industries. Enhanced efficiency was typically found in the cotton textile industry as a result of rationalization during the previous 1928–31 deflationary period.

After all ties with gold had been severed, the value of the yen dropped. By the end of 1932, the foreign exchange had fallen 42.4 percent from the previous year, and it was over this point that many countries condemned Japan for "dumping." However, the value of the yen in 1931 was already overvalued—by 21 percent over the 1925 level—in an effort by the government to restore the gold standard. Before the government's purchase of yen abroad, ¥100 in 1925 was equivalent to US$40.75. Four years later, in 1929, it equaled US$46.5, up 12.4 percent. When Japan went back to the gold standard, ¥100 appreciated to US$49.368 in 1930, up 17.5 percent. It dropped to an equivalent of US$28.120 at the end of 1932, after Japan had left the gold standard. If 1925 instead of 1929 (the year chosen by Statistics of the League of Nations) is used as the base year to compare rates of devaluation, Japan's rate of devaluation would be 30.9 percent of the 1925 level, not 42 percent as in the statistics of the League of Nations mechanically states. The statistics of the League of Nations states Japan's yen currency was depreciated by 66 percent in relation to gold in March 1935 based on the January 1929 levels.[7] Opinions and statements condemning Japan for its expansion of exports always stressed the high devaluation rate and unanimously ignored the economic efficiency that had been achieved by 1930 in parts of Japanese industry. The influence of these deflationary policies was apparent in the area of cost.

Table 1.1 shows that Japanese exports in dollar terms started to fall early in 1930 because of the Inoue deflationary policy in 1928 and the resultant strong appreciation of the yen. Japanese exports in 1932 fell much deeper to 41 percent than what had been experienced elsewhere in the world to 54 percent of 1926 levels. The Japanese economy bottomed out in 1932, two years earlier than the world economy did. Japanese trade also started recovering earlier than world trade; its exports in 1934 were 66 percent of 1926's, but world exports were still sinking at 32 percent.

We cannot bypass one thing in this respect. Statistics of the League of Nations could not pay enough attention to a small country's situation (in distributive shares in world trade), such as Japan's, and therefore failed to consider what had happened in Japan's economy. The statistics ignored Japan's previous strong appreciation of its currency, which had been progressing well during 1928–29. Thus the use of 1929 by the League of Nations as the base year was irrelevant to those who understood the Japanese adopting the gold standard. Or we can say at least that the base year was arbitrarily and roughly chosen for the cross-country comparison of the rate of currency depreciation. (It might also be said that the League's statistics were based on statistics from the Japanese government. Then Japanese officials bear some responsibility for explaining the large appreciation of the yen that took place under the deflationary policy implemented in 1927–28.) But these comparisons that used 1929 as the base became the salient reason why many countries blamed Japan for surging exports and thus discriminated against Japanese products.

There was great transition, both in components of Japanese trading commodities and in which countries were trading with Japan. Although Japan's trade did not recover to its pre depression equivalent by 1937, the rate of recovery was higher than in the rest of the world, as table 1.1 shows.

After the Imperial Economic Conference held at Ottawa in 1932, British India was the leader in imposing restrictive measures on Japanese products. Canada and Australia, also members of the British Commonwealth, adopted prohibitive quotas or tariffs on imports from Japan.

After the failure of the London Economic Conference in 1933, the world economy, led by Great Britain, was confirmed in moving toward a bloc economy.

When the Sino-Japanese War started near Peking in July 1937, it signaled the termination of Japanese participation as a "free" trade partner in the "free" world economy.

5. Foreign Trade as a Substitute for "Prerequisites"

As a fundamental system of an island country, the Japanese economy relied a great deal on international trade. Exports and imports each accounted for some 17 percent of Japan's GNP in the 1926–37 survey period. However, foreign trade had vast historical significance to the entire Japanese economy, more than what the quantitative figures generally suggest.

Technology and the absence of modern indigenous industries

In its initial stage of industrialization, Japan manufactured products by imitating imported commodities. Imports allowed Japan to constantly borrow a high standard of technology, which was absorbed by traditional Japanese artisans and bureaucrats (the elite of that time) to forge pertinent improvements and even to create small innovations as they made use of it in everyday life.

Imports also permitted Japan to turn the disadvantageous absence of any modern indigenous industries to an advantage through the adoption of the most advanced technology on a large scale. International competitiveness in some manufactured products, notably in the cotton textile industry, had been acquired by the period of our research.[1]

Japan's import substitution while lacking tariff autonomy

Because of the unequal treaties of 1854, Japan lost tariff autonomy and thus was banned from tariff protection until 1911.

Under this condition, Japan's first modern industry, cotton spinning, developed a system to become internationally competitive. In an earlier period Japan had imported cotton textiles and piece goods from advanced Great Britain and British India. These imports had constituted about 45 percent of the total Japanese import value during the initial decades from 1858, when Japan's ports were opened.

The Japanese government first attempted to establish an import-substituting cotton-spinning industry, but failed because of small-scale factories and the use of domestic materials. To survive, it was of the utmost necessity that Japanese cotton-spinning companies achieve a cost advantage and quality improvement at the initial stage of production because they had to compete with foreign products imported freely from advanced countries in a domestic market without tariff policies.[2] This became possible by borrowing the most modern technology and creating large companies and enterprises at the initial stage of industrialization. When the Japanese industry overcame its difficulties in the internationalized and no tariff autonomy domestic market, it became strong enough to compete in the world market. The Japanese cotton textile industry started to export its products soon after it conquered the domestic market.

RESOURCE-POOR JAPAN

Foreign trade enabled resource-poor Japan to make the best cost selection of the most suitable raw materials for its industrial circumstances. This was possible through imports from the world market, where cheap materials were available. Production costs were further reduced by the bulk importation of good-quality raw materials, used in place of domestic products of nonstandardized quality and produced locally on a small scale. Large-quantity purchases also benefited the Japanese because sellers offered materials to volume buyers at lower prices. Foreign trade promoted Japan's incentive to turn its scarcity of resources into an advantage: wide-scale resource selections worldwide. Could Japan now be industrialized at today's

level if it had then depended on only the small amount of domestically produced raw cotton and iron ore?[3]

A testing ground

Exports were critical not only in helping to balance imports, but
also in serving as a testing ground for exported products. After
having passed domestic consumer evaluation and testing, exported
commodities were continually judged in regard to cost and quality as compared with foreign products on the world market. As a
result, constant pressure was extended to production in the home
market, and this brought about adoption of the most advanced
technologies, better selection of materials, progressive marketing, and improved management. All were reflected in the cost and
quality of the products, and domestic consumers could benefit
from feedback on the products as they were tested on the world
market.

The size of the domestic market for many primary export commodities, except for tea and silk, in the interwar period was four
times larger than the foreign market.[4] The interdependent expansion of the domestic and foreign markets contributed to the scope
of the division of labor and the economies of scale, thus generat-
ing additional feedback that further improved competitiveness.

A keen domestic and overseas competition encourag-
ing the speedy diffusion of improved technology

Easy access to the sea and constant exposure to the world market often prevented a few industries from monopolizing new technology and thereby promoted the dissemination of innovations
throughout the economy. The speedy diffusion of improved technology brought keener domestic competition. The same factors
gave the Japanese economy a swift, flexible, and adaptable character, which enabled it to change quickly to adjust to world economic conditions.[5]

"THERE IS NO ROOM FOR THE NEWCOMER"

During the 1926–37 period, Japan emerged as a newly industrialized competitor on the world's stage, the first non-Western nation to do so. However, by this time the world market had been divided among the advanced Western countries. Consequently, world trade networks and patterns had reached a certain static stage of balance. The competition Japan then presented in some manufactured products, notably cotton textiles, elicited the judgment that "there is no room for the newcomer" in the world market.[6]

From the viewpoint of Western producers and traders and the vested interests they represented, Japan was disturbing the established harmony in many local and world markets. But the disturbance could be understood and labeled as a "creative destruction" of the old-market equilibrium; old value systems and old price mechanisms were giving way to new ones.[7]

EXPANDING THE SIZE OF LOCAL MARKETS BY COST REDUCTION

In textiles, especially, Japanese merchants were able to carve out a share in the old market. But not only did they take a piece of the established market: they also contributed to expanding local markets (or they prevented the market's size from deteriorating further during the Great Depression) by supplying manufactured consumer goods at lower costs. Furthermore, products were introduced into new markets where most people had hitherto found such items prohibitively expensive. These activities were true in the second half of the period of this study, notably in new, remote markets. Given the above, one might ask, "Why did Japan open new markets in distant continents rather than nearby?"

IMPORT RESTRICTIONS

This period found Japanese products subjected to severe discriminatory practices in Japan's chief foreign markets. These actions were implemented because of Japan's historically unprecedented challenge to vested Western trade and industrial interests—Japan was the first non-Western nation to emerge from backwardness to confront advanced Western countries in the economic sphere.

The delayed economic recovery from the Great Depression adversely affected world trade expansion in the second half of this survey. The main trade conflicts stemmed from companies in exporting industries in the advanced countries wanting to prevent their established market shares from being encroached upon by exports from newly industrialized enterprises in backward countries such as Japan.

THE BRITISH TEXTILE INDUSTRY

One significant element that contributed to the British Commonwealth-Japan trade conflicts during this period was the decline in Britain's textile industry, which was experiencing diminishing returns on marginal investments. The declining profit rates of the textile industry in advanced countries spurred protectionism. Even without Japanese textile competition, the British economy had been experiencing record high rates of unemployment, especially in the Lancashire textile industry. A main factor in this was the strong overvaluation of the British pound sterling.[8] The situation was exacerbated by the international competition from Japan when, in 1931, Japan surpassed Britain in output volume of cotton textiles and in their exports, thereby emerging as the world's primary textile producer and exporter.

CHINESE BOYCOTTS

Meanwhile, the anti-Japanese boycott movement in China intensified after 1927, climaxing in 1931 and 1932. It then spread to Japan's main overseas markets: South Asia, Asia, North America, and Europe. The exports of light industrial products, especially cotton textiles, increasingly became the target of trade barriers, and these exports sharply declined in those markets. The underlying reasons for this were twofold. An anti-Japan boycott appealed first to the interests of Western manufacturers who wanted to protect their established shares in colonial markets, second to the interests of local cotton textile manufacturers who relied on infant industry protection in regions more backward than Japan.

Chapter 2

Anti-Japanese Boycotts as Trade Barriers in China

1. THREE FACTORS IN THE DETERIORATION OF JAPAN'S TRADE WITH CHINA

I discuss the anti-Japanese boycotts in China early in this chapter because they produced effects similar to prohibitive trade barriers. Their influence in this period (1926–37) generated significant, direct, and long-term consequences that affected Japan's trade with China. Furthermore, the publicity surrounding them and the worldwide sympathy extended toward China as a nation displaying nationalistic resistance ultimately influenced Japanese economic development in the ensuing years.

My interest is confined to the economic consequences of the boycotts. I do not question whether they were internationally illegal actions by a modern nation, as one Japanese representative had argued.[1] Neither do I investigate whether the boycotts were prolonged, supported, and fomented by the Chinese government.[2]

Nor do I question the nature of the boycotts: whether they resulted from Chinese self-defense and national sentiment provoked purely by Japan's military operations in Chinese territory, or vice versa.[3] Other questions, such as why Japan's representatives did not complain about the boycotts to the League of Nations, or why Japan did not present problems caused by the boycotts to the League of Nations, as the United Kingdom did in 1927 regarding China's boycotts against U.K. goods, are also outside the scope of this study. This chapter analyzes the economic implications of the boycotts and does not intend to pass any political judgments on them. I consider them understandable as a result of the Japanese military presence in China.

China was among Japan's most reliable and most important trading partners. For two decades, until 1926, it had absorbed some 20 percent of Japan's commodity exports, and Japan was relying on China for some 12 percent of all its imports. Except for 1918, Japan annually earned surpluses from China's trade, and net earnings increased sizably after 1920. These surpluses had contributed to redressing Japan's constant trade deficits with advanced Western countries. In 1926 alone, Japan's surplus with China totaled US$85 million, and its deficit with the rest of the world was US$329 million.[4]

However, Japan's trade with China deteriorated throughout the period of my research. The surpluses in trade with China *proper* (see next subsection) dropped year by year, and from 1933 onward they were negligible. Table 2.1 shows that the absorption of Japan's exports by China proper rapidly declined to only 5.6 percent in 1937, from 20.6 percent in 1926. Imports over the same period showed a similar trend: The share fell to only 3.8 percent, from 10.1 percent.

At least three factors in China proper contributed to this deterioration:

1. The anti-Japanese boycotts that developed into a significant obstacle as the Japanese occupied more and more of China.
2. The development of the Chinese and the Japanese cotton textile industries there.
3. The 1931 tariff reform in China.

These factors will be investigated from the view of whether trade barriers were erected as a long-term influence on Japan's trade.

The statistical separation of China into three regions

Before presenting my analysis, I must clarify the classification of China as it pertains to my investigation. I statistically classified China into China proper, Kwantung leased territory, and Manchukuo (after 1931) purely for analytical purposes in accordance with the Japanese statistical data because the Kwantung and Manchukuo regions had been under heavy Japanese influence or outright occupation during the period of my survey.

Table 2.1 Share of Japan's exports in the three Chinese regions, 1926–37, compared with the rest of Asia

(percent)

	1 China proper	2 Kwantung	3 Manchukuo	4 = 1+2+3 All China	5 The rest of Asia
1926	20.6	4.8	—	25.4	18.8
1929	16.1	5.8	—	21.9	20.7
1931	12.5	5.7	0.9	19.1	34.9
1932	9.1	8.5	1.8	19.4	30.0
1935	5.8	11.9	4.4	22.0	27.9
1937	5.6	12.4	6.8	24.9	26.9

Source: Statistical table 1, appendix I, of this book.

It is noteworthy that the aggregate share of "All China" (China proper, Kwantung, and Manchukuo) remained nearly the same, 21 percent to 25 percent (except for 1931–32), throughout the 1926–37 period, as shown in column 4 of this table. The more that exports to China proper (column 1) declined, the more those to Kwantung (column 2) and Manchukuo (column 3) increased. Thus when the figures of these three areas are combined (as League of Nation statistics were), increases in trade with Kwantung and Manchukuo balance the drop in trade with China proper.

As presented in column 1 of table 2.1, exports to China proper declined after the "independence" of Manchukuo; therefore by 1935 they represented only 5.8 percent of Japan's total exports, 28 percent of the 1926 level. The table reveals that Japan's trade in the three areas in 1935 was quite different from that in 1926. The relative importance of Kwantung also increased enormously, as shown in the table. In 1926 this region absorbed 4.8 percent of Japan's total exports; in 1934 it absorbed 13.6 percent (not shown in the table); in 1935, nearly 12 percent.

Of all exports, those for Manchukuo grew at the highest rate from 1933 onward, as column 3 reveals. The value of commodities sent to Manchukuo surpassed those sent to China proper in 1937, and from 1931 to 1935 the decline to China proper accelerated. The years 1931–32 marked a watershed for the decline in China proper and for the growth in Kwantung and Manchukuo. Despite the enormous increases in exports to Kwantung and Manchukuo, Japan faced an ever-increasing dilemma because trade surpluses in these regions were settled in Japanese currency instead of U.S. dollars.

Japan's Asian trade

Besides China, the relative importance of the rest of Asia is shown in column 5 of table 2.1. Japan's total exports to it expanded to nearly 27 percent in 1936 and 1937—one time to more than 34 percent in the peak 1931 period—from 18.8 percent in 1926. The expansion of Japan's trade to Asia from 1926 to 1937 was therefore almost solely attributable to increases outside China.

Table 2.1 shows that nearly 25 percent of Japan's total exports in 1937 went to all of China (column 4), with increased shipments to Kwantung and Manchukuo; nearly 27 percent went to other Asian countries (column 5). Therefore the remaining 48 percent went to other world markets.

Japan's share of China's import statistics

Chinese data reveal that Japan's relative position in China's imports also greatly deteriorated in comparison with China's other main trading countries; this is shown in table 2.2. In 1935 and in 1937, Japan's share of China's imports (column 3) fell to about 15 percent (it was only 9.7 percent in 1933), from 30 percent in 1926.[5]

China's cutback in the total imports corresponded to two changes in the Chinese economy during the 1935–37 period. The prices of foreign goods rose to more than counterbalance an appreciation of the silver-based Chinese currency vis-à-vis gold in 1934 and 1935. Furthermore, the value of the Chinese currency fell after China abandoned the silver standard in 1936, although world prices and Chinese tariffs remained nearly the same.[6]

In comparison, Chinese data indicate that the drop in imports from Japan was larger than the drop in total imports from the rest of the world, as is clear comparing them with those from Britain (column 1) and the United States (column 4).[7]

Table 2.2 Share by main trading countries and total value
         of China's imports in selected years from 1926 to 1937

					(percent)
	1 Britain	2 Hong Kong	3 Japan	4 U.S.	Total import value (in millions of gold dollars)
1926	10.3	11.1	30.0	16.7	1,124
1929	9.4	16.9	25.5	18.2	1,265
1932	11.3	5.5	13.9	25.5	1,634
1935	10.6	1.8	15.1	19.0	919
1937	11.7	1.8	15.7	19.8	953

Sources: League of Nations, *International Trade Statistics 1929* (Geneva, 1930), 337, and *1937* (1938), 309; Maritime Customs, *The Trade of China* (Shanghai, 1939), published by order of the Instructor General of Customs.

This table shows that the biggest loser in the China market was Hong Kong, followed by Japan.[8] The U.S. share rose to nearly 25.5 percent in 1932, from 16.7 percent in 1926, as the shares of Japan and Hong Kong declined.

Chinese imports via Hong Kong
Table 2.2 also shows that Hong Kong's share (column 2) was the first to swell (to 21 percent in 1927), but it then declined steeply to a negligible amount from 1932 onward.

About 80 percent of the cargo sent to Hong Kong from Japan in the 1920s was said to be destined for southern China, only passing through Hong Kong en route. When boycotts in China proper hit Japanese products in 1929, Chinese imports from Hong Kong were high, about 17 percent of China's total. Hong Kong's share fell to 5.5 percent in 1932 when Japanese goods, which were being transshipped via Hong Kong to China, came under scrutiny and inspection and were confiscated by boycotters.

Thus I object to counting Japanese exports to Hong Kong as Chinese imports from Japan. This view opposes Professor Charles F. Remer's calculation of trade statistics.[9] Only acceptable are his calculations before September 1931, which include imports from Hong Kong as imports from Japan; that period was before the start of anti-Japanese boycotters' inspections of cargo to China from Hong Kong. Because of this inclusion, his estimates of trade figures after September 1931 are flawed.

(In the Japanese statistics, Hong Kong absorbed only 2.58 percent of Japan's total exports in 1926, an amount that increased to 2.8 percent in 1929. This slight rise appears much smaller than Hong Kong's gain in table 2.2 [Chinese statistics] because Hong Kong's relative share was small in the total Japanese data.)

The Chinese tariff reform and the anti-Japanese boycott

Was the deterioration of Japan's exports to China proper especially because of the change in China's stance toward tariffs? The Chinese had turned their tariff policies into a protectionist vehicle at the beginning of 1931. Average tariff rates on Japanese commodities were raised above common tariff rates because most Japanese goods were classified as in the "general category" of daily staples.[10]

Japan's exports to China, though, did not register much immediate decline in response to the revisions.[11] Rising tariffs had already induced Japanese cotton textile companies to invest in China and to expand their affiliates there before 1931.[12] Furthermore, the expansion of production capacity in Japanese-owned textile companies in China accelerated after 1931.[13]

This point is important. At the beginning of 1931, Chinese tariffs had been raised on Japanese goods in the "general category," but the higher tariffs had little direct effect on imports from Japan. This clarifies why the decline of China's imports from Japan after the Manchurian Incident of September 1931 was due to the boycotts.

The deterioration of Japanese exports to China proper was more pronounced in 1927, in 1929, after the Manchurian Incident, and in the seven ensuing years. Anti-Japanese boycotts increasingly intensified during these years, growing into a nationwide movement. Therefore the best explanation for the deterioration was the anti-Japanese boycott movement in China.

2. The Anti-Japanese Boycotts in China

The frequent exercise of antiforeign boycotts by the Chinese revealed a nationalism with a long historical background. The foremost reason for this was the imposition since 1842 of unequal treaties that affected China's economic relations with Western powers. These treaties accorded extraterritorial rights and foreign concessions to foreigners and fixed the tariff rates at approximately 5 percent ad valorem for China's international transactions. Although the rates were revised four times, the average remained lower than 5 percent until the 1920s.[1]

Being a backward country, Japan imitated the Western powers to obtain extraterritoriality in China in the Treaty of Shimonoseki in 1895. Ironically, Japan itself did not have tariff autonomy because of the unequal treaties it had concluded starting in 1858 with Great Britain, the United States, France, Russia, Switzerland, and Belgium. Not until 1911 did Japan acquire the tariff autonomy that became effective in 1913.

The first large-scale boycott in China took place in 1905 and was related to a United States immigration law. Several instances of anti-British boycotts followed.[2] Chinese boycotts against Japan occurred several times before the period under study: in 1908, 1909, 1915, 1919–21, 1923, and 1925–26.[3] All were caused by specific incidents, and confrontations that included physical clashes often followed. China's boycotts against Japan developed after the Chinese government accepted Japan's ultimatum of the Twenty-One Demands in 1915, although the boycotts were poorly organized. After the demands, the Chinese felt they had been humiliated nationally and that Chinese rights and the nation's economic interests had been encroached upon. When roused, these feelings overrode other China-Japan relationships.

The development of boycotts in China and their effect on Japan's trade before 1926 can be summarized as follows:[4]

40

1. The Chinese were eager to recover tariff autonomy by shaking off the unequal treaties concluded with the Western powers and Japan.
2. Students and merchants initiated the boycotts in the early 1920s. The boycotts demanded also the removal from the Chinese government of certain "corrupt" officials, a demand called by one writer a "moral wakening" of the Chinese.[5]
3. The boycott movement was revitalized by Chinese nationalism.
4. A temporary anti-Japanese boycott took place in June and July of 1925, but it was soon overtaken by an anti-British boycott. A Russian adviser to the Kuomintang Party seemed to have succeeded in directing the boycott against Great Britain, both in Hong Kong and in China, for nearly one-and-a-half years from June 1925 through October 1926.[6] Chinese workers and union members actively participated in the boycotts and became aware of their effectiveness. They learned through their experience in this anti-British boycott how to organize and effectively use the boycott movement.
5. After 1926, the Kuomintang took over leadership of the boycott movement against Japan.[7]

In preparing this work, hundreds of volumes of declassified documents dealing with anti-Japanese boycott practices in Japan's principal foreign markets were consulted at the Archives of the Ministry of Foreign Affairs in Tokyo.[8] The following seven subsections summarize my lengthy and time-consuming analysis of these declassified materials.

   I. The 1927–28 anti-Japanese boycotts in central China and south China
  II. The boycotts in Hankow, 1928–29
 III. Shanghai, after the Manchurian Incident in 1931
 IV. The boycotts in other regions after 1931
  V. The boycotts as trade barriers in three regions of China
 VI. Substitutes for Japanese products
VII. After the first Shanghai Incident in 1932

I. THE 1927–28 ANTI-JAPANESE BOYCOTTS IN CENTRAL CHINA AND SOUTH CHINA

The boycott of 1927 began against Great Britain, but the landing of Japanese marines at Hankow that April caused a shift in the target from Britain to Japan. Meanwhile, the British left Hankow, relinquishing the British concession there. Serious anti-Japanese demonstrations took place in Soochow, Changsha, and Shanghai. Japan's announcement of its intention to dispatch troops to Tsinan to protect Japanese living in the Shantung area rekindled Chinese emotions against the Twenty-One Demands and against Japanese interests in north China and Manchuria. The Peking government and the Nationalist government protested.

In June, public organizations in Canton joined the boycott movement and stevedores refused to unload Japanese cargo. The Chinese Stock Exchange stopped dealing in Japanese shares, and the anti-Japanese boycotts restarted in Amoy and Swatow. At news of the additional landing of Japanese troops to protect the Shanghai Railroad (especially from Tsinan to Tsingtao), the boycotts became vigorous in the Shanghai and southern coastal regions, where the Chinese refused to sell food to the Japanese. They then spread to Kuikiang, but the agitation disappeared by the end of September with news of the Japanese government's withdrawal of troops from Shantung and because Chinese authorities had suppressed the anti-Japanese boycotts. After October, the boycotts turned to Britain.[9]

Although the 1927 anti-Japanese boycotts lasted about half a year, Japan's share declined only slightly in Chinese import statistics; this was shown in the same data in table 2.2 in section one of this chapter. But the British share fell nearly 3 percent, reflecting the first three months of the anti-British boycott that year. Hong Kong gained an increase of 70 percent in exports in 1927 over the previous year, most of it at the expense of Great Britain.

In Japanese export data, China's share fell 4 percent because of the 1927 boycott. The decline was principally attributable to a 17 percent fall in exports to central China from the 1926 level. The first period of the decline was due to a fall in shipments to the Yangtze Valley during April and May; the second, in July, was due to the boycott in Shanghai. Five hundred thousand bales of Japanese cotton yarn were held in Osaka warehouses because of the boycotts, and Japan's exports of cotton yarn fell to 118,000 bales in 1927, from 206,000 in 1926.[10] Japanese cotton-spinning mills cut operations from full capacity to prevent yarn prices from falling.[11] The summer was a depressed one for the Japanese cotton industry; Chinese mills, however, were said to reap profits as a consequence of the boycotts. Japan's exports to south China declined sizably at this time, though the distributive share of that region was originally quite small.

Local boycotting against Japan was renewed once again at Amoy in March 1928 because of clashes between Japanese marines and Chinese pickets following the arrest of Koreans attached to the Japanese consulate there. Japan's exports to central China and south China greatly declined, but those to north China and Manchuria hardly dropped.[12]

The boycotts were further stimulated by another clash between Japanese troops and the Nationalist army at Tsinan on May 9, 1928, one that involved a greater number of soldiers on both sides than at Amoy. This event resurrected Chinese feelings associated with the Twenty-One Demands, this time causing it to spread to the countryside. The Chinese turned again from general antiforeign feelings to specific anti-Japanese emotions. By this time the Nationalists also definitely understood that Japan was blocking their way to north China. The boycott movement became more concentrated on cities of the upper Yangtze Valley.

II. THE BOYCOTTS IN HANKOW, 1928–29

When a Japanese marine killed a Chinese laborer in a motorcycle accident in the midst of the boycotts in January 1928, Hankow[13] became the center of a violent boycott. This boycott generated a new pattern and methods that a few years later were implemented by the Anti-Japanese Association in Shanghai to frame an organized, nationwide boycott.

The general character of the Hankow boycott differed from those in previous years. It became well organized and progressively more severe without destroying Japanese goods in Chinese hands.[14] In Changchow alone, more than 70 associations supported the boycott and stopped selling food to the Japanese.[15]

The Anti-Japanese Association's boycotting methods became extremely refined, avoiding direct violence against the Japanese. The association inspected and detained Japanese goods as "enemy goods," levying a fine or penalty as a contribution to the association or to the National Salvation Fund. Several instances of confiscation and detention of Japanese goods in Chinese merchants' hands were reported every day. By strikes and by punishment of Chinese workers who served the Japanese, the association immobilized all means of carrying, unloading, transporting, and shipping Japanese goods. Imports from Japan to Hankow, which had almost reached a standstill since August 1928, now completely stopped. Even private mail parcels containing Japanese goods were detained.[16]

The boycotters also banned all exports to Japan of such commodities as raw cotton, hemp, and cereals from the beginning of 1929 by forcing a 50 percent ad valorem contribution to the National Salvation Fund. From then on, all loading of exports was stopped. Furthermore, the boycotters oppressed the operation of Japanese shipping companies by demands for large penalty sums and by extended longshoremen's strikes. Japanese steamers had no cargo. Chinese banks, money brokers, and dealers in Japanese goods closed their operations; the number of jobless Chinese workers increased; and the Chinese decided not to sell food to the Chinese who worked for the Japanese.[17]

Products of Japanese-owned factories were also subject to boycotts. This has been almost unrecorded in foregoing written accounts, which have wrongly been accepted as factual, as I will discuss later. The Japanese-owned factories stopped operations because of huge stockpiles of output and tried to sell accumulated goods in north China regions and in Hong Kong.[18] The Anti-Japanese Association declared that it would pay wages of 20 or 30 Chinese cents daily for the strikers, but this was not done.[19]

By the end of January 1929, Japanese commodities were piled high in Japanese storehouses, more than 215,000 cases that mostly contained sugar and cotton cloth. Their prices increased as the Chinese New Year approached.[20] Some signs of relaxing the boycott appeared as the negotiations surrounding the Tsinan Incident made progress after March. But the pickets and inspectors of Japanese goods were ever present. Chinese merchants, curiously enough, stopped transactions not only in Japanese goods, but also local ones, even in mid-April, because they were concerned about the future of the Anti-Japanese Association. Radical association leaders in the Hankow district were shaken and worried at news of the Wuhan army's defeat and the expected arrival of the Nanking army.[21]

Japanese factories restarted operations in April 1929, but some had lost workers and customers during the nearly yearlong boycott. The provincial government declared a termination of the boycott, but the Anti-Japanese Association rejected this, and some Chinese merchants and professional boycott leaders maneuvered against it. The boycott in this region finally stopped at the end of May 1929.

The prevailing uncertainty caused by the 1928–29 boycott and civil war so discouraged Hankow merchants that the local economy fell into a depression that lasted for years. Two years later, Hankow's merchants guilds were said to be reluctant until the last stage to join the anti-Japanese boycott movement of 1931 because of the experience of this previous severe setback.

III. SHANGHAI, AFTER THE MANCHURIAN INCIDENT IN 1931

On the arrival of news about the Wanpaoshan Incident of July 1931, a furious anti-Japanese boycott movement ensued in Shanghai and in many port cities in the area of the Yangtze River. The Chinese were resurrecting all their anger against Japan.[22] The Anti-Japanese Association in Shanghai allowed the importation only of Japanese coal, iron products, and chemicals to fulfill domestic industrial necessities for economic development as specified by a "Five-Year Boycott Plan" and a "Five-Year Self-Sufficiency Plan."[23]

1. Shanghai as the center of a nationwide boycott

The Manchurian Incident of September 18, 1931, took but 20 days to incite regions along the Yangtze into the strongest form of the boycott. Within a month, the movement entered an acute nation-wide phase by members and ardent supporters of the Nationalist party, student organizations, merchant guilds, and worker unions. This time Shanghai became the center and the model of the boy-cott.[24] Depending on declassified documents of the Ministry of Foreign Affairs, my research, which focused on the boycott in Shanghai and its results, can be summarized as follows.[25]

The Anti-Japanese Association at this time resolved to sever all economic relations with Japan through systematized boycotts. It determined not only to sever trade with Japan, but also to pro-hibit Chinese from working for Japanese enterprises and factories or in domestic services. The boycotters imposed the prohibitions with the threat of disciplinary punishment, including death pen-alties to traitors and confiscation by the association of private property.[26]

Thus Chinese banks and money exchangers stopped correspon-dence with Japanese banks, and compradors left Japanese banks by the beginning of October. Chinese compradors and accountants in the Western companies in Shanghai refused bills and checks issued on Japanese banks, and Chinese bargemen stopped han-dling Japanese cargo. Furthermore, Chinese citizens were forbid-den to use Japanese ships, currency, banks, and insurance compa-nies, to read or to refer to Japanese journals, and to visit or invite Japanese people formally or privately to any social or business affair. Because of the widely penetrating boycott, all transactions involving Japanese merchandise were completely suspended at this time, including coal and chemicals (mainly acid and bleaching agents), which until August had been but loosely boycotted.[27]

2. Japanese shipping businesses

Japanese shipping companies moored more than half their steamers and reduced the frequency of sailings. Japanese ships ran with no cargo or passengers on the routes from Shanghai to Hankow, to Canton, and to Tientsin and also on the Taiwan-Tientsin route, the European line, and the United States line in the Yangtze River. In addition, the Chinese canceled contracts with Japanese-owned marine and fire insurance companies.

3. Japanese factories

Japanese-owned factories in Shanghai primarily consisted of 21 cotton-spinning mills, and 9 were large companies. The cotton spinners employed some 66,700 Chinese workers, or 89 percent of the total in Japanese-owned factories in Shanghai.[28]

All forward contracts—14,617 tons of cotton yarn and 4,830 tons of cloth—until April 1932 were canceled because of the boycotts after the incident of September 18 (1931). Goods produced in Japanese-owned factories were subject to the boycott the same as imported goods from Japan. The affected Japanese-owned companies therefore increased exports to the south Asian market to more than twice the normal level, a maximum of 44 percent of the total output, and then curtailed production by 30 percent in October. Nevertheless, unexpected inventories—3,178 tons of cotton yarn and 76,260 tons of cotton cloth—accumulated during October alone, and continued to pile up.[29] Chinese cotton-spinning mills were either reactivated to operate at full capacity or resuscitated from suspended operations. Some Chinese workers were hired from Japanese companies by Chinese spinning factories.

Japanese owned 136 factories in Shanghai then that were not cotton-spinning factories. Most were small operations established after 1930. By the end of October 1931, sixty plants had shut down, discharging 2,496 Chinese workers. The main reasons for their failures were the inability to collect bills and to get credit. These closed plants had engaged mainly in the manufacture of rubber, hides and skins, soap, ice, and thermos bottles. At least 10 factories that survived slowed their operations to 10 percent to 30 percent of normal.[30]

IV. THE BOYCOTTS IN OTHER REGIONS AFTER 1931

1. Central China

The boycott movement flared up again in September 1931 in Nanking, Hangchow, Wuhu, Hankow (for the second time), Iching, Chungking, and Chengtu and grew more serious day by day. The systematic and drastic methods of the boycott in Shanghai were imitated by boycott leaders in many cities throughout China. In some of those cities, the Chinese claimed Japanese concessions and refused to sell food and other living necessities to Japanese, or even to rent houses to them.[31]

Exports to central China sizably declined from October 1931 to March 1932, to about 16 percent of what they were a year earlier. This astonishingly large fall was unmistakably due to the boycott even if we take into account the 1931 summer flood and resultant lower level of per capita income of the Chinese in this region.[32] This six-month blockage (October 1931–March 1932) was a blow to Japan, since its export earnings here had previously been the largest of all regions in China proper.

2. South China

The coast of south China rapidly resumed the severest form of boycott within 20 days after September 18, and the acute situation continued. Foochow, Amoy, Swatow, and Canton became local centers led by Kuomintang party members. Because of its thoroughness, the boycott had a depressing effect on local economies, and the Japanese residents evacuated Hangchow and other cities along the Yangtze River in moves to safer regions.[33] The fall in Japan's exports was most pronounced in south China.

3. Hong Kong

In Hong Kong, some members of a Japanese family were massacred and some seriously wounded by Chinese mobs in the

Kowloon settlement at the end of September; British troops fired on the mobs.[34]

4. North China

In Tientsin and in Shantung Province in north China, Japan's exports declined to a lesser degree because the boycotts were much less vigorous.[35] They fell only slightly in Tientsin, and it was in this region, in Chingtao, that they first started to recover. The expansion in exports spread in local markets in Shantung Province as a repercussion of the boycotts in Shanghai and cities along the Yangtze River.[36] Thus exports to north China increased monthly after February 1932 over what they had been a year earlier.

5. The boycotts and the decline in Japan's exports

Table 2.3 compares the trend in imports from Japan and other leading countries in three main Chinese ports in 1930 and 1931: Shanghai and Hankow in central China and Tientsin in north China. Hong Kong has been added to the table, since it exhibited a strong decline because of the Chinese anti-Japanese boycotts. The declines in Japan's import share in these three ports is associated with the degree of severity of the boycotts. The United States expanded its share at Japan's expense.

Table 2.3 Japanese declining share of imports in three main ports of China

(percent)

Port	Year	Japan	Britain	U.S.A.	Germany
Shanghai	1930	19	12	25	5
	1931	14	11	31	7
Hankow	1930	28	9	20	11
	1931	17	5	31	6
Tientsin	1930	45	7	17	5
	1931	43	8	17	8
Hong Kong	1930	12	9	7	5
	1931	9	11	8	5

Source: Ministry of Foreign Affairs, Gaiko Monjo (unpublished diplomatic documents in Japanese—hereafter cited as The Documents), A 110, 21-5, XI, Commercial Confidential No. 327: 1841–43.

V. THE BOYCOTTS AS TRADE BARRIERS IN THREE REGIONS OF CHINA FROM SEPTEMBER 1931 TO FEBRUARY 1932

1. Immediate effects of the boycotts in Shanghai

Here is a summary of the immediate effects of the boycotts in Shanghai during the 20 days after the Manchurian Incident in 1931:

   i. After the incident, about 28 percent of the 1930 monthly volume of imports from Japan was either canceled, unshipped, or blocked in Shanghai. Moreover, other losses occurred, caused mainly by a fall in the value of the yen.[37]
   ii. The immediate loss in exports to Japan was about 22 percent of the 1930 monthly export transactions to Japan.[38]
   iii. Japanese trading companies suffered large losses, about 26 percent of value more than in 1930.[39] However, the value of international transactions between China and third countries carried on by Japanese trading companies in Shanghai was at least twice as much as the value of direct trade between Japan and China.
   iv. Country substitution for Japanese goods started immediately; this will be examined in subsection VI.

Table 2.4 An estimate of Japanese losses in Shanghai, principal commodities, September 19–October 18, 1931

(thousands of dollars)

	Imports from Japan	Exports to Japan	Trade with third countries	Total
Transaction values in 1930 (monthly average)	37.6	7.5	95.3	141.5
Losses: Forward contracts	54.3	1.9	284	340.7
Unexpected inventories	56.3	.8	39	96.2
Other losses*	31.1	.6	35	66.8
Total	141.7	3.3	358	503.7

Source: *The Documents*, A 110, 21-5, XI, Commercial Confidential No. 327.

Notes: 1. The figures of twenty items in imports from Japan cover 76 percent of total transaction values.

2. The trade figures with third countries cover five principal items only. If values of silk, ramie, sugar, matches, glassware, hides and leather, cotton knitting, iron products, and other Japanese products were added, the total transaction value and the loss would be larger.

* Commodities that did not arrive: Does not include such costs as interest, storage, shipments, storehouses, wharves, business operations, banks, and Japanese wholesalers and retailers.

2. Exports to Japan from Shanghai

During 1930, most exports to Japan were foodstuffs (*fu*, coleseed, cotton seed, and sesame) and raw cotton. All were shipped only from Shanghai to Japan. All shipments to Japan were completely shut off by the middle of October 1931.[40]

Table 2.5 shows rates of decline in Japan's exports to regions of China and to Hong Kong from September 1931 to April 1932, as compared with the same months in the previous year. A 97 percent fall as shown in the table meant almost no exports to south China after October 1931, though the value of exports to this region was small even before the boycotts.

Table 2.5 The decline in Japan's monthly exports to three regions of China and to Hong Kong

(percent)

Year	Month	North	Central	South	Hong Kong
1931	September	−27	−44	−72	28
	October	−50	−68	−91	−79
	November	−73	−80	−97	−83
	December	−66	−88	−97	−75
1932	January	−32	−87	−94	−67
	February	29	−96	−97	−72
	March	114	−83	−99	−74
	April	52	−31	−88	−62

Source: Ministry of Finance, *Nihon Gaikokuboeki Geppo 1931–1932* (Monthly Returns of Trade of Japan) (Tokyo: Ministry of Finance, 1932–1933).

VI. SUBSTITUTES FOR JAPANESE PRODUCTS

1. Shanghai from October to December 1931

Table 2.6 shows the decline of Japan and the rise of competitors in imports of principal commodities into Shanghai from October to December 1931. All main exports from Japan, except for machinery and parts, drastically dropped each month in comparison with the monthly average in 1930.

Several comments can be made on table 2.6:

- Under a complete blockage of imports, cotton cloth declined to only 4 rolls in December 1931, from 620 rolls, the monthly average in 1930.

Among imported commodities from Japan, cotton cloth represented 33.7 percent of all imports into Shanghai in 1930. More than 28 percent of the equivalent value of the previous year's cotton cloth sales was canceled and not delivered in the month after the Manchurian Incident.

The decline in cotton cloth was primarily due to substitution by local products: China's imports of cotton cloth were reduced sharply to 102 rolls in December 1931, from an average of 770 rolls a month in 1930. British products did not

Table 2.6 Japan's exports to Shanghai and their substitutes

(units as noted)

Item	Country	1930 monthly average	1931 October	December
Cotton cloth	Japan	620	229	4
(1,000 rolls)	Britain	148	56	93
	Total	770	289	102
Sugar	Japan	84	14	0
(1,000 piculs)	Dutch E. Indies	290	310	477
	Total	416	369	539
Seafood	Japan	59	3	0.7
(1,000 piculs)	Canada	17	0	4
	Total	83	11	52
Paper	Japan	63	31	26
(1,000 piculs)	U.S.A.	24	14	48
	Total	150	144	155
Chemicals and	Japan	13	12	1
medicines	Britain	40	8	2
(1,000 piculs)	Total	75	30	28
Coal*	Japan	78	37	17
(1,000 tons)	Total	103	56	23
Raw cotton	Japan	13	15	7
(1,000 piculs)	U.S.A.	80	137	319
	Total	242	328	424
Machinery and	Japan	216	517	365
parts (1,000	Britain	849	310	589
Haikwan teals)	U.S.A.	290	68	244
	Total	1,592	1,218	1,409

Sources: "The Influence of Chinese Boycotts on Trade," July 1932. In Department of Foreign Trade, Ministry of Commerce and Industry, *The Documents, The Manchurian Incident*, II, 1852–1860.
Original source: Maritime Customs, *The Trade of China* (Shanghai: 1940).

Note: Total figures include imports from other countries.

* Japan exported high calorific coal for ferrous furnaces in China, Japanese investments.

substitute well because imports from Britain also fell from the 1930 monthly average during the same three-month period, as shown in table 2.6.

- Products of Japanese-owned cotton textile factories were strictly *boycotted* in the Shanghai region during the same period,[41] and total imports of raw cotton to China, all from the United States, increased greatly, reflecting the brisk activities of the Chinese cotton textile industry.[42]

This point is clearly counter to passages in Yen Chung-p'ing's book—and also in many writings by Japanese scholars—on this issue, such as the following: "The decline in Japanese cotton textile imports to China was due to the substitution by the products of Japanese-owned cotton textile factories in China."[43] Japanese scholars excessively generalized their passages as in "even the boycott was powerless," or "the anti-Japanese boycott, as a whole, was *temporarily* effective"(author's italics).[44]

- Paper, marine products, and metal products contributed 9.8, 6.3, and 3.7 percent, respectively, to the value of 20 principal import items from Japan in 1930.

All Japanese products faced country substitution, also presented in table 2.6: Products of the United States, Switzerland, Norway, and Canada substituted for paper; of Britain, the United States, and Germany for metal products; of the Dutch East Indies for sugar; and of Britain and Germany for chemicals. Chinese restaurants decided not to use Japanese seafood; thus, for example, trout and sardines from the United States, Canada, and the U.S.S.R. substituted for these products from Japan.[45]

2. China proper from October 1931 to February 1932

I developed a detailed analysis for China proper in table 2.7 to see which commodities declined most markedly and which countries, if any, supplied substitutes to China. The table shows the same trend as the one for Shanghai. All exports from Japan declined very rapidly, now even including machinery. This table presents the results for only five months, but later I will examine whether the substitution of Japanese products by other countries continued or was a short-lived phenomenon.

The trends in the fall of Japanese exports and in substitutions in the China proper market were similar to what occurred in Shanghai:

    i. *Cotton cloth:* The share in cotton cloth declined 46 percent within a span of only five months. The Japanese share was reduced to 46 percent, from 80, and the British share increased to 44 percent, from 15, during the same period. However, a large decline in the total volume of imports of cotton cloth showed a substitution by Chinese products, instead of by British products, for Japanese imports.[46]

    ii. *Sugar:* In 1931, China's intake of refined sugar declined to only 32 percent of the 1929 peak.[47] Japan's share fell to some 13 percent, from 25, in the five-month period presented in the table. The major supplier was the Dutch East Indies, which is now Indonesia.

Table 2.7 Import share of principal trading countries in China proper, October 1931–February 1932

(percent)

Item	Country	October 1931	February 1932
Cotton cloth	Japan	80.0	46.3
	Britain	15.4	44.4
Sugar	Japan	25.0	13.8
	Dutch E. Indies	53.9	50.6
Machinery/Parts	Japan	34.9	13.0
	Britain	22.5	32.3
	U.S.A.	13.9	18.3
Paper	Japan	37.6	9.2
	Germany	4.1	18.3
Seafood	Japan	54.7	14.9
Flour	Japan	61.3	14.6
	U.S.A.	27.4	80.9

Source: *The Documents*, A 110, 21-5, II, Commercial Confidential No. 1852–1860.
    Original source: Maritime Customs, *The Trade of China* (Shanghai: 1940).

iii. *Paper:* Japan's share of paper imports also sharply declined to only 9 percent, from about 38.

iv. *Flour:* Japan's relative position in flour imports dropped to 15 percent, from 61, during the same five months, as the United States became the predominant flour exporter to China. The total value of flour imports more than tripled in February over October, and in 1932 they were 36 percent higher than the 1931 volume. However, the increase was temporary. Flour mills comprised the most important industry in China after textiles, and their numbers were expanding. Therefore the imported volume of wheat flour was reduced during the period from 1926 to 1937.[48]

v. *Marine products:* Japan fell to the position of a minor supplier of marine products, despite increased Chinese purchases.

vi. *Machinery:* Even though the total amount of machinery and parts imported during the October-February period remained nearly stationary, Japan's share declined to 13 percent, from 35, while Britain and the United States saw their shares expand.

VII. After the first Shanghai Incident

On January 28, 1932, serious fighting between Japan and China started in Shanghai. Trade was paralyzed and all Japanese-owned factories were closed until April.[49] After this first Shanghai Incident, an agreement to cease hostilities between the two nations was concluded at the beginning of May 1932. The National Salvation Association in Shanghai, however, immediately announced that it rejected the agreement and passed a resolution to continue the bitter boycott. Passages in the Lytton report and in Japanese official documents stress that the Nationalist government encouraged the boycott.[50]

In the beginning of 1933, the boycott in China became still more violent because of further Japanese military operations and later again at Japan's withdrawal from the League of Nations.

This time it involved such regions as Tientsin, in the north, where the movement had previously been less intense.[51]

Unfortunately, the Japanese military and government authorities failed to appreciate the depth of Chinese nationalism and continued military involvement in Manchuria and later in China proper throughout the period. As a result, imports from Japan definitely deteriorated below what they were in 1931, which had already represented a drastic situation. Japan's relative share of China's imports was hit severely, falling to only 9.9 percent in 1933, from 30.0 in 1926.

At the time of the boycott movement's success, the Chinese economy was pushed into a deflationary spiral that lasted until 1935. Two factors besides the boycott and the war were the cause of this: The U.S. silver purchase policy at the end of 1933 brought on an exodus of silver from China, and also floods and the prolonged influence of the Great Depression resulted in poor agricultural performance.

3. Japan's Export Distortion: Japanese Exports to Six Regions of China

Regional distribution

Table 2.8 presents the development of Japan's exports to regions of China as indices in U.S. dollar terms.

Table 2.8 Indices of Japan's exports to various regions in China, 1926–37

(1926 =100)

	1 Kwantung	2 Manchuria	3 North	4 Central	5 South	6 China proper
1926	100	100	100	100	100	100
1929	123	93	82	82	15	80
1931	69	18	53	40	18	35
		(Manchukuo)				
1932	72	27	44	14	0.6	18
1933	119	64	30	11	0.7	13
1935	183	112	39	21	13	21
1937	214	136	49	25	7	26

Source: Ministry of Finance, *Nihon Gaikokuboeki Nenpo 1926–38* (Annual Returns of Foreign Trade of Japan) (Tokyo: Ministry of Finance, 1927–39).

Note: China proper (6) includes 3, 4, and 5.

The declines in exports to different regions varied by the degree of severity of the anti-Japanese boycotts, as noted in the previous section. Total exports to China proper in the last column dropped to 18 percent of the 1926 level in 1932, and to only 13 percent in 1933.

South China registered the most pronounced decline of all of China proper, to only 15 percent of the 1926 level by 1929.

Japan's exports to this region hardly existed in 1932 and 1933, as shown in the above table.

In central China, where the anti-Japanese boycott was very rigorous, Japan's export earnings especially declined after 1931, to only 14 percent and 11 percent in 1932 and 1933, and to a quarter of the 1926 level in 1937.

In north China, where the boycott movement was less severe than in south China and central China, the decline was sharp in 1933, dropping to 30 percent; it then recovered to about half the 1926 level during the ensuing years. In 1931 and 1932, Japan suffered a blow in exports to Manchuria; however, exports to this region after 1933 grew to more than in 1926.

The next table presents the development in distributive shares of each region in China proper and in Manchukuo, clarifying how these regional falls and rises affected Japan's trade. Exports to Kwantung are excluded for analytical purposes.

Table 2.9 The regional distribution of Japan's exports to China

(percent)

	Manchuria	North	Central	South	Total
1926	16.1	24.0	53.6	5.0	100
1929	18.3	24.7	54.5	0.9	100
	(Manchukuo)				
1932	16.7	48.7	34.6	0.1	100
1933	43.0	30.6	25.5	0.1	100
1935	45.9	24.0	28.4	1.2	100
1937	45.7	24.9	28.8	0.7	100

Source: Ministry of Finance, *Nihon Gaikokuboeki Nenpo 1926–38* (Annual Returns of Foreign Trade of Japan) (Tokyo: Ministry of Finance, 1927–39).

Japan's exports had declined a great deal in south China. But the relative share there was 5 percent at its maximum in 1926; therefore the fall was not as hard as the declining indices in the previous table indicated. The south China share became negligible after 1929.

Central China was important because this area alone absorbed more than half the total of Japan's exports to China in 1926. That importance declined as Japan's exports there fell to a third of the overall total in 1932 and further deteriorated to 25 to 28 percent in the 1933–37 period. The boycotts spread tightly over this region.

North China maintained about a quarter of the total weight throughout our survey; this well reflected the relatively loose boycotts in this region. Contrary to the effective boycotts in central China and south China, exports to north China boomed in the first six months of 1932 as a repercussion of the severe boycott in central China after September 1931. The north China share increased to more than 48 percent in 1932 because of this.

In comparing these four regions, it seems fair to state that declines in central China and south China were largely attributable to the effective anti-Japanese boycotts.

In 1926, Manchuria absorbed about 16 percent of all of Japan's exports to China, and its relative importance grew to more than 43 percent after 1933. In trade with Manchuria/Manchukuo after 1932, Japan's balance showed a surplus every year. Because of the great surge in exports to Manchukuo, the total of net earnings from this region was equivalent to $4.24 billion from 1931 to 1937.

A significant aspect of this surge was that all exports were financed by Japan's net foreign investment.[1] This caused a precarious external financial position for Japan because the earnings were paid by inconvertible Manchurian and Japanese currencies. In this sense, the increase in net exports to Manchukuo from Japan was similar to an "immiserizing growth" because the export-expanding country became worse off.[2] Japan was unable to gain any foreign exchange benefits; it merely exported products (mostly infrastructure-related items and factory equipment) that were largely made up of imported materials requiring payment from foreign exchange earnings from other countries.

Japan tried to offset losses incurred by the boycotts in its central and south China markets by expanding exports to Manchuria. The ambitions of Japanese militarists and policymakers also supported the idea of future gain from Manchukuo trade as a direct compensation for the boycott barriers.

This idea was poorly conceived, even from an economic viewpoint, because of Manchuria's limited natural resources and small market.[3] It mainly offered soybeans and low-quality iron ore and demanded few Japanese manufactured products because of its low population density and low income level. The "desire" was encouraged by military, political, and (misconceived) economic needs, and the needs exerted pressure in such a way that the Manchurian route should work complementarily to the Japanese economy as a substitute for the lost markets of south China and central China for Japanese exports of manufactured goods and imports of raw materials.

Japan's national economic gains stemming from trade also disappeared. Worldwide optimal resource allocation for Japan as a trade-based nation was lost concerning China. Japan needed to find outlets outside China for the products of its "young" and rapidly growing manufacturing abilities.

COMMODITY DISTRIBUTION IN TRADE

Commodity distribution will be analyzed in three steps. In the first and second steps, original Japanese data are followed, including Manchukuo, although this blurs what happened in exports to different regions in China. Increases in exports of certain commodities in Manchukuo and north China statistically hide their falls in central and south China. But using these data is handy for the preliminary steps.

Table 2.10 highlights which commodities deteriorated more, that is, which ones were the major subjects of the boycotts. It shows indices of Japan's exports of principal commodities to China in value terms for selected years. Table 2.11 shows the relative weights of principal commodities in value terms.

Among declining commodities, manufactured goods (cotton cloth, cotton yarn, knitted goods, sugar, flour, paper, and china/porcelain) in total contributed 56.9 percent of the total exports to

Table 2.10 Indices of principal commodities in Japan's exports to China, 1926–37

(percent)

	Cotton yarn	Cotton cloth	Sugar	Marine products	Flour	Coal	Paper	Iron products	Rayon
1926	100	100	100	100	100	100	100	100	100
1929	26.9	82.9	80.1	79.4	133.7	61.7	132.8	90.9	27.5
1932	4.0	17.7	13.5	20.6	62.0	10.6	36.8	40.6	33.3
1935	17.5	19.5	30.1	42.9	55.0	3.2	67.6	126.7	383.3
1937	24.7	30.3	32.7	52.3	92.4	1.1	118.2	196.7	550.0

Source: Ministry of Finance, *Nihon Gaikokuboeki Nenpo 1926–38* (Annual Returns of Foreign Trade of Japan) (Tokyo: Ministry of Finance, 1927–39).

Note: China in this table includes Manchuria/Manchukuo.

Table 2.11 Comparisons of commodity distribution (percent) in Japan's exports to China

	1926	1929	1932	1935	1937
Declining exports					
Manufactured goods					
Cotton Cloth	37.5	35.5	22.2	10.9	12.2
Yarn	5.2	1.6	0.7	1.3	1.3
Knitted goods	0.5	0.6	0.3	0.2	0.7
Subtotal	43.2	37.7	23.2	12.4	14.2
Sugar	6.4	5.8	2.9	2.9	2.2
Flour	3.8	5.7	8.0	5.4	3.7
Paper	2.8	4.3	3.5	2.8	3.3
China/porcelain	0.7	–	–	–	–
Subtotal	13.7	15.8	14.4	11.1	9.2
Primary goods					
Coal	5.8	2.7	1.5	0.2	0.0
Marine products	2.6	2.3	1.8	1.6	1.0
Subtotal	8.4	5.0	3.3	1.8	1.0
Expanding exports					
Manufactured goods					
Iron products	1.2	1.2	1.7	2.3	2.6
Rayon	0.5	1.5	0.5	2.8	2.9
Canned goods	–	–	–	0.4	0.6
Subtotal	1.7	2.7	2.2	5.5	6.1

Source: Ministry of Finance, *Nihon Gaikokuboeki Nenpo 1926–38* (Annual Returns of Foreign Trade of Japan) (Tokyo: Ministry of Finance, 1927–39).

Note: In this table, China includes Manchukuo.

China in 1926. Their contribution declined sharply, to only 23.4 percent, in 1937. Two other declining commodities in the list are coal and marine products, which are primary products.

A number of comments can be made concerning table 2.11:

Declining products:
- *Manufactured goods:* The deterioration in Japan's exports was most pronounced in manufactured goods, with cotton textile products (yarn and cloth) and sugar being the biggest losers.
- The declines of cotton textile products during the 1926–37 period were the largest of all exports to China. The total of cotton textiles alone (cloth, knitted goods, and yarn) contributed 43.2 percent of all Japanese exports to China in 1926, but it fell to only 12.4 percent in 1935 (even if we add the cotton textile exports to Kwantung). If we include the small values of diverse other cotton products, the contribution would be higher. Cotton cloth and cotton yarn accounted for 75 percent of all Japanese manufactured exports to China in 1926.

  Of all shipments from Japan to the world, China purchased 47 percent of cotton cloth, 9.6 percent of knitted goods, and 38 percent of cotton yarn in 1926 volume terms.[4] In 1937, the exports to China drastically shrank to roughly half these levels, accounting for only 26 percent, 5.6 percent, and 14 percent, respectively. Sales of cotton knitted goods to China actually doubled in volume; thus the fall apparently was due to a deterioration in value. The unit price dropped in 1937 to only a quarter of what it was in 1926.

  The deterioration of exports in the China market was comparable to their expansion in the world market: 180 percent each for cotton cloth and yarn and 280 percent for cotton knitted goods in value terms in 1937 over the 1926 level.

  Earnings in exports to China in cotton cloth, knitted goods, and yarn dropped to only $16.3 million in 1932, from $105.7 million in 1926. They did recover somewhat, to $30.8 million in 1937, or 29 percent of the 1926 level. Therefore, Japan's reliance on the China market for exports of cotton textiles became smaller and smaller during the 1926–37 period, as shown in tables 2.10 and 2.11.

The substitution in cotton textiles was made first by Chinese lower-count cotton textiles. The boycott was effective protection for the Chinese cotton textile industry, which restarted development. Moreover, China's developing domestic cotton textile industry made a rigorous boycott against Japanese cotton textiles possible and easier.

- Collective shares of exports of sugar, flour, paper, and china/porcelain declined 4.5 percent during the 1926–37 period.

   The relative position of sugar fell to 2.2 percent in 1937, from 6.4 percent, in the total exports to China.[5] Products of the developing local industry and of the Dutch East Indies substituted for sugar.[6]

   Products of the United States and Germany substituted for paper as indicated in table 2.6.

   After increasing in 1929, sales of flour and paper similarly declined from 1932.

- All exports mentioned so far were consumption goods, easily substituted for by local products and products of other countries. Therefore they could be severely boycotted.

- *Primary products:* The deteriorating primary goods were marine products and coal.

   Coal was another big loser, but this was due more to Japanese policy than to the boycotts. (Since Japan was a net coal importer from China, a 6 percent contribution of this commodity to the total exports to China in 1926 rapidly shrank to zero by 1936). Of coal exports to central China during the 1926–30 period, two thirds were products of Japan's Kyushu islands (because of their high calorific power necessary for ferrous furnaces built in Manchuria by Japanese investment), and the rest were reexports of Manchurian products.[7] However, the annual net imports of coal from China were small, $1.2 million in 1926, for example. From 1926 to 1937, Japan's net imports of coal from China totaled less than $13 million.[8]

Marine products also lost sales in central and south China, where products from the United States and Canada were substituted for Japanese salted fish and dried fish, as presented in table 2.6.

Seaweed was not substituted by other countries because it was considered a special Japanese product; therefore the decline was less pronounced in the original data.[9]

Expanded exports:
Shipments of three manufactured products (iron products, rubber tires, and rayon) were increased, but their contribution in value terms to total exports was small.

After rayon suffered a heavy drop in the 1931–33 period, and though it was a consumption good, it grew to 380 percent in 1935 and to 550 percent in 1937 over the 1926 level. Its annual export value, however, was small.

The growth of rayon was in high contrast to the tremendous declines of cotton yarn and cloth within textile exports. Comparing cotton exports with rayon exports, we find cotton was the product of an age-old industry and severely boycotted, with its exports sizably deteriorating; but rayon was a new product, and it registered growth after 1935. Both products, however, were very often manufactured in the same companies in Japan in that period.[10] These companies produced cotton staples with a certain percent being blended with synthetic materials, which was the product growing at the fastest rate among Japanese manufactured goods and also among exports to the China market.

In the third and final step of our analysis of commodity distribution, table 2.12 brings us a clear-cut view of the degree of decline in each principal Japanese export in the four regions of China.[11]

Table 2.12 Regional/commodity distribution in Japan's principal exports to China

(millions of dollars)

Item	Region	Year/ 1926	1929	1932	1935	1937
Cotton:						
yarn	Manchuria	1.9	1.1	...	...	...
	North	3.6	0.4	–	–	1.0
	Central & South	6.5	1.5	–	–	1.0
Cloth	Manchuria	25.0	16.2	...	...	...
	North	27.3	12.2	4.7	2.2	0.5
	Central & South	48.0	35.2	2.7	2.2	6.5
Piece	Manchuria	–	1.2	...	...	...
goods	North	0.3	2.4	2.0	1.2	0.9
	Central & South	0.3	1.1	0.1	1.0	1.5
Sugar	Manchuria	0.3	0.7	...	...	...
	North	2.5	2.2	0.5	1.0	0.8
	Central & South	11.6	6.4	0.2	1.7	1.5
Flour	Manchuria	...	2.9	...	...	...
	North	...	4.9	1.7	–	4.3
Paper	Manchuria	0.1	–	...	...	...
	North	1.8	2.2	1.2	1.5	1.0
	Central & South	3.1	5.3	0.2	0.3	1.0
China and	North	0.1	0.3	0.1	0.3	0.3
porcelain	Central & South	0.9	0.7	–	0.3	0.3
Chemicals and	Manchuria	...	0.1	...	...	...
explosives	North	...	0.1	0.3	0.9	0.8
	Central & South	...	1.3	0.3	1.1	1.1
Metal	Manchuria	0.1	–	...	...	...
products	North	0.8	1.1	0.7	2.3	3.3
	Central	1.0	2.0	1.5	1.5	1.4
Spinning and	North	0.3	0.4	0.3	0.2	0.4
weaving	Central	0.9	1.1	0.5	0.4	2.0
machinery						
Rubber tires	North	0.3	0.4	0.3	0.2	0.4
	Central	0.4	0.5	–	0.2	0.2
Marine	North	1.4	0.7	0.5	0.4	0.2
products	Central	4.1	3.2	0.2	1.4	0.7
Coal	Central & South	9.3	5.7	1.0	0.3	–

Source: Ministry of Finance, *Nihon Gaikokuboeki Nenpo 1926–38* (Annual Returns of Foreign Trade of Japan), (Tokyo: Ministry of Finance, 1927–39).

Note: China in this table includes Manchuria as a region up to 1929 and thenceforth no data are available for Manchuria, as is indicated by three dots (...), since after 1931 Manchuria did'nt exist in the Japanese data; the region was classified under the name of Manchukuo, not China. The figures have been collected from the Japanese customs office statistics of the relevant years. Figures near zero have been indicated with a dash.

Conclusions

We can draw several conclusions based on tables 2.10, 2.11, and especially table 2.12.

1. The declines in Japanese exports of consumption goods to China shown in table 2.12 were the heaviest of any in all previously presented tables. Among export items, goods exported primarily to central and south China registered pronounced declines. Notably, cotton cloth, $48 million of which was sold to central and south China in 1926, was reduced to only $2.2 million worth in 1935.

2. Once Japanese commodities had lost their markets in central and south China in 1929 and again in 1931–32, they never recovered. The loss of markets suffered by most Japanese manufactured consumer goods in central and south China followed this pattern. One essential reason was the availability of substitutes, especially from local sources.

3. The development of the Chinese cotton textile industry to a great extent made possible the boycott and the exclusion of Japanese cotton textiles. The development of this industry was then accelerated by the boycotting of Japanese products, notably in the central China market.

4. The gravest of export declines were in cotton yarn and cotton cloth. Here the detailed statistics of Japanese customs reveal the rapid improvement of quality in cotton textile products associated with changes in their export volumes, which reflects technological improvements in this Japanese industry.

   For example, cotton cloth, gray (unbleached) and narrow width of 27–29 inches, had been exported in large volume in 1926, but fell from 1932 onward. In these exports, bleached, dyed, and printed cloth in widths of more than 34 inches, though in the beginning only in small quantities, replaced previous ones.

Thus the decline in Japanese cotton textile exports actually involved a shift of emphasis from the lower-count, unbleached, and narrow width cloth to the fine-count, dyed or printed, and wider cloth. The Chinese cotton textile industry caught up with the Japanese in the lower-count exports via the boycotting protection, although the Japanese industry still kept a competitive edge in quality-cum-price in bleached, dyed, and printed cloth vis-à-vis Chinese and British cloth.

The Chinese demand for coarse cotton goods was high; Japan had been exporting them in quite large quantities before large-scale boycotting started, as shown in table 2.12. After 1932, the volume exported became very small because of a large fall in coarse, unbleached cotton textiles, though the quality was refined. The Chinese demand for refined cloth was not high, and probably would not have been high even without the boycotts. In central and south China, products of Japanese-owned factories were boycotted as imported "enemy goods." The fall in cotton product exports in central and south China markets was due to the boycotts.

In north China, the situation was different. After 1932, Japan's exports in cotton cloth further deteriorated until 1937 because of the vigorous activity of Japanese-owned cotton textile makers based in this region. Here is one piece of evidence to prove this: The average rate of profit of seven large Japanese cotton-spinning companies in China was increasing in the second half of 1936.[12]

Therefore, in the staggering drop of cotton cloth exports in the period of our survey, about a quarter was attributable to the statistical separation of Manchukuo, a quarter to the substitution effect on products of Japanese-owned factories, and half to the boycott-cum-development of the Chinese cotton textile industry. The war and resultant economic depression in central China and south China provided a backdrop.

Also, among cotton products, imitation nankeens, drills, and twilled shirtings had not been exported to Manchuria; thus the statistical separation of Manchukuo in general little affected the sharp downward trends of these products in exports to China.

5. An increase in exports of textile machinery to north China (and some to central China) brought a boomerang effect. Their increase was inversely correlated with Japanese sales in cotton goods, which deteriorated.

6. Some manufactured goods, mainly for industrial use (chemicals and iron products), increased in shipments to north China and even to central China, to some extent. The increases, however, were too small to offset irreversible factors influencing the definite deterioration of Japan's exports to China proper over the period.

The Nationalist government eased the policy somewhat against Japan by suppressing the boycott, which in Shanghai, central China, subsided from the second half of 1935 to the beginning of 1936. But the economic tie that had been almost completely severed during these boycott years could not be recovered. The routes and channels of Japanese commodities to reach Chinese users were cut, and Japan's products were replaced by domestic and foreign products; Chinese consumption patterns had changed. Japan's trade with China was thus distorted, putting more weight in exports and imports only in Manchukuo and north China.

4. Distortion in Japan's Imports from China

The Chinese boycotts also banned exports to Japan. Imports from China and thus China's share of Japan's import market were curtailed year by year: Imports followed in the wake of the sharp downward trend in exports.

Before 1926, Japan had imported a large variety of commodities from China, mostly primary products, but the flow of merchandise from China increasingly changed in 1926–37.

The weight of imported merchandise shifted from raw cotton to foodstuffs (beans and grains) and heavy industrial materials (coal and iron). Chinese raw cotton fell to a negligible amount in Japan's total imports of this commodity over the period of this study.

Table 2.13 was constructed from Japanese customs office trade statistics in a manner similar to the method used for table 2.12 to show the values of principal commodities imported from China.

Several comments can be made on table 2.13:

1. *Major imports besides raw cotton:* In 1926, beans and bean oil cake for feed and fertilizer (soybeans and soybean cake) shipped from Manchuria comprised 35 percent of Japan's imports from China. Other main imports that year were raw cotton and ginned cotton (19 percent); coal, iron ore, and tin ingots and slabs (7 percent); flax, hemp, and jute (3 percent); and salt (0.1 percent). These principal commodities covered 64 percent of the total imports from China in 1926, but in 1937 this figure dropped to 48 percent.[1] The products were diversified into small amounts of minor products in a continual reduction of total imports.

2. *Foodstuffs:* Beans (excluding bean oil cake) represented 10.2 percent of the total imports, including Manchuria and the

Kwantung leased territory in 1926, and provided 78 percent of all imported beans to Japan.[2] Bean imports from China increased to provide 95 percent of foreign beans in Japan in 1929, and from then on they held the predominant position in the bean import market until Japan's defeat in World War II. Thus the share of this commodity rose to about 20 percent of annual imports from China from 1929 onward.

Table 2.13 Japan's principal imports from China

(millions of dollars)

Commodity	Region	1926	1929	1932	1935	1937
Foodstuffs						
Soybeans	China proper	6.1	3.9	-	-	-
	Manchukuo			5.1	15.3	21.5
	Kwantung	1.0	1.7	0.3	0.2	0.2
Wheat bran	China proper	4.8	4.0	1.3	-	-
Other grains	China proper				6.6	5.7
	Manchukuo			-	5.3	13.5
Fertilizers						
Bean cake	China proper	9.1	14.3	-	-	-
	Manchukuo			11.7	6.7	8.0
Other fertilizers						
	China proper	3.8	4.0	-	-	-
Industrial materials						
Raw cotton	China proper	21.1	15.5	5.3	5.9	6.8
Coal	China proper	1.7	3.5	0.8	2.2	4.7
	Manchukuo			6.3	8.8	8.6
	Kwantung	8.7	12.8	0.8	-	-
Iron ore	China proper	1.8	3.9	1.0	3.1	3.4*
	Manchukuo			-	0.4	-
Pig iron	China proper	-	1.3	-	-	-
	Manchukuo			1.2	5.4	4.3*
Tin	China proper	1.4	0.8	0.3	0.9	1.0*
Other minerals						
	China proper	-	-	-	5.4	5.2
	Manchukuo			-	6.2	11.2
	Kwantung	-	-	-	0.3	0.9

Source: Ministry of Finance, *Nihon Gaikoku Boeki Nenpo* (Annual Returns of Foreign Trade of Japan) (Tokyo: Ministry of Finance, 1927–38).

* The figures for iron ore, pig iron, and tin are for 1936, since figures are not available for 1937, not even in Japanese customs data.

Japan imported bean oil cake for fertilizer and feed. In 1926 it accounted for about 14 percent of Japan's imports from China, a large share as a single commodity group. These imports steadily declined, as shown in the table, to 3 percent in 1937, largely because of developments in the Japanese chemical fertilizer industry and to some extent because of imports from Germany. Fertilizer imports from China covered a third of Japan's fertilizer imports in 1926, but that value fell to 14 percent by 1936.[3]

In Chinese statistics, bean oil cake, soybeans, and soybean oil, mostly shipped from Manchuria, had replaced the importance of traditional exports, including silk and tea, by 1930.[4] The shares of these latter two traditional goods fell to 17 percent of China's exports in 1930.

Flax, hemp, and jute together amounted to 2 to 3 percent of the total imports from China throughout the 1926–37 period. They covered 30 to 40 percent of Japan's imports of these commodities. The rest was bought from British India and the Philippines.

Salt imports in 1926 comprised only 0.1 percent of the total imports from China, but 58 percent of total Japanese salt imports. Despite a 70 percent increase of salt in the volume of imports from China, salt shipments from African countries grew faster than those from China in response to Japan's increasing industrial requirements and in order to reduce Japan's trade surplus, a surplus resulting from the rapid growth in Japan's exports of cotton textile products there from 1933 onward.[5]

3. *Chinese raw cotton*: Japan's purchases of raw (ginned) cotton were reduced to 5.4 percent of the total imports from China in 1937, from 19 percent in 1926.[6] The value of Chinese raw cotton in 1926 provided only 6 percent of Japan's total raw cotton imports and had tapered off almost entirely by 1937, dropping to 0.8 percent. This sharp fall reflected anti-Japan export boycotts-cum-developments in the cotton industries

in China and Japan, which led to country diversification in raw cotton imports.

4. The following aspects of the development of the Chinese cotton textile industry are relevant to the Chinese boycotts as import and export barriers.

   i. China's cotton textile industry had achieved remarkable growth from 1920 to 1929 and was continuing to grow.[7]
   ii. China became a net importer of raw cotton (mainly long staple) by 1920 and a net exporter of cotton yarn by 1928. About a third of raw cotton consumption by the Chinese textile industry was imported in 1930.[8] Raw cotton output in China tended to grow slowly from 1926 to 1936, despite a higher price inducement relative to the prices of other goods.[9]
   iii. Under the assistance of the League of Nations, in 1933 the Nationalist government designed a plan to encourage and to control raw cotton and cotton textile production to achieve self-sufficiency in these products.[10]

Related to the boycotts of exports to Japan, the Japanese government had shown an interest in increasing output and improving the quality of Chinese raw cotton, because most of it was short staple. Mitsubishi Co. Ltd. distributed American cotton seeds in a contract with Chinese farmers that called for the output to be sold to this company. This practice ended up in failure because of the boycotts and local wars.

Shipments of many kinds of products to Japan from central and south China had been stopped. Toward 1937, Japan's imports from China were regionally distorted, coming more and more from Manchukuo and north China. In commodity terms, the imports were concentrated in only a few products: soybeans, bean cakes, coal, and iron. Their shares in the Japanese market were quite large, as shown in table 2.14.

5. *Results:* The distortion in China trade and huge export financing to Manchukuo resulted in the Japanese balance of payments going into a sizable deficit within a few years.[11]

The long-term influence of China trade distortion drove Japan to seek new markets worldwide in manufactured exports and in imports of foodstuffs and industrial materials.

Table 2.14 Chinese commodity shares in the Japanese market

					(percent)
Commodity˙	1926	1929	1932	1935	1937
Soybeans	78.3	95.9	96.2	92.1	96.6
Bean cakes	95.6	97.0	91.5	96.4	94.4
Coal	82.5	79.0	79.9	76.8	78.0
Iron	6.0	6.4	14.6	10.5	14.4
Raw cotton	6.2	5.9	4.2	2.9	2.8

Source: The same as in table 2.13.

Note: China here includes the Kwantung leased territory and Manchukuo.

Chapter 3

THE DRASTIC DECLINE OF JAPANESE EXPORTS TO THE UNITED STATES

1. INTRODUCTION TO JAPAN-U.S. TRADE RELATIONS

From 1926 to 1937, Japan's exports to the United States registered an astonishing change. They fell so much that it was as if a torrential rain had swept the harvest from the paddy fields.[1] The shift from a large annual trade surplus, which had nurtured Japan's economic growth, to a grave annual deficit aggravated Japan's global balance of payments in this period and raised concern among students analyzing Japanese economic development. The issue has been described repeatedly in many writings on Japanese political and economic history. The causes of this change, however, have never been scrutinized by economists applying modern economic instruments. This chapter attempts to use these instruments to analyze the causal factors that provoked the shifts in trade patterns. This study will clarify the specific relations between these factors and examine the link, if any, to protectionism in the United States against Japan. First, let us survey Japan-U.S. trade relations around the period of this study.

The United States had generally proved to be the greatest and most reliable customer for Japanese exports, offering a stable and ever-growing market from the opening of Japanese ports in 1858 until 1929. The Japan-U.S. trade balance had most often been favorable for Japan, a situation that had contributed greatly to redressing Japan's global trade imbalance. From 1926 to 1929, the United States annually absorbed as much as 42 percent of total Japanese exports. During the same period, Japan enjoyed a U.S. trade surplus at an annual average of $94 million, or 23 percent of the annual total value of exports to the United States.

In contrast, Japanese exports to the United States from 1932 to 1934 plunged to an annual average of $122 million, only 40 percent of the 1926–29 level. Japanese imports in the same period also declined, although far less than exports did, averaging $174 million annually, a reduction to 57 percent of the earlier level. The trade deficit increased yearly thereafter. The annual average level of Japanese exports to the United States from 1926 to 1937 was $196 million, but the imports from the United States reached $280 million annually. In 1937, the Japanese trade deficit with the United States was 49.6 percent of the value of Japan's total exports to the United States.

The smaller reduction in Japanese imports than in exports was due to three major factors. First, the Japanese need for U.S. raw cotton did not diminish as the Japanese cotton industry strove to surpass the British cotton industry and to lead world production and exports in 1932 and 1933. Of total imports from the United States in 1935, raw cotton accounted for 48.5 percent.

The second factor was the need for imported industrial equipment and raw materials as the Japanese economy launched its fourth stage of industrial upsurge, from 1935 to 1936.[2] The increase in crude oil, gas and fuel oil, sulfate wood pulp, iron and steel scrap, aluminum ingots and bars, and refined copper was due to this upsurge. In 1935, of total Japanese imports from the United States, metals and metal products (excluding machinery and vehicles) constituted 19.37 percent; crude oil, gasoline, gas and fuel oil, 12.4 percent; machinery and vehicles, 10.0 percent; wood and paper, 5.7 percent; and chemicals and related products, 3.3 percent.[3]

Third, munitions imports played an increasing role in Japan-U.S. trade after war broke out between Japan and China in 1937. After 1929, there were reductions in imports of foodstuffs, leaf tobacco, sawmill products, rubber tires, sulfate of ammonia, tin-plate, steel sheets, and other products, but these reductions did not counterbalance the strong incentive to import generated by the three needs described: for raw materials (especially a good quality U.S. raw cotton—fine long fiber), for industrial equipment, and for munitions products.

The Japanese trade deficit with the United States after 1934 increased at a rate that shocked the Japanese. It became nearly three times the size of Japan's global trade deficit in the 1934–36 period, overriding by a great margin Japan's favorable worldwide trade performance (appendix I, table 1). The rate of U.S. importance as a recipient of global Japanese exports sharply fell to only 18 percent in 1934, from 42 percent in 1926, and did not return to the earlier level. It remained at 20 percent of global Japanese exports in the ensuing years; this process is presented in table 1.3 in chapter one.

The sharply diminished trade with the United States was an unprecedented issue in Japanese history. For decades, Japan had relied on the opportunity for increased trade with the United States to develop its economy. The problem of the collapse of this trade was national in scope: It had major repercussions on the Japanese economy as a whole. In 1934, U.S. trade figures, as shown in table 3.1, reveal that the import index from Japan fell more sharply than from the rest of the world, a decline to 29 percent versus 37 percent. The recovery of imports in 1937 from this low 1934 level of trade was also much weaker for Japan (50 percent) than for the world (69 percent).

Further, table 3.2 illustrates the decline of Japan's relative rate of importance in U.S. imports to 6.6 percent in 1937, from 9.8

Table 3.1 Indices of U.S. trade

(percent in value terms)

	Exports		Imports	
	World	Japan	World	Japan
1926	100	100	100	100
1929	81	108	97	107
1932	51	51	27	33
1934	39	80	37	29
1937	127	110	69	50
1939	118	89	52	39

Sources: Statistical table 1 in appendix I of this book. League of Nations, *Statistical Yearbook, 1930/31* (Geneva: League of Nations, 1931), 162; *1939/40* (1940), 182.

percent in 1929. The small 3.2 percent fall of Japan on the U.S. side in 1929–37 was nevertheless considered by the Japanese as a staggering fall because Japan had lost 24 percent of total export earnings in the most-profitable U.S. market. (The small 3.2 percent drop in imports from Japan in the U.S. statistics was due to Japan's small share in total U.S. imports.)

Table 3.2 Geographical distribution of U.S. imports, selected countries, 1926–37

(Percent)

	1926	1929	1932	1934	1937
Japan	9.0	9.8	10.1	7.2	6.6
British Malaya	n.a.	5.0	2.0	6.0	8.0
Philippines	n.a.	2.8	6.0	5.0	4.0
British India	3.	3.	2.	3.	3.0
Italy	2.0	2.0	3.0	2.0	1.0
United Kingdom	8.0	7.0	5.7	6.0	6.0
Canada	10.0	11.0	13.0	14.0	13.0
Germany	4.0	5.0	4.0	4.0	3.0
World	100.0	100.0	100.0	100.0	100.0

Geographical distribution (%) of U.S. exports to Japan

	1926	1929	1932	1934	1937
Japan	5.4	4.9	8.4	9.8	8.6
World	100.0	100.0	100.0	100.0	100.0

Source: League of Nations, *International Trade Statistics 1930* (Geneva: League of Nations, 1932), 323, 345; *1938* (1939), 296, 318.

To return to the Japanese perspective, three factors are considered the most probable cause of the staggering fall in Japanese exports to the United States. The principal one was the Great Depression in the United States, which had led to unprecedented levels of unemployment, of business bankruptcies, of production decline, of low income, and of the value of the U.S. currency vis-à-vis gold. The shrinkage in U.S. trade was also astonishing: In 1934 it was only a third of its level in 1929. This was surely one of the causal factors, but it does not sufficiently explain the sharper decline of Japan's exports to the United States compared with other world exporters, as shown in tables 3.1 and 3.2.

Even in the 1930s, when Japanese exports to the United States declined, the No. 1 Japanese export commodity was raw silk. Raw silk earnings constituted 82 to 83 percent of the total value of its exports to the United States from 1926 to 1935. The importance of raw silk, however, declined to only 53 percent of total Japanese exports in 1937. Therefore the decline in the total value of exports to the United States followed in the wake of changes in the use of raw silk. This should be remembered as the second factor when causal relationships between the fall in Japanese exports and U.S. protectionism are examined.

Finally, a third factor was the relative weakness of Japan's export growth and recovery in the U.S. market, from 1926 to 1937, in commodities besides raw silk, in comparison with stronger performances in other world markets.

Although the effect of the first factor, the Great Depression, is inseparable from changes in U.S. demand for Japanese products, our attention will focus on the second and third factors to examine why Japanese exports did not recover in the U.S. market to the same extent as they did in the rest of the world. Analyses of these two factors, the shocking decline in silk exports and the weak export recovery in commodities other than raw silk, will be presented after a short review of the U.S. boycott movement against Japan. The effect of the Great Depression on Japanese exports, however, will be treated as a function of U.S. demand for Japanese raw silk in the third section of this chapter.

2. U.S. Intellectuals Support the Boycott

The movement to boycott Japan by not wearing silk dresses and hosiery made of Japanese silk had started in the United States during the 1920s.[1] The "Buy-American" sentiment merged and supported this movement from the beginning of the 1930s,[2] but the boycott movement drew more public attention after the Manchurian Incident in September of 1931.

The Twentieth Century Fund, headed by Dr. Nicholas Murray Butler, president of Columbia University and the 1931 Nobel prize winner in international peace, organized the Committee on Economic Sanctions against Japan in 1931. Intensive investigations by members of the committee resulted in the fund declaring a boycott against Japan: "Even boycotting raw silk alone would deprive 3,000,000 Japanese farmers of their sericultural revenues.

The American movement to boycott Japanese silk in dresses and stockings (circa 1935).

It would inflict an immense damage on the Japanese economy, while creating 300,000 jobless in hosiery and other silk manufacturing industries in the United States."[3]

Appeals to the president of the United States and to the U.S. Congress to impose the embargo came from such people as Dr. Lawrence A. Lowell, president of Harvard University; Newton De Baker, former secretary of defense; presidents and faculty members of several other universities; and groups of correspondents. The aim was to support the position of the League of Nations to stop Japan's military actions in China. This appeal was printed in almost every daily U.S. newspaper on February 20, 1932. Dozens of professors at Princeton University and establishments in Princeton, N.J., and all members of the Rockefeller Foundation signed a statement calling for the severance of economic relations with Japan. Almost all newspapers printed this statement on February 26, and by the end of that day, five thousand Americans had already become active participants. The movement progressed and continued to receive publicity for several months.[4]

The boycott's effect on finance and business activities

The Chinese-American community had been active in boycotting Japanese products in the United States, and these activities intensified after the Manchurian Incident. Their protests were centered in Boston, New York, Washington, and many other cities on the East Coast. The Chinese held meetings to appeal to the public for a boycott of Japan, distributing pamphlets, entitled "Embargo Japan: Silk, Cotton and Munitions," in downtown and residential areas in these cities. The Chinese Students Association took the initiative in the boycott movement in the northwestern United States.[5]

Anti-Japanese sentiment in Boston became keen by the end of February 1932, responding to the Chinese activity and the appeals of American intellectuals. Nearly a hundred members resigned from the Japan Society in Boston.[6] American banks in New York had tightened credit to Japanese banks after the Manchurian Incident, and it became impossible for Japanese banks in New

York to get new credit, even with the collateral of Japanese government bonds. American banks hesitated to discount bills for the
Japanese. The Morgan Guarantee Trust by this time had become
cautious in dealing with Yokohama Specie Bank (a Japanese government bank), Mitsui Bank, and Mitsubishi Bank, even though
Mitsui and Mitsubishi were among the best private Japanese
banks.

Some 40 to 50 percent of Japanese exports had been financed
by letters of credit from American banks, but these credit lines
were tightened to discourage trade dealings. American bankers
were nervous because of the uncertainty of the Asian situation.
They were also psychologically depressed by the state of silk sales
in New York. Silk manufacturers felt hopeless doing business.
After the Shanghai Incident, the trend further intensified.[7]

The Pacific Commerce Bank, a financial institution for the
Japanese in Seattle, closed down in October 1931 because a great
many Chinese customers withdrew their deposits.[8] About 8,400
Japanese lived in Seattle in October 1931; the Chinese population was estimated to be about 1,300. This ratio of Chinese to
Japanese was among the lowest of all West Coast cities, but about
30 Japanese small shops (foodstuffs, barbers, and hotels) and restaurants dealing with Chinese and Filipinos lost all their Chinese
customers after the Manchurian Incident. The Mitsui Trading
Company and the Mitsubishi Trading Company both suffered
a drastically reduced volume of shipments for China because of
unloading difficulties in Shanghai. Foreign cargo ships were substituted for Japanese cargo ships running the Asian routes. A shipment of 15 million bushels of wheat from the United States to
China for relief purposes was contracted excluding Japanese shipping companies at the request of the Chinese government.[9]

Public opinion on the Japanese boycott
Public opinion in the United States about boycotting Japan was
divided into those pro and con, but the former had a much larger
voice. The intellectuals who appealed for economic sanctions as part

of a worldwide public opinion drive believed these sanctions would be sufficient to terminate the crisis in Manchuria and to cause the cessation of hostilities between Japan and China. They said that to threaten Japan, the embargo had to be defined in more concrete and limited terms than stated in Article 16 of the Covenant of the League of Nations. On the other hand, they preferred economic sanctions against Japan over American military intervention in China.[10]

Weaker groups opposed the boycott. They said that the embargo's sanctions were not specific enough, nor was it possible to decide the priority status of embargo items among munitions, credit, raw materials, and foodstuffs. They believed instead that any partial embargo would tend to become a complete one and would be very effective against the Japanese because of the particular weakness of its economy. Therefore the embargo might create a threat of a war between the United States and Japan. Some people argued that an embargo would spur Japan toward war in desperation and thereby aggravate the situation in China. Others said that Japan might retaliate by invading American possessions in China, which would lead the United States into war.[11]

Since in 1931 Japan had purchased 40 percent of total U.S. raw cotton exports, or 12 percent of the cotton produced in the United States, some consideration also had to be given to cotton producers in regard to the boycott. Raw cotton exporters opposing the boycott said that opening up new outlets at existing price levels would be extremely difficult in the current world market conditions.[12]

The administration of the United States at this time rejected the idea of the embargo, in a judgment that it was extraordinarily punitive.[13] However, the notion of applying economic sanctions against Japan was later revived, and an embargo was imposed by the U.S. government in 1940.

3. Analysis of the Catastrophic Collapse of Silk Exports

I. The significance of silk exports to the Japanese economy

The reasons why silk exports receive attention here are threefold. First, silk represented a great proportion of Japan's total exports in the period under study. Silk was the prime foreign exchange earner for Japan even in the 1920s, although its relative importance in total exports had steadily declined since the turn of the century as other products expanded rapidly with Japanese industrialization. Silk exports still accounted for about 36 percent of Japanese total commodity exports in the 1920s, though this ratio went down sharply in the 1930s, to 15.5 percent in 1935 and to 12.8 percent in 1937. Silk was exceptional for Japan: Because the country had few natural resources, an expansion in production for exports usually required an increase in imports of raw materials. But such was not the case for silk.

The U.S. market's importance to Japan's raw silk trade can not be overestimated. About 85 percent of all raw silk output in Japan prepared for foreign manufacturers was shipped abroad from 1926 to 1929. Of the remaining 15 percent, most was consumed domestically, and a very small quantity was fabricated for exports as manufactured silk products. The United States absorbed 98 percent of total Japanese raw silk exports to the world. A predominant amount of raw silk (as materials for U.S. silk manufacturers), together with a very few manufactured silk products, comprised 82 to 83 percent of total Japanese exports to the United States from 1926 to 1935.

The second factor in the significance of the silk industry to the Japanese economy was its link to the livelihood of Japanese farmers. Silkworm raising by millions of Japanese farmers became the most important revenue of all byproduct earnings after Japan opened its ports to the world. This cash flow sizably assisted the farmers in paying off their burdens of rent in kind (33 percent) and taxes (33 percent) while retaining a minimum level of subsistence.[1] Japanese farm women were deeply involved and took special care in handling the worms, which required patience and delicate methods. They refined age-old traditional skills and improvised small inventions in raising and reeling. By the turn of the century, Japan had become the world's leading silk exporter, surpassing even China in product quality relative to price.

Despite a steady growth in overseas demand, the output of silk responded very slowly because raising cocoons and growing mulberry required exacting and hard work. The work was usually dependent on the women in the family, and the total hours of labor depended on the weather and the year-round farming cycle. In the long run, increases in demand had continually pushed the price of silk upward since Japan had become a monopolistic supplier to the U.S. market. As described earlier, silk nurtured Japan's rapid industrialization by earning foreign exchange to meet the country's import needs of machinery, technology, and raw materials. It involved a wide range of the farming community, from landowners to peasants, and was a great help financially for the 2.21 million Japanese farming families involved in sericulture in 1929.[2]

For Japanese farmers, the working hours of family members involved in sericulture (mulberry picking and silkworm raising) were considered as being cost-free. Sericulture farmers earned only a fractional profit above the cost (that is, counting only expenses to buy silkworm eggs), even in 1929[3] when the total value of Japanese silk exports reached a historical peak. In 1930 the total value of silk exports drastically decreased. A recent study shows that in 1932 the cost of production for superior quality cocoons per *kan* (a Japanese unit of weight equal to 3.75 kilograms, or

8.25 pounds) was on average 63 percent higher than the market price of cocoons in Japan because of record low price quotations in the raw silk market in New York.[4] By the fall of 1932, at least 13 million peasants, or 40 percent of Japanese farm families, were gravely hit by heavy losses in the sericulture industry, and many were forced into bankruptcy. Silk-producing areas such as Nagano, Gunma, Tochigi, Ibaraki, and Fukushima Prefectures were especially damaged. Countless news articles in the press reported frequent famines, suicides, and other tragedies in these rural areas.[5]

The government implemented financial policies from 1929 to 1931 to save poverty-stricken sericulture farmers, but they were insufficient. The agriculture sector had already been in a prolonged, deep recession caused by a poor harvest in 1927. The damage inflicted on sericulture farmers made the situation worse. The effect of the decline of the value of silk exports was significant as the first step toward weakening the financial status of the independent landowner class in rural areas. Members of this class were often political leaders in village life, and most of their political beliefs had been brewed in democratic thought in the Taisho period (1912–26).[6] The damage also triggered destruction of the Japanese farmer class, creating many landless and hunger-stricken people who would soon become factory workers. Therefore it also led Japan to reorganize the agriculture sector, on which its economy at that time still heavily depended.[7]

Third, the damage in silk exports influenced Japanese life by ultimately reorienting the social value system of Japan. The farmers' hunger and their desire to escape from this hopeless plight nourished the growing ambition of militarists and expansionists. Democratic factions were losing power because a succession of democratic cabinets had failed to improve the terrible condition of the depressed farmers. A trend to turn the nation's eyes from domestic problems to possible conquest outside Japan's territory, namely in China, was quickly gathering force, and it became an inexorable tide sweeping national sentiment toward the belief that Japan needed to expand outside its territory to save the farmers, the agriculture sector, and the country. The militarists and expansionists seized power in the first half of the 1930s, first the power to influence public opinion, then the power to control the cabinet and the nation. The decline of silk and the absence of expansion in other exports to the U.S. market further aggravated Japan's ongoing agrarian crisis.

Next, we will look at the factors that contributed to such a heavy decline in Japan's silk exports to the United States. What effect, if any, did the boycott of Japan, especially of silk, have on the decline of silk exports?

II. ANALYSIS OF THE FACTORS THAT CONTRIBUTED TO THE DECLINE IN SILK EXPORTS

Rates of U.S. tariffs on silk

Japan's silk exports to the United States[8] were divided into two groups of commodities: The first group contained raw silk and silk waste. U.S. tariffs on that group were classified as nonmanufactured in U.S. government statistics and duty-free in the period of our survey. Raw silk production meant the reeling of silk from cocoons, a process that required an extremely low degree of fabrication. The production was carried out in thousands of farmers' homes and in cottage industries. Raw silk and silk waste earned very small profits even without counting implicit wages for the farmers' families as a part of the cost.

The second group was Japanese-manufactured silk, such as silk cloth (processed silk, not raw silk), lace, handkerchiefs, underwear, and hosiery. U.S. tariffs on manufactured silk goods were high. They varied from 55 to 95 percent per pound, depending on the degree of fabrication and the competitiveness of foreign silk manufacturers vis-à-vis domestic ones.[9]

Although Japanese silk manufacturers started to produce 37-inch-wide silk fabrics for export by substituting modern machines for traditional tools (which wove only 17-inch-wide silk fabrics for Japanese kimono), they were unable to continue this new fabric production. Traditional Japanese patterns and colors of silk fabrics also did not suit the Americans. However, it might have been only a matter of time and experience if Japanese producers could have supported themselves during the catch-up period to respond to U.S. consumer demand, as Japanese chinaware and porcelain makers such as Noritake had done in an earlier period. Japanese silk manufacturers were unable to respond quickly enough because to do so they had to buy imported machinery that they couldn't afford. But to meet an increased raw silk demand, they simply worked harder to produce a greater amount of raw silk. A U.S. high-tariff policy efficiently shut out manufactured Japanese silk products, thwarting any ambitions to modernize production processes and to develop exportable manufactured silk goods for the United States at this time.

On the other hand, the free-tariff policy of the United States on the nonmanufactured group effectively stimulated Japan to become specialized as a raw-silk exporter, a raw-materials supplier to the advanced country, the United States. In other words, with the use of raw silk Japan lost the incentive to promote the further industrialization of modern silk manufacturing. Thus raw silk accounted for 95.5 percent of total Japanese silk exports to the United States by 1926. This rose to 99.2 percent in 1932.[10]

The boycott's effect on imports of Japanese silk

The effectiveness of the boycott movement in the United States on reducing the level of imports of Japanese raw silk can be assessed by observing two relationships. First, if it were effective, the importance of Japan should have fallen in the U.S. silk import market compared with the importance of other countries, notably China and Italy. To the contrary, though, Japan's position in the market expanded over the period of our survey, as shown in table 3.3. Imports from Japan were 84 percent and from China 13 percent in 1926, when the boycott movement was still insignificant in the United States. However, imports from Japan rose to 93–97 percent during the 1932–37 period, when the idea of economic sanctions against Japan was being loudly promoted by

U.S. intellectual leaders and the press. In other words, no replacement of Japan with another country occurred at this time in the U.S. silk import market, despite the boycott. Therefore we can reject the view that the boycott directly affected the imports of Japanese silk to the United States.

Table 3.3 Shares of major exporters in the U.S. raw silk market

(percent)

Year	Japan	China	Italy	Rest of the world
1926	84	13	2	1
1929	83	14	2	1
1932	93	3	3	1
1934	97	2	0	1
1937	93	5	2	0
1939	88	10	2	0

Source: U.S. Dept. of Commerce, *Foreign Commerce and Navigation of the United States* (Washington: U.S. Dept. of Commerce, 1926, 1929, 1932, 1934, 1937, 1939).

Secondly, the boycott might have taken the form of discrimination against all of Japan's raw silk imports, since nearly all raw silk purchases of the United States were from Japan. It is noteworthy, however, that in the boycott years of 1929 to 1933 and in the period of the "Buy American" campaign after 1931, the volume of imported Japanese raw silk rose by 24 to 30 percent higher than the 1926 level, as shown in the next table:

Table 3.4 Indices of Japanese raw silk exports to the United States

Year	1926	1929	1932	1935	1937
Unit price	100	79.8	25.3	25.7	31.9
Quantity	100	130.8	124.3	125.5	107.6
Value	100	104.4	31.3	32.3	34.3

Sources: Toyo Keizai Shinposha, *Nihon Boeki Seiran* (Foreign Trade of Japan: A Statistical Survey), *The Supplement* (Tokyo: Toyo Keizai Shinposha, 1975 rev. ed.), 24–28.

Kajinishi Mitsuhaya et al., ed., *Nihon Sen'i Sangyo-shi Soronhen* (History of Japanese Textile Industries), (Tokyo: The Association of the Japanese Textile Industry, 1958), 941.

Thus we can conclude that the boycott movement induced no quantitative decline in the United States of silk imports from Japan, either in market share or in absolute amount.

Rather the drastic decline in the value of raw silk exports to the United States stemmed from a sharp fall in unit price, down to only 25 to 32 percent of the 1926 level in the 1932–37 period, as shown in table 3.4. A 25 percent higher volume in exports did not compensate for this severe fall in unit price during the 1929–37 period. In 1932, the production cost for superior quality cocoons was on average 63 percent higher than its market price in Japan, as mentioned earlier.[11]

A regression analysis

Regression analysis was used to determine the influence of the six independent factors below on the decline of Japanese raw silk exports to the United States. The period of the regression models begins with 1925 and continues through 1939, instead of 1926 to 1937, to obtain a broader statistical base. The data and sources of the models are presented in statistical table 3 in appendix I.

In all, a dependent variable *(MPT)*, six independent variables *(USIC, USC, USRP, WSP, PR, RELP)*, and three models (I, II, III) are included. Most statistical figures are expressed in index numbers, which are denoted in table 3.5 by adding *I* (Index) at the beginning of the variables; for example, *IUSC* is for the index of the *USC*, U.S. consumption level.

MPT: The dependent variable was the value of raw silk exports to the United States in dollar terms. In volume terms Japanese raw silk exports there did not decline but increased during the period when the value of raw silk exports had sharply fallen, except for small year-to-year changes mentioned earlier. It should be in dollar terms because the yen was overvalued in the early phase of the model and undervalued during the latter period of this time series vis-à-vis the U.S. dollar.

The quality of exported raw silk in fact changed, although a homogeneous product was assumed over the period of the model. The fineness of filament shifted yearly from a lower to a higher denier in the following progression: Raw silk up to 12 denier comprised almost all Japanese silk exports to the United States in 1926. Most raw silk exports shifted to more than 12 denier and up to 17 denier in 1929. Then 85 percent of all silk shipped in 1932 exceeded 17 denier, with the rest being of higher denier. By 1937, nearly 95 percent of the total was around 24 denier. This dramatic shift in raw silk exports from a lower to a higher denier, within only 12 years of Japan's long sericultural history, reflected efforts by Japanese farmers to prevent silk being replaced by rayon in the United States.[12]

The *dependent variable, MPT,* is Japanese raw silk exports to the United States. The independent variables detailed below provide the specifications of the regression models.

The null hypothesis in each of these three models was tested, that the change in the dependent variable was the result of changes in the independent variables.

Model I

The *independent variables* are *USIC, IUSRP,* and *IWSP.*

USIC: The substitution effect on a product theoretically entails the income effect; thus we used a variable *USIC,* the per capita income of the United States. Did a falling U.S. income level because of the Great Depression induce Americans to buy less silk, a luxury item? Or did it accelerate the substitution of rayon for silk because of rayon's lower price?

USRP: U.S. rayon production. Rayon was a new product used as a silk substitute. After being introduced from Europe, the rayon industry in the United States rapidly grew throughout the 1920s. Although setting up factories in the industry required a great amount of fixed capital, rapid progress in technology had been made and the quality of the product was quickly improving. The industry soon proved to be a beneficiary of the economies of scale. It expanded and flourished in the 1920s and 1930s under the protection of a U.S. high-tariff wall, insulated from the competition of European rayon producers.[13]

When Japan's raw silk exports hit a record high in 1929, silk imports in the United States also registered an all-time high.

However, the consumption of rayon in the country grew dramatically and had already surpassed that of silk by 1927. By 1937 the volume of rayon output in the United States had increased five-fold over the 1926 level.[14] Thus the variable *USRP* was employed, the volume of rayon output in the United States. A homogeneous quality of product over the period of the regression model was assumed, though the substitution effect for silk accelerated coincident with the technological progress that inevitably improved quality.[15]

WSP: We included the variable *WSP*, the index of world silk production with a one-year time lag. We used the time lag because raw silk imported in the United States consisted largely of products of sericultural countries from the previous year.

Model II

The independent variables are *USIC, IUSRP, IWSP,* and *IPR.*

PR: Price of rayon. Because of scale economies, the cost and the price of rayon products in the United States declined so rapidly that the manufacturers created a price guarantee system to protect inventory losses of rayon yarn purchasers from 1930 to 1937. U.S. rayon producers were conscious of the price of silk yarn. The price of 150-denier rayon yarn (one denier means 450 meters of silk filament weigh 0.05 grams) fell to 59 cents a pound in 1934, from $1.25 in 1929, or by more than half.[16] The price of raw silk fell 53.5 percent over the same period.[17] Therefore the variable *PR,* the unit price (index) of rayon in the United States, is used for model II. However, *USRP* and *PR* represent quantity and price; both are inversely correlated to each other under pure competition. One or the other must later be eliminated.

Model III

The independent variables are *USC, WSP,* and *RELP.*

USC: A variable for the level of consumption in the United States, the *USC,* could alternatively be used for the variable *USIC,* the U.S. per capita income. The *USC* would have been a better explanatory variable for our analysis if there had been no problem with it, but there were no recorded data before 1928. Thus the third model employing *USC* has a shorter period because of the available data.

RELP: The variable *RELP* is the ratio of the unit price of silk to USRP. This ratio drastically declined from 1925 through 1934, indicating that the unit price of silk declined as the production of rayon increased in the United States.

Results of the regression analysis

The statistical results for the cross-section regression models are presented in equations 1, 2, and 3 for models I, II, and III in table 3.5.

In model I and II *USIC* and *IUSRP* are both significant at the 0.01 level in equations 1 and 2 as proven at the high ratios in the last column. This means that changes in per capita income and in level of rayon output were significantly influential on the fall of Japan's raw silk exports to the United States. When the U.S. income level fell, the value of raw silk exports to the U.S. market also fell. When U.S. rayon output increased, raw silk exports fell because the *IUSRP* and the *IMPT* are negatively correlated.

Table 3.5 Determinants of Japan's raw silk exports to the United States

Eq.	Dependent	Constant	USIC	IUSC	IUSRP	IWSP	IPR	RELP	$\sqrt{R^2}$
1.	IMPT	−6.361	1.1812		−0.2357	−0.1592			0.9429
t		(7.803)	(7.808)	(0.057)					
2.	IMPT	7.960	1.2061		−0.2525	−0.1109	0.5232		0.9377
t		(6.766)	(3.191)	(0.258)	(0.301)				
3.	IMPT	15.67		0.2063		−0.1865		0.7933	0.9788
t				(1.727)		(0.732)		(10.548)	

Source: See table 3 in appendix I.

Note: Each t denotes the result (in parentheses) of a student's t-test.

The value of *IUSC* in equation 3 is small because of the short period of the available data; however, the nature of this variable is similar to that of *USIC* in equations 1 and 2. *RELP* is significant

in equation 3 at the 0.01 level also. The R ratio in equation 3 (on the fifth line) is the highest. Thus model III shows that Japan's raw silk exports were influenced greatly by the level of U.S. consumption and the ratio between unit silk prices and U.S. rayon output. Of the three models, model III best explains the fall in raw silk exports.

Judged on high ratios, *USIC, IUSRP,* and *RELP* largely explain the change in *IMPT* over the subject period. Among the tested factors, the U.S. per capita income level (and the level of consumption) and the rayon output level explain well the fall in the value of Japanese raw silk exports to the United States.

IWSP is not significant in all three equations: Increasing world silk production did not much affect the fall in sales of Japanese raw silk in the U.S. market.

The inclusion of IPR, the price of rayon, in equation 2 only raised the value of the residual. Thus we discarded this variable.

To sum up: The fall in Japanese raw silk exports to the United States after 1930 was not directly influenced by the anti-Japanese boycott movement in the early 1930s. An increased volume of imports of Japanese raw silk in the U.S. market and an increase in Japan's share of this item in the U.S. import market prove this. The fall in raw silk exports was primarily accounted for by a lowered U.S. income level and the growth of rayon as a silk substitute in the United States.

4. U.S. Tariffs on Manufactured Japanese Products

In the previous section we concluded that no effective discriminatory pressures existed against Japanese silk imports in the United States, but this only applies to imports of Japanese silk. Besides raw silk, the rest of Japan's exports to the United States did not expand enough to make up even partially for the fall in silk earnings over the period of this survey. This was a conspicuous feature of Japanese export performance of the U.S. market in contrast to the strong recovery of Japanese exports in the world market during the 1934–37 period from the 1932 level, as shown in table 1.2.

Exports excluding silk comprised 17 to 18 percent of total Japanese exports to the United States during the 1926–35 period. Nonsilk exports included china/porcelain, stoneware, straw-hat materials, tuna, menthol, and decorative articles and sundries (as listed in order of value in 1926). Except for tuna, these exports consisted of miscellaneous goods, and most were produced in extremely labor-intensive, small-scale cottage industries in Japan.

The U.S. tariff system relevant to Japanese nonsilk exports
Until 1923, the U.S. tariff system had adhered to a *conditional* most-favored-nation (MFN) policy for 144 years. This policy had been discriminatory against third countries because it limited the reciprocal benefits reached under the agreement to the two nations involved, prohibiting their extension to a third party. Even though retaining a conditional MFN, U.S. tariff policy for most of its history had been generally nondiscriminatory in practice.[1] But this nondiscriminatory principle had some exceptions.

A few are relevant to our subject and were still in effect in the 1930s. These were penalty duties and contingent duties provided by the Tariff Acts of 1890, 1897, and 1909.[2]

Penalty duties were more inexcusable than the conditional MFN from the viewpoint of U.S. nondiscriminatory practices. This was a striking measure because penalty duties were to be applied to the exports of offending countries. Furthermore, in 1909 a double-column tariff was enacted—for example, a specific duty in the first column plus an antidumping duty in the second—which marked the first departure from the historic U.S. single-column practice based on the nondiscrimination principle. Despite maintaining the conditional MFN, the United States single-column tariff by this time did not discriminate against the products of other countries, except for a few situations when reciprocity agreements were concluded. The penalty and double-column tariffs were levied on some Japanese products, notably on electric lamps, in the 1934–37 period, which will be shown in the subsection on ad valorem incidence of U.S. specific duty on Japanese products, below in table 3.6.

The U.S. Tariff Act of 1922, known as the Fordney-McCumber Tariff, raised U.S. tariffs to a high and protective level. The lack of any provision in the 1922 act for reciprocity agreements also led to a major deviation from the principle of tariff negotiability. The nonexistence of reciprocal agreement measures was due to the following U.S. understandings: Negotiations of agreements on tariffs were preferential in nature, and they conflicted with the nondiscrimination principle. Finally, Section 315 of the act provided measures to equalize foreign and domestic production costs.[3]

The United States considered that tariffs were a domestic problem and should be of no concern to foreigners. "The prosperity of the United States economy is attributable to the tariffs that thereby protect the domestic market for American products" was stated in an address by President Calvin Coolidge, justifying the U.S. tariff policy at that time.[4]

Section 317 of the Tariff Act of 1922 authorized the president to impose penalty duties of up to 50 percent ad valorem on any product of any country discriminating against the United States. The original purpose of this section was to obtain nondiscriminatory treatment for U.S. exports by threat of penalty duties.

In 1923, the United States adopted a policy of unconditional MFN customs treatment, which established the basis for U.S. commercial policy in the ensuing three decades. But the policy was not applied equally to all countries at that time. By 1933, the United States had *un*conditional MFN pledges from 29 countries. However, it still retained a conditional MFN policy with 15 others, and Japan was one of them.[5]

The Hawley–Smoot Tariff Act of 1930 reinforced the high and protective nature of the U.S. tariff system. Any provisions to make reciprocity agreements were still absent in this act, and the very heights of the tariffs were in many instances redundant. Protected by previous tariff acts, 96 percent of U.S. consumption of manufactured goods was produced domestically by that time, and agricultural products were already covered under the 1922 act.[6] The advocates of the 1930 act emphasized that the United States needed to improve its trade balance and employment. This goal was not fulfilled because implementation of the act produced a much heavier fall in exports than in imports resulting from foreign repercussions. U.S. exports were severely curtailed just when the economy most needed their earnings. U.S. trade declined to nearly a third, and the U.S. share fell in the world market, thereby inducing a great fall in the size of world trade and finally sending the world economy into a depressionary spiral. Thus the strong protectionist nature of the Hawley–Smoot Act and its far-spreading deep effect on the world market contributed to transforming and worsening the U.S. recession into the Great Depression that followed. As the United States withdrew into its own domestic markets, so did countries around the world.

Before 1930, U.S. tariffs were conspicuously high for most competitive Japanese manufactured products.[7] The U.S. progressive tariff system was structured according to the degree of product processing, embodying a high degree of tariff escalation. This also generated heavier tariffs on Japanese products, since most

Japanese manufactured exports depended greatly on the processing of imported raw materials. The tariff act of 1930 raised many
rates further. This act also imposed specific duties levied as a fixed
amount of money per unit of the subject goods, that is, cents per
unit. They were increased after 1933 when the dollar prices of
Japanese goods fell. I have converted the rates into ad valorem
incidences (meaning ad valorem tariff rates) in the next section,
in table 3.6. In this sense, specific duties protected the U.S. market
against the effect of yen depreciation.

U.S. tariff policy toward Japan under the New Deal

In the New Deal policies undertaken by the Franklin D. Roosevelt
administration, foreign trade policy dispalyed a dual nature.
Secretary of State Cordell Hull had been on the side of tariff
reduction. When he served as the U.S. delegate at the London
Conference and at the Seven American Countries International
Conference in Montevideo in 1933, the U.S. government affirmed
its resolution to work toward a reduction of tariffs and the
removal of quantitative restrictions via international agreements.
All these agreements were to include unconditional MFN clauses.

By embarking on the New Deal program, the Roosevelt administration made an all-out effort to extricate the U.S. economy
from the depression. A reduction in tariffs was consistent with the
New Deal to alleviate the malaise caused by the Hawley-Smoot
Act. However, the National Industrial Recovery Act (NIRA) and
the Agricultural Adjustment Act (AAA) enacted in the New Deal
were designed with domestic economic recovery as the highest
priority. Through these two acts, the U.S. government determined
to support domestic industries by raising the domestic prices of
industrial and agricultural products. The government then authorized the imposition of higher tariffs and quantitative restrictions on imports if they interfered with these domestic recovery
programs. It was said that the Roosevelt administration, for its
political stability, needed to mitigate increasing congressional
opposition to the New Deal, especially to Secretary Hull's tariff
reduction program.

Consequently, the government compromised on its original trade objectives of a reduction in tariffs and a removal of quantity restrictions, with a selective increase in tariff rates for some products when their importation interfered with a domestic recovery program by the NIRA and the AAA. The Roosevelt administration decided that the U.S. government was able to selectively raise tariffs to a prohibitive level if this would serve the depressed domestic economy, instead of stimulating foreign trade.

The Trade Agreements Act of 1934 laid down the following three principal features of U.S. commercial policy:

1. The retention of the unconditional MFN policy, which had started in 1923. However, the United States kept a conditional MFN with Japan during the period covered by this study.
2. The prohibition of quantitative restrictions.
3. The negotiability of high U.S. tariffs.

The retention of the unconditional MFN policy (except for 15 countries, including Japan) determined the selective character of the negotiating procedure. This dictated that most negotiations had to be on a bilateral, reciprocal basis because of the impractical complexity of negotiating product-by-product on a multilateral basis at that time.[8] The products, the subject of trade agreement concessions, were exempted from the "flexible" cost-equalization provisions (Section 336) of the 1930 trade act.

The United States made efforts to stimulate its exports through negotiations of agreements for the mutual lowering of trade barriers. Through bilateral and multilateral negotiations after 1934, tariffs were sizably reduced. Tariff reductions made under these agreements were to be generalized to third countries.[9] However, an extension of the reduction of tariffs to third countries was possible only if they had an *un*conditional MFN clause with the United States. But Japan had none.

The 1934 Trade Agreements Act also delegated to the president the power to change duties in trade agreements with foreign countries. Thus a great power to discriminate against any country belonged to the president and to the tariff lawmakers in Congress.

None of these improvements in U.S. tariffs, however, was real-ized for Japanese products at that time. Contrary to Secretary Hull's tariff reduction program, after 1933 the tariff policy on Japanese products was tightened. Washington directly acted after March 1933 to impose new import restrictions on several goods of which Japanese shipments to the United States had been rapidly growing. Under the "flexible" cost-equalization clause (Section 336) of the 1930 tariff act, duties were raised on tuna packed in oil, canned clams, frozen swordfish, and wool knit gloves valued at not more than $1.75 per dozen pairs. Fees were levied on vari-ous types of imported cotton rugs under section 3 (e) of the NIRA. Shipments of cotton rugs and wooden lead pencils were limited by agreement with Japan, specifying maximum amounts.[10] The U.S. reasoning for these actions had a stronger coloring of an overall scenario of anti-Japanese boycotts than may initially be imagined.

With Japan, the United States maintained a conditional MFN policy. Therefore, neither tariff reduction nor escape from the "flexible" cost-equalization provision was possible for Japanese products unless Japan concluded a reciprocal tariff concession agreement with the United States. In short, the protective side of the inconsistent trade policy during the New Deal worked against Japan. The strong pressures laid on the importation of Japanese manufactured goods could possibly be interpreted as repercus-sions to Secretary Hull's trade policy. Tariff reductions were not always totally welcomed by persons who shortsightedly sought only the recovery of the domestic economy. The Roosevelt admin-istration had responded to the criticisms of groups dissatisfied with the policies of lowering tariffs in foreign trade and the New Deal in general. But why were these reactions against tariff reduc-tions directed primarily at Japanese trade?

What were the underlying reasons for these U.S. policies toward Japan's trade? The first one that comes to mind that may have influenced them was Japan's small share in the U.S. export mar-ket. During the 1926–37 period, Japan imported only about 3 percent of the total value of U.S. exports to the world, which constituted 33 percent of the total Japanese import value. Thus the United States was the most important trading partner for Japan, but Japan occupied an unimportant portion of U.S. exports. The importance of trade with the United States was not only in the total trade value, but also in the effect on its own economy; Japan was unable to substitute any other country for the United States in purchasing such goods as finer staple raw cotton and high-quality machinery. In short, if the United States wanted, it could ignore Japan in trade policy considerations, but the reverse was not true. Furthermore, trade with Japan from the U.S. viewpoint could be ignored without imposing any hardship because Japan's trade share was small.

The United States did however conclude concessional tariff agreements with other low-economy countries that were not its eminent trading partners. Therefore the hypothesis that the United States regarded small countries as not important enough to conclude trade agreements does not conform to the reality, and we should look for another reason. The question still remains why the United States imposed trade restrictions which specifically affected Japanese commodities imported in increasing quantities.

Japanese products became the selective targets of an increase in tariffs among the general stream of reduction. This came about because of a few conceivable reasons. Firstly, the U.S. government knew that Japan was unable to shift the purchase of industrial goods from the United States to other countries, although Japan represented a small 3 percent of U.S. trade. Secondly, the Roosevelt administration demonstrated its political and economic power in trade and was not blindly reducing tariffs for every foreign product. Thirdly, imports of the above-quoted Japanese goods had rapidly grown, and the phenomenon was conspicuous. The quick growth of imports was concentrated in a few items. The showering type of concentrated export growth caused damage to specific U.S. producers, who strongly protested. Japan was only a backward country that had started to challenge the West economically for the first time in the history of the world. And finally, it was the common understanding then that Japan had invaded China. Did the influence of the Chinese appeal to the president of the United States and Congress to impose economic sanctions on Japan continue on to the decision to levy higher tariffs on selected Japanese goods at this time, although the idea was formally rejected by the U.S. government in 1931?

Ad valorem incidence of U.S. specific duty on Japanese products
I have made an attempt to weigh rates of U.S. tariffs for selected Japanese manufactured products. The tabulations in table 3.6 compare rates of U.S. tariffs on Japanese goods and changes of Japan's relative importance in the U.S. market in 1934 and 1937. It would have been preferable if the same kind of comparison were possible for earlier years, but the improved methods of compiling statistical data of the U.S. government started only after 1934.

U.S. statistics have two kinds of tariffs: ad valorem and specific. The rate of tariffs of *ad valorem duty* is expressed as a percentage of the value of the commodity. *Specific duty,* as mentioned before, is levied as a fixed amount (by cents) per unit of commodity. A specific duty is very often accompanied by an ad valorem duty, to be called a *compound duty.* For example, the compound duty for Japanese special eyeglasses valued at not more than 65 cents a dozen (item number 9145 in 1934) was 20 cents a dozen (specific duty) plus 15 percent (ad valorem duty), as shown in table 3.6. Japan had a 100 percent market share of this item in 1934. Many Japanese nonsilk exports to the United States during the period of our survey were miscellaneous manufactured products. Specific duties were levied on most of these goods.

To measure the weight of specific duty on selected goods imported from Japan, I converted the specific and compound duties into ad valorem incidence (rate) for each of the tabulated 36 items. Item selection was made by import value of more than US$20,000 in 1934, and the method of conversion employed was as described in a U.S. government publication.[11]

The nominal rates of specific duties of selected items and their ad valorem incidences in 1934 and 1937 are listed in column 2 of table

3.6. Average ad valorem incidences that applied to all countries on an egalitarian basis on the subject item are presented in parentheses to compare with the ad valorem incidences applied to Japanese products in the same item number in column 3 of table 3.6.

The following two findings can be observed in the table:

1. When tariff rates were levied as specific duty plus ad valorem duty on each item, the nominal rates were the same for products of every country. When the specific duty rates are converted into ad valorem incidences, however, they vary by country in respect to unit value and volume of imported goods. Unit value and numbers of pieces imported are quite different, depending on the country of origin. In this sense, a country such as Japan that frequently exported cheap goods in great quantity to the United States was levied higher rates of ad valorem incidence of specific duties than those from advanced countries, such as Great Britain and Germany, which exported more expensive goods in smaller volume.

2. Japanese miscellaneous products were cheap and numerous in line with Japan's stage of economic development. In other words, Japan could compete only by offering cheap and numerous miscellaneous manufactured products in the U.S. market as an underdeveloped country rapidly catching up with the advanced countries. U.S. specific duties, though nominally fair to every country, unfavorably affected Japanese competitiveness in these cheaply priced and voluminous exports.

For example, in table 3.6, earthen crockery and stoneware (no. 5371.1, listed as item 12) was levied a specific duty of 10 cents a dozen plus 50 percent of the ad valorem duty. The ad valorem incidence of this compound duty was 65.2 percent on average for all countries in 1934, as shown in the parentheses in column 3, but for Japan it was 75.6 percent in the same year because Japan exported a great many cheap goods under the same-item category in U.S. tariff classifications. With this higher rate of compound duty, the Japanese market share of this item showed no growth and remained at 45 percent in 1934 and 44 percent in 1937 (column 4).[12]

The compound duty on combs (item 31 in the table), a value of more than $4.50 per gross (no. 9760.5), was 2 cents for each comb plus 35 percent. The ad valorem incidence of this duty in 1934 was 84.4 percent for all countries on average (in parentheses), but for Japan it was 121.1 percent in column 3. Japan's market share was 95 percent in 1934, but declined to 69 percent in 1937, as shown in column 4.

Japan was competing with Great Britain and Germany in exports of pencils (no. 978.02, item 33) to the United States, and this item was levied 50 cents per gross of goods plus 25 percent ad valorem. The ad valorem incidence was 180.6 percent for all countries, but it was 288.0 percent for Japanese commodities as shown in column 3. Mechanical pencils (no. 978.07, item 34) were levied a specific duty of 45 cents per gross plus 40 percent ad valorem; the ad valorem incidence was 58.3 percent on average, but a higher 85.6 percent for Japanese goods as shown in column 3. Japan's market share for these two kinds of pencils was 74 (Item 33) and 81 (Item 34) percent respectively in 1934, but had dropped to zero by 1937 when British and German pencils were substituted for the Japanese products, as shown in column 4.

Electric incandescent lamps (no. 7064.0, item 14), were levied double-column duties of 50 percent; a 30 percent antidumping duty was added only on Japanese products to the 20 percent ad valorem duty common for all countries in 1934. The antidumping duty was repeatedly exercised only on Japanese products in 1937. Even with these additional antidumping duties specifically applied to Japanese products, Japan's market share was unaffected and stayed at 100 percent of total U.S. imports of these lamps during the 1934–37 period. The constant application of these antidumping duties was to penalize Japan and to discourage its growing competitiveness against U.S. products, but they could not depress its import market share of the item.

Japan monopolized the U.S. market in buttons made of pearl or freshwater shell (no. 9724.0, item 28 in the table), even with a prohibitive ad valorem incidence of compound duties of 174 percent in 1934 and 159 percent in 1937. Duties were imposed on similar Japanese buttons, pearl or shell, ocean (no. 9724.1, item 29), equivalent to 135.5 percent ad valorem incidence in 1934 and 119.6 percent in 1937. The Japanese market share of this item fell to only 23 percent in 1937, as shown in column 4, from 91 percent in 1934, yielding to imports from the Philippines, which had free duty. The Philippines' share rose to 75 percent from a few percentage points during the same period, enjoying the absence of any duties in the U.S. market as shown in column 2.[13]

Several remarks can be made concerning these duties:

1. Antidumping duties in these instances were based on section 315 of the 1922 act to equalize foreign and domestic costs of production, as already mentioned. Costs of production are measurable when they are applied to a specific product and for only a limited time. Dumping in the sense of selling at a price lower than the domestic cost of production cannot last for many years because the Japanese producer would go into bankruptcy unless his profits in the domestic market were high enough to sustain his dumping losses in markets abroad. Even if dumping is interpreted as selling products cheaper abroad than in the home market, the producer would before long cease to sell abroad because it is less profitable.

2. To measure the cost of production for international comparisons, one must also consider the purchasing power parities of the United States and Japan. However, this concept implies measurement problems, which are complicated and even dubious in the depth of their theoretical meaning including index number problems.

3. In regard to electric lamps, Japanese companies did not stop exporting them, even after being levied double-column duties, because these enterprises were highly specialized in producing lamps by exploiting economies of scale to sell to the masses. One company was Matsushita Electric. It succeeded in satisfying

the demand of the masses both at home and abroad in a narrow field of electric home appliances. Later, using profits stemming from economies of scale in the original field, the company also expanded production into other fields. It grew to become the company that today is known worldwide.

4. The application of antidumping duties can seldom be found in U.S. documents during the subject years except for these Japanese instances.

5. Other findings from table 3.6:

i. Japan's market share of 16 items declined in 1937 from the 1934 levels.

ii. Of the 16 items, specific duties and ad valorem duties were levied on 11. The other 5 had only ad valorem duties, but the rates were high at 90 percent or more for rayon apparel (no. 384.09, item 8), and at 70 percent for microscopes and magnifiers (no. 915.01, item 18), for example

iii. When the ad valorem duty was less than 70 percent, Japanese exports of these items grew, as the table indicates (no. 9701.2, item 22).

iv. When specific duties (on quantity) were added to ad valorem duties, the higher the difference between the average ad valorem incidence (rates) and the real effective rates applied to Japanese commodities, the heavier the discriminatory pressures on Japanese competitiveness. These duties could be said to be discriminatory against Japan. The documents of the U.S. Department of Commerce in 1934 and 1937 did not mention discrimination against Japan's products; however, specific duties added to ad valorem duties were discriminatory against any country that exported numerous low-unit-price products. Japan was the most competitive developing country in some manufacturing fields, exporting to the United

States a great many cheap products, which fell into the same item category in U.S. tariff classifications to compete keenly against products from advanced countries (or from the duty-free Philippines). In producing these items, Japan had just caught up with the advanced countries in comparative cost advantages by producing numerous low-priced products— which probably was one unavoidable stage of economic development in an industrially backward country. In this sense, among all exporters of the above-listed manufactured products, Japan suffered most from the effective rates (ad valorem incidence) of the U.S. specific duties.

The decline in market share of these products may in some ways be a reflection of other market factors, that might include changes in American preference from cheap to better products as U.S. income levels recovered slightly in 1937. Nevertheless, the comparisons of average ad valorem incidences of specific duties applied to all countries, and those applied on Japanese products, provide a new approach, so far unexplored, for an examination of the effect of U.S. specific duties that were nominally fair for every country. The approach makes clear that the country suffering the most was Japan in regard to these export products. Besides these products, Japan was trying to expand trade in manufactured goods (other than cotton textiles) to gain foreign exchange for importation of U.S. products. By this time, the Japanese realized they could no longer rely on raw silk exports to the U.S. market to accomplish this.

In 1937 U.S. duties were high on categories in which Japanese exports were clustered. Japan's market share was 72.2 percent for total pottery (nos. 5350.1–5374.9) under a 73.5 percent average rate of duty. Japan's market share was 74 percent for silk manufactures, under a 54.5 percent average rate of duty. Japan's share for rayon and other synthetic products was 84.7 percent, and the average rate of duty was 50.0 percent.

Table 3.6 Ad valorem incidence of specific duty of U.S. imports from Japan, selected product values, tariffs, and market shares in 1934 and 1937

	1		2		3		4	
Brief description of item (Item no. in 1934)[a]	Total value ($1,000)		Tariffs (%)		Ad valorem incidence of specific duty (%) (figures in parentheses for all countries)[b]		Market share (%)	
	1934	1937	1934	1937	1934	1937	1934	1937
1. Tuna fish in oil or other substances (0065.2)	701	1,913	45				91	94
2. Rubber-soled footwear with fabric upper (2020.1)	299	202	35.2				90	93
3. Rubber balls and toys (2033.3)	262	135	70				97	95
4. Cotton floor coverings, "hit-and-miss" rugs (3225.1)	272	1,729	3¢/lb. + 51.2%		(75.0)	(75.0)	100	98
5. Rugs not wholly or chiefly made of cotton (3225.7)	91	887	5¢/sq. yd. + 35%		(71.0)	(35.0)	100	83
6. Silk manufactured, woven, not jacquard (3710)	490	745	55				49	93
7. Silk handkerchiefs, hemmed (3762)	160	479	60				71	81
8. Manufactured rayon wearing apparel, embroidered (384.09)	307	848[c]	90				98	98
9. Straw hat materials (3900.2)	833	1,116	45				87	89
10. China & porcelain, vitrified and nonabsorbent, decorated (5350.2)	2,004	2,770	10¢/doz. + 70%		94.1 (88.1)[b]	89.0 (84.8)	68	67
11. Earthenware: articles & items other than sanitary wares, decorated (5360.2)	586	518	70				74	44

Brief description of item (Item no. in 1934)[a]	Total value ($1,000)		Tariffs (%)		Ad valorem incidence of specific duty (%) (figures in parentheses for all countries)[b]		Market share (%)	
	1934	1937	1934	1937	1934	1937	1934	1937
12. Earthen crockery & stoneware, nonvitrified, decorated (5371.1)	1,042	1,189[d]	10¢/doz. + 50%		75.6 (65.2)	78.9 (66.4)	45	44
13. Earthenware, other (5373)	354	484	10¢/doz. + 50%		(64.4)	(63.5)	58	46
14. Electric lamps, incandescent, metal (7064.0)	352	536	50% for Japan with 30% antidumping duty[e] (20% for common)				100	100
15. Electric lamps, metal filament & other (7064.2)	479	369	20				99	99
16. Menthol, natural (8127.0)	797	980[f]	5¢ lb.		25.0	21.3	94	100
17. Special eyeglasses not valued over 65 cents per dozen (9145)	79	145	20¢/doz. + 15%		70.3	83.5	100	100
18. Microscopes, magnifiers, reading glasses, and loupes (915.01)	113	54	70				84	68
19. Mechanical toys (941.20)	72	404	70				80	88
20. Toys & parts of cellulose compounds having movable parts (941.70)	97	268	1¢ each + 60%		101.9	98.0	100	100
21. Toys and parts of china and porcelain (941.80)	277	172	70				100	96
22. Beads & beaded ornaments (9701.2)	54	147	60				92	97

(continued)

Table 3.6—*Continued*

112

Brief description of item (Item no. in 1934)[a]	Total value ($1,000)		Tariffs (%)		Ad valorem incidence of specific duty (%) (figures in parentheses for all countries)[b]		Market share (%)	
	1934	1937	1934	1937	1934	1937	1934	1937
23. Toothbrushes having handles or backs of cellulose compound (9710.0)	253	279	2¢ each + 50%		132.6	127.0	98	99
24. Toothbrushes not having backs or handles of cellulose (9710.1)	92	145	1¢ each + 50%		101.4 (92.8)	97.5 (92.5)	80	87
25. Hairbrushes (9714.1)	44	95	1¢ each + 50%		65.0 (61.9)	66.7 (63.4)	77	76
26. Other toilet brushes having backs or handles of cellulose compound (9714.2)	41	29	2¢ each + 50%		105.4	(113.7)	100	92
27. Handles or backs of brushes of cellulose compound for toothbrushes (9714.4)	36	73	1¢ each + 50%		146.1	155.5	100	100
28. Buttons, pearl or shell, freshwater[g] (9724.0)	1	52	1 3/4¢ line per gross + 25%		174.0	159.0	100	100
29. Buttons, pearl or shell, ocean[h] (9724.1)	62	87	1 3/4¢ line per gross + 25% (duty free for the Philippines)		135.5 (130.7)	119.6 (116.5)	91	23
30. Combs, except wholly metal or rubber not specifically provided for (9760.0)	264	170	1¢ each + 25%		88.8	83.5	99	99
31. Combs, value $4.50 per gross (9760.5)	20	9	2¢ each + 35%		121.1 (84.4)	80.0 (70.6)	95	69

Brief description of item (Item no. in 1934)[a]	1 Total value ($1,000)		2 Tariffs (%)		3 Ad valorem incidence of specific duty (%) (figures in parentheses for all countries)[b]		4 Market share (%)	
	1934	1937	1934	1937	1934	1937	1934	1937
32. Matches having stained, dyed, or colored stems (9765.0)	222	2		40			67	91
33. Pencils, stamped other than manufacturer's name or trademark (978.02)	25		050¢/gross + 25%288.0		(180.6)	74	0	
34. Other, mechanical pencils (978.07)	73		045¢/gross + 40%85.6		(58.3)	81	0	
35. Pipes & smoker's articles not specifically provided for (9800.9)	241	233		40 (for 1934)	60 (for 1937)		71	68
36. Umbrellas (9820.0)	53	82		40			76	99

Source: U.S. Dept. of Commerce, Foreign Commerce and Navigation of the United States (Washington: U.S. Dept. of Commerce, 1934 and 1937).

Notes:
a. Some item numbers are different in 1934 and 1937.
b. Figures in parentheses are ad valorem incidences of specific duty for all countries, and those without parentheses are for Japan's products. For the conversion of specific and compound rates to ad valorem incidences of specific duty, see Conversion of Specific and Compound Rates of Duty to Ad Valorem Rates—Report to the President on Investigation No. 332–99 Under Section 332 of the Tariff Act of 1930, as Amended, 896 (Washington: USITC, July 1978), 20436. Item no. 10.
c. 384.18, U.S. Dept. of Commerce, Foreign Commerce and Navigation of the United States (Washington: U.S. Dept. of Commerce, 1937), Item no. 8.
d. Ibid., 190. Item no. 12.
e. Antidumping duty (3,416). Item no. 14. Common 20 percent duty plus antidumping 30 percent (3,416) duty, 50 percent (20 + 30 = 50) for Japanese lamps.
f. 8127.1, Ibid., 156. Item no. 16.
g. The same products from the Philippines were duty-free; therefore a total of $235,000 worth of these products was imported from there in 1937 and none from Japan. Item no. 28.
h. Buttons of pearl or shell, freshwater (9724.0), comprised Japan's monopoly in the market. But for similar articles from the ocean (9724.1), the United States imported $87,400 worth from Japan (23% of total imports) at 1.75 cent line per gross + 25% (ad valorem incidence of 116.5%), versus those from the Philippine's, $284,839 worth (75%) with free duty, in 1937. U.S. Dept. of Commerce, Foreign Commerce and Navigation of the United States (Washington: U.S. Dept. of Commerce, 1937), 286. Item no. 29.

Japanese cotton textiles in the United States

By 1931, Japan had become the best customer for U.S. raw cotton, but for U.S. cotton exporters, this meant only a shift of the best buyer from the United Kingdom to Japan.

Japanese cotton manufacturers expanded sales worldwide in 1932, and the market in the United States was no exception. Most trade friction occurred over imports of certain types of Japanese cotton cloth, which competed with American products at a lower price. U.S. imports of Japanese cloth grew from 1 million square yards in 1933 to some 7.3 million in 1934, to 36.4 million in 1935, and to 75 million in 1936.[14] The corresponding value rose to $1.7 million in 1936, from some $363,000 in 1934. The higher value of cotton product exports was, however, a minimal contribution to Japan's total trade with the United States in terms of balancing the drastic fall of silk export earnings in the same period.

The share of Japanese cotton products in the U.S. domestic market was only a negligible fraction of the total U.S. cotton product output. But the U.S. cotton textile industry could not tolerate even this small invasion. A special cabinet committee appointed by the U.S. president to investigate the cotton textile industry recommended the negotiation of an informal quota with Japanese textile manufacturers. "Voluntary" limitations on exports, a device created by the Japanese, were imposed by the Japanese industry in 1935.[15] Voluntary export restrictions (VERs) on Japanese cotton cloth were repeated often thereafter throughout the latter half of the 1930s. The VER was rediscovered and pushed by the United States later in the mid-1950s and quickly became widespread among Japanese trading partners in the West. The application of VERs—for example, the "quota" system used for Japanese automobiles—continued untill March 1994.[16]

Dissatisfied with the VER mechanism, the American textile industry sent a mission to Tokyo and concluded a quota agreement with Japanese manufacturers toward the end of 1936. The quota for 1937 was 155 million square yards with the condition that it would be reduced to 100 million for 1938.

In 1937, U.S. imports of Japanese cotton cloth were only 0.4 percent of total cotton cloth import value.[17] Japanese cotton cloth (no. 304.000 in 1937), unbleached, not containing silk, rayon, or other synthetic textiles with average count number not exceeding 10, was levied a specific duty of 5.5 cents a pound, which was equivalent to a rate of 32.1 percent, compared with an ad valorem duty of 13.5 percent for the same item imported from the United Kingdom and Czechoslovakia.[18] Japanese shipments of this item were again characterized by a huge quantity relative to the total value compared with U.K. products. This was because the unit price of British cloth was 13 times higher than the price of Japanese cloth. In other words, the Japanese quantity of this item was 31 times more than that of U.K. products, but the total value was only about 4 times the value of the United Kingdom's cloth.[19] Japanese cotton cloth of the same item number, but with average count number not exceeding 32, was levied a specific duty of 17.6 percent a pound, which was equivalent to 62.0 percent of ad valorem duty; the effective rate for the same U.K. products was equivalent to 25.0 percent. This was analogous to the situation in the effective rates of U.S. tariffs on Japanese manufactured products discussed earlier, when a large quantity of Japanese products with a cheap unit value was imported to the United States.[20]

By 1933, many countries had changed their trade policies to the bilateral trade equalization scheme (discussed in the following chapters). Each of the raw-cotton-producing countries demanded that Japan buy more raw cotton from them to meet their purchases of cotton products from Japan; otherwise they would reduce the amount of their purchases. Under this scheme, Japan was compelled to import raw cotton from such countries as India, Brazil, and Egypt regardless of its quality, because these were substantial customers for Japanese cotton products.

A downhill trend in the Japanese cotton textile industry in quality and quantity became inevitable, but this was not yet apparent. In 1937, with stored good-quality U.S. raw cotton, Japanese cotton yarn production reached a prewar peak, 1,586 million pounds.[21] It fell precipitately thereafter as low-quality raw cotton began to enter Japan from several developing countries.

The case of the Philippines

One problem faced by U.S. cotton textile manufacturers was Japan's invasion of U.S. third-country markets, which had been good customers. However, cotton textiles represented only a small portion of U.S. exports, 1.9 percent of the total in 1936.

Exports of U.S. cotton cloth to the Philippines declined from an average of 540 million square yards in the 1925–27 period to 226 million in 1934 and 187 million in 1935, most likely because of Japanese competition.[22] Japanese exports of cotton cloth to the Philippines expanded rapidly after 1932. Japan's supplying of cotton piece goods in 1935 also rose to some 58 percent of the Philippine market and the U.S. share dropped to 38 percent, from 57 percent in the years 1930–33.

An agreement for "voluntary" export restrictions to the Philippines was concluded between Japan and the United States in early August 1935. It limited Japanese exports to 45 million square meters annually for two years thereafter, with the elimination of a threatened increase of Philippine duties on the commodity. Japanese exports of cotton piece goods were given 42 percent of the Philippine market at its 1931–34 level. Thus the U.S. State Department defended the Philippine market, which was considered to rightfully belong to U.S. producers.

Chapter 4

BRITISH COMMONWEALTH DISCRIMINATION AGAINST JAPANESE TRADE

British Embassy.

Tokyo.

No. 18 (1/95/33)   *Dictated by H.G.*   10th January, 1933.

TYPED

SENT

Sir,

Mr. Fitzmaurice, His Majesty's Consul-
General at Batavia, was recently kind enough to send
to this Embassy an extract from a Confidential Report
on political events in the Netherlands East Indies which
he had furnished to the Foreign Office. This Report
raises questions of both political and commercial
importance which have long engaged the attention of
this Embassy; and I accordingly requested Mr. Sansom,
Commercial Counsellor, to make some comments on the
matters dealt with.

2.   I have the honour to transmit herewith
copy of a Memorandum drawn up by Mr. Sansom which
merits careful study. I would especially draw your
attention to the erroneous impression which still
prevails, that the danger of Japanese competition to
British trade lies in such artificial methods as
subsidies and dumping. If this were the case, we
should have much less to fear than we have.

3.   A copy of this despatch and its enclosure
has been sent to His Majesty's Consul-General at Bat

I have the honour to be,
With the highest respect,
Sir,
Your most obedient,
humble Servant,

The Right Honourable
Sir John Simon, G.C.S.I., K.C.V.O.,
etc., etc., etc.

A 1933 letter from the British Embassy in Tokyo, found by the author in the British Public Record Office in Richmond, noting that the Japanese threat to British trade did not lie in Japanese subsidies or dumping.

1. Historical Background

Great Britain imposed a heavy strain on world trade by concluding the Imperial Preference Agreements with its Commonwealth dominions and colonies at the Ottawa Conference in 1932. Britain hoped that the change would (1) improve its balance of payments through a stronger bargaining power of the British Empire, and (2) thus increase employment in the depressed economy. The British economy suffered from problems as consequences of two reforms in the monetary system: a deep deflation caused by a readoption of the gold standard in 1925 and inflationary pressures after the 1931 devaluation.[1] Conclusion of the Imperial Preferential Agreements marked a turning point in world trade, from laissez-faire policies to protectionist policies.

In 1933, Japan's leading export industry shifted to cotton textiles from silk; the contribution of the former became 24 percent of total trade earnings, outstripping the 21 percent of the latter. This was a change of Japan's export-leading sector to a manufactured product, cotton textiles, from a primary product, raw silk. Japan's cotton textile exports also reached the world's highest volume that year, surpassing Great Britain's, the former world leader.[2] Among Japanese cotton textiles, the largest foreign exchange earner was cotton cloth. Its export volume in 1933 reached 2,090 million square yards, the world's largest that year. Because of the achievements of Japanese exports, acute trade conflicts ensued between Japan and Britain, especially in Commonwealth markets where strong discriminatory pressures on Japan's trade were being openly imposed.

2. THE JAPAN-CANADA TARIFF WAR

Canada had acquired tariff autonomy through the 1846 Enabling Act of the United Kingdom. The Japanese-Canadian trade relationship was opened with the conclusion of the Japan-Canada Commerce Treaty of 1906, at which time Japan had still not recovered its tariff autonomy. Japan finally did recover it by means of the Japan-United Kingdom Commerce and Navigation Treaty in 1911, which regulated Japan-Canada economic relationships that had been under the 1906 Treaty. The 1911 treaty in general had more detailed regulations than the Japan-U.S. Commerce and Navigation Treaty. The most significant difference was exemplified in the detailed regulations of the 1911 treaty, which did not permit Canada to establish any racial discriminatory measures, such as those in the 1924 Immigration Act of the United States.

Canadian trade policy from the 1910s to the 1930s had three features. First, it was generally amicable and aimed at trade expansion. Second, it seemed to oscillate between two opposite directions: free trade under Liberal Party governments and protectionism under Conservative Party governments. These oscillations in policy straightforwardly influenced revisions of the tariff system. Third, major tariff reforms after the late 1920s were targeted to favor the mother country and the Commonwealth areas over the United States (until 1935) and the rest of the world.

Canada's dependence on trade with the British Commonwealth and the United States together had never been lower than 87 percent of total imports and 78 percent of total exports from 1913 through 1937. Other countries' shares of the total were the remaining 13 percent in imports and 22 percent in exports. The Japanese-Canadian trade relationship belonged to these relatively small shares of 13 to 22 percent of Canadian trade worldwide.

Japan shared only 0.4 percent in Canadian imports and the same in exports from 1913 to 1925.[1]

After World War I, Canadian trade growth was rapid, expanding to 240 percent by 1929 over the 1919 level because of large-scale access to British Commonwealth and U.S. markets. The growth of Canadian trade was the second highest in the world, trailing only Japan's, which reached 440 percent during the same period.[2] Canada's exports to Japan accounted for only 2.7 percent at most of its total exports.

Canadian trade policies and Japanese exports up to 1929

Japan, having most-favored-nation treatment, maintained a friendly relationship with Canada until 1929. On conclusion of a reciprocal agreement, the Canada-France Treaty, in 1922, Canada extended the beneficial tariff reductions stemming from this treaty to include Japanese products. Five other countries, including Italy, Belgium, and Holland, received similar treatment.

Canadian tariffs thus became generously lower for major Japanese exports: raw silk, silk textiles, china and porcelain, and tea. The tariff rates for Japanese goods were at special agreement rates and lower than the medium-level tariffs applied to non-Commonwealth areas, including the United States. For instance, Canadian tariffs on Japanese silk fabrics were lower than those levied on American silk fabrics, inducing a strong competitiveness of Japanese silk fabrics versus American products in the Canadian market. This low competitiveness of the United States was due to the use of imported Japanese raw silk for American silk fabrics exported to Canada.

In 1926, the Liberal Party government in Canada lowered general tariffs that had been raised after World War I. The purpose was to strengthen the Imperial ties to Britain. Imperial privilege in tariff policies could be strengthened in two ways: One was to lower the tariffs for Britain and the Commonwealth, and the other was to raise tariffs for the rest of the world. Favoring freer trade for expansion, the Canadian government at this time lowered general rates for 46 items, medium rates for 98, and Imperial preferential rates for 270. It raised general rates for 54 items, medium rates for 35, and preferential rates for only 11. The same Liberal government again lowered tariffs in May 1930 for a very short period. The Liberals, however, lost cabinet positions in the election, and the new government replaced the free trade policy with a protectionist policy.

Major Japanese imports from Canada that increased until 1926 were wheat, flour, dried fish, and foodstuffs, besides such industrial materials as wood pulp, lead, and lumber. From 1919 to 1926, Japanese trade with Canada expanded to $11.6 million in exports, from $2.4 million, and to $30 million in imports, from $380,000. Japanese exports to Canada grew constantly until 1929.

Among Japanese trade partners, Canada absorbed only one percent of total Japanese export value to the world in 1926, even with these rapidly expanded figures. The Canadian share in Japanese exports was small, but it was sharply reduced to only 0.3 percent in the 1932–35 period. The fall in Canada's share in Japanese exports after 1930 was due to the trade rivalry of the two countries.[3] This fall stands out against the trend of growing Japanese exports elsewhere. Japanese exports to Canada recovered somewhat, to 0.6 percent, in 1937 after the improvement in commercial relations between the two countries.

Canadian tariffs on Japanese goods during the 1930–36 period
In 1929, the United States absorbed 46 percent of total Canadian exports. British Commonwealth areas, including the mother country, absorbed 34 percent. In the same year, Canada's trade balance turned to a deficit from annual surpluses during the previous 16 years. In 1930, the U.S. absorption of Canadian goods fell dramatically, to only 30 percent (60 percent in 1928) of total Canadian exports; this drop widened the trade gap, which gravely affected the Canadian economy. The large Canadian trade deficit was in the main caused by the U.S. Hawley-Smoot Tariff, which imposed high tariffs on major Canadian exports, especially agricultural goods. The Canadian government immediately retaliated

by imposing high tariffs on American imports. The Canadian Liberal Party lost the general election in August 1930, and repercussions of prohibitive tariffs on the trade of both countries were accelerated by the spread of the Great Depression. The result was a further shrinkage in the size of trade between the United States and Canada. But the influence of the Hawley-Smoot Tariff on trade did not stay within the relationship of the two countries. The damage in trade with the United States pushed Canada further to favor the Imperial alliance, to embark on strict import measures and protectionism. This change in trade direction adversely affected Japanese exports to Canada from 1930 onward.

Imperial preferential treatment for British Commonwealth areas
In September 1930, the new Canadian Conservative government embarked on new trade policies to mitigate trade difficulties. This time it took up protectionist measures to widen the margin of the Imperial Preference; it raised tariffs on more than 130 items that originated outside the British Empire, thus according further preferential treatment for the Commonwealth countries. Many Japanese products not included in the 1922 French-Canadian reciprocal agreement were subject to these upward revisions.

At the tariff revision in September 1930, Canada revised regulations for two reasons: (1) to prevent the dumping of imports and (2) to secure the right to preclude at any time the importation of goods from nonmember countries of the League of Nations. The purpose as explained was to control imports from Germany and the U.S.S.R.[4] To further meet these politico-economic objectives, in November 1930, after the London Conference, the Canadian government again raised tariffs for some 630 non-British articles; thus the general level of tariffs was raised. It further implemented a new tariff act to change regulations on the following three major points:

1. Ad valorem duties for foreign products regarded as "identical" to Canadian products.

2. Dumping duties to widen the margin of the Imperial privilege. The application of dumping duties henceforth had significant effects on Japanese exports, as detailed below.

3. An arrangement to reduce preferential rates at any time by Imperial Order.[5]

These tariff reforms became effective in July 1931, and the changes were difficult for non-Commonwealth countries, especially Japan. After the Imperial Economic Conference held at Ottawa in 1932, Canada raised general tariffs on 225 articles and medium rates on 80 articles (all non-British products); leading Japanese exports became the subject of this upward revision. Under the agreement, Canada extended similar preferential treatment for 30 to 60 articles in 1932 to dominions and other areas of the British Commonwealth, notably Australia, New Zealand, and the Union of South Africa.[6]

In response to the Japanese government's complaint, the Canadian government stated that the application of Imperial preferential treatment for Commonwealth countries did not conflict with the most-favored-nation (MFN) clause concluded in the Japan-United Kingdom Commerce and Navigation Treaty and the Japan-Canada Commerce Treaty.

The 1931 Canadian tariff reforms and Japan
Several of the 1931 Canadian tariff reforms had an impact on trade with Japan.

1. *Canada's official rate of foreign exchange for Japanese currency:* The Canadian government legislated a new act to adopt a special tariff system to levy ad valorem tariffs based not on world market prices at prevailing foreign exchange rates, but on prices converted at Canada's officially fixed exchange rates. The new regulation stated that if the value of foreign exchange of the exporting country fell more than 5 percent over the fall in the value of the Canadian currency vis-à-vis the U.S. dollar, the

Canadian government could set its own foreign exchange rates for the currency of that country. When Japan left the gold standard system in December 1931, Canada immediately fixed the value of the yen at the level of the old gold parity, 100 yen equaling C$49.85.

The purpose of this official exchange rate was to apply a higher ad valorem duty. The Canadian customs values of Japanese goods that were converted at this official (artificial) exchange rate became much higher than their transaction values. Meanwhile, the prevailing worldwide value of the Japanese currency was declining very rapidly. It fell on the one-year average as follows: 100 yen was valued at C$28.12 in 1932, C$25.227 in 1933, and C$29.511 in 1934.[7] In comparison, in 1932 the customs value was 64 percent higher on average than the transaction value of the same Japanese goods; it was 81 percent higher on average in 1933 and 71 percent higher in 1934. Excluding freight and insurance costs for shipment, an average Canadian customs valuation of Japanese products was roughly 72 percent higher than the transaction price during the 1932–34 period.

It was on these extremely high customs valuations of Japanese goods that the Canadian government levied ad valorem duties. Therefore the effective rates of ad valorem tariffs on Japanese goods were artificially increased, but nominal ad valorem rates were the same for Japan as for every other country. Furthermore, the general tariff rate also was raised. The higher the value of customs valuation, the higher the effective rate of ad valorem duty. The effective rates of consumption and other domestic taxes, charged after customs duties, rose to much higher levels than what would have been levied on the original transaction value.[8] The effect of the depreciation of the Japanese currency from 1932 was more than offset by this measure. Further, the margin between the Canadian official exchange rate at gold parity and the current value of the Japanese currency was imposed as a *foreign exchange dumping duty* on Japanese goods, as examined below.

Moreover, Canada implemented another dumping duty under the 1931 reform, a special official Canadian *price-dumping duty* based on Canada's customs valuation at the highly appreciated value of the yen. The artificial customs valuation at the gold parity for Japanese goods lasted from the end of 1931 through the beginning of 1936.

By 1934, the value of the Japanese yen had fallen to 35.6 percent and of the Canadian dollar to 60.2 percent from the levels of their old gold parities. By March 1935, eighteen countries depreciated their currencies more than 5 percent lower than the fall in the Canadian currency vis-à-vis gold.[9] However, Canada applied the foreign exchange dumping duties on the products of only six countries. Besides Japan, they were Finland, Denmark, Switzerland, Norway, and Spain. The aggregate value of exports of these five countries to Canada was smaller than Japan's in 1932.

2. *A foreign exchange dumping duty (foreign exchange equalization surtax):* A foreign exchange dumping duty was added to the newly increased ad valorem duty for the products of countries judged as depreciating foreign exchanges more than five percent of the fall of the Canadian currency vis-à-vis gold. Therefore this duty was applicable to the goods of the countries that were the subject of Canadian official exchange rates. Such products were from the same six countries, including Japan.

The margin between the customs value (converted at C$49.85 per 100 yen) and the original transaction value was added as a foreign exchange dumping duty on Japanese products. If the transaction value of the goods was C$25.20 (=100 yen) in 1933, the *foreign exchange dumping duty* for the goods would be C$24.65 (C$49.85 – C$25.20). The original purpose of this duty was to defend against losses caused by the depreciated value of the currency of other countries. This Canadian exchange equalization surtax effectively more than offset the loss caused by the depreciation of the Japanese currency at the end of 1931, because from 1929 to March 1935, the Canadian dollar depreciation averaged 41 percent, and that of the Japanese yen averaged 66 percent.[10]

The Canadian government explained that the foreign exchange dumping duty was not discriminatory because it was applicable to products of any foreign country in which the value of the currency of the country had depreciated more than five percent in relation to the fall in the value of the Canadian dollar vis-à-vis gold. The Japanese were concerned about three points:

> i. The currencies of 18 countries met this criterion, though no explanation was found in the documents for the omission of the other 12. The Canadian customs valuation could have been applied to products of these omitted countries, which should have led to the application of the foreign exchange dumping duty on them.
>
> ii. The aggregate number of goods from the other five countries subject to this surtax was very small, compared with the number of goods from Japan.[11] Therefore this foreign exchange dumping duty was primarily applied to Japanese products in the Canadian market.
>
> iii. The Canadian government lowered its official foreign exchange values for five currencies of these six to adjust the inflated costs of production in these exporting countries. A downward adjustment was not considered for the value of the yen, despite the inflation in Japan. The prices of leading Japanese export goods had already risen to 145 percent in 1933 over the 1931 level. The wholesale price index was up 38 percent in Japan, but in Canada it had increased only 3 percent during the 1931–35 period.[12] Until the end of the Japan-Canada tariff war of 1936, Canada's official value for the yen had never been lowered.

But the foreign exchange dumping duties were not applied if the Japanese products were subject to special *official Canadian customs price-dumping duties* (explained below) because the effective rate of the latter was much higher than that of the former.

To illustrate: The foreign exchange dumping duties were in general applied to Japanese goods if they were *identical* to products of *non*protected Canadian industries. (The importance attached to *non*protected goods will be discussed later.) When an item of Japanese goods arrived at a Canadian port, if its original transaction price as described on the Japanese shipping document was equivalent to C$30.03 in 1932, its Canadian customs price became C$49.85 because of conversion at the old gold parity. If the rate of ad valorem duty was 35 percent, as commonly practiced in Canada in those days,[13] the amount of duty on the item was C$17.44 instead of the C$10.51 that would have been levied on the original transaction price. The effective rate of the ad valorem duty then becomes 58.08 percent instead of the nominal 35 percent for the transaction value.

The full margin between the customs value and the original transaction value was C$19.82 (C$49.85 – C$30.03), which was levied as the foreign exchange dumping duty and added to the already increased effective ad valorem duty. The total of these two duties reached as high as C$37.26 (C$17.44 + C$19.82), the effective tariff rate being 124.07 percent of the original transaction price. The f.o.b. price of this Japanese product with the duties at the entering port became C$67.30, more than double the original transaction value. Furthermore, consumption and other domestic taxes at higher effective rates were added to this high after-duty price when the product reached Canadian consumers.

3. *The special official Canadian (customs) price-dumping duty:* The foreign goods to which Canadian customs valuations were applied at appreciated official exchange rates were divided into two categories:

> i. Goods *identical* or *similar* to products of protected Canadian industries subject to the Canadian official price-dumping duty;
> ii. Goods *identical* only to products of nonprotected industries subject to the foreign exchange dumping duty.

Foreign products *identical* to products of *protected* industries were selected by the Canadian authority as being subject to official pricing. Official Canadian exchange rates (the value of the old gold yen for Japan) were applied for the official pricing. Products subject to this price-dumping duty were again products of the same six countries, including Japan.

The Canadian government designated the official prices for 35 Japanese items that were considered to be *"identical"* to products of *protected* domestic industries. The customs estimation of official prices for those "identical" Japanese goods was based on two factors: a highly appreciated official exchange value for the yen set at C$49.85, and the official "norm" price, which was the factory price of the "identical" Canadian product. In the estimation of "norm" prices, differences in costs of production in both countries and thus comparative cost advantages on which international trade took place were ignored. The main Japanese goods that now became subject to official pricing had been increasingly imported from Japan for a long time before the yen's depreciation. This meant that these products were competitive with "identical" Canadian products long before 1931—if Japanese goods were more expensive in comparison with their quality, they would not have been increasingly imported and thus become subject to the official pricing. Because of the application of the "norm" price and the old gold parity for the value of the yen, the official Canadian prices of Japanese products became extremely higher than their original transaction prices from Japan.

The "norm" prices for Japanese goods were based on high factory prices of *"identical"* products of Canadian *protected* industries. (The unit price and the cost for goods of Canadian protected industries had been higher than the original transaction price of imported Japanese goods; otherwise importation did not take place.) The official prices of Japanese goods after the Canadian customs valuation very often became more than double in comparison with the prices of "identical" products of protected Canadian industries. Then, again, Canadian customs levied the full margin between the official and the transaction prices as the special official price-dumping duty.

4. *The effective ad valorem and the f.o.b. price:* After the effective ad valorem rates were applied, the f.o.b. price became much higher. Because of an application of "norm" prices that were much higher than the transaction prices, the effective rates of the special

official price-dumping duty became much heavier than those of the foreign exchange dumping duty. This duty was added to the ad valorem duty.

An ad valorem duty itself for this subject product was also calculated on this "norm" price, not on the transaction price. The effective rates of the ad valorem duties again became much higher than their nominal rates and were heavier than rates on the subject Japanese products for customs valuation of the transaction price. This resulted because Canada not only used the foreign exchange at the gold parity; it also used Canadian "norm" prices as criteria. Finally, Canada imposed this high and effective ad valorem duty in addition to an extremely high official price-dumping duty (the margin between the official and the transaction prices of the product) for the Japanese goods involved.[14]

The Canadian authorities selected 35 Japanese items as being subject to official pricing, and 10 of these were major Japanese exports. In decreasing order of value, they included raw silk, silk fabrics, rayon fabrics, electric bulbs, china and porcelain, cotton fabrics, umbrellas, and canned seafood.[15]

This special official price-dumping duty proved to be the heaviest of all Canadian tariffs levied against Japan. The rate of ad valorem duty for the same kind of products was the same for every country. When the "norm" price was exercised, however, its effective rate went up much higher than the nominal tariff on the original transaction price. After Canadian customs valued the official price of a product, the official price-dumping and ad valorem duties were added: the resultant f.o.b. price was extraordinarily high. It formally replaced the original transaction price from Japan at the Canadian port.

As a whole, Canadian tariffs were prohibitive, much higher than necessary to protect domestic industries.

The Japanese protest
I uncovered the following in a document sent by the British Embassy in Tokyo to the Foreign Office in London.[16] The Japanese government proposed to redress the balance of trade

between Japan and Canada by modifying the exchange equalization surtax in 1934. It repeatedly protested that "the application of these dumping duties was inconsistent with the most-favored-nation treatment in the 1911 Japan-United Kingdom Commerce and Navigation Treaty." But the Canadian government's reply was the same as always: "The practice was not contradictory." The negotiation focused on the Canadian treatment of the value of the yen at a gold parity for customs valuation purposes. The Japanese government suggested in May 1935 that "it would prohibit the importation of various kinds of Canadian goods and Japan would substitute to import them from other countries."

However, the imposition of these exorbitant duties continued from 1931 through mid-1936, until the Japanese government finally applied prohibitive countervailing tariffs on Canadian goods.

Consequences of the new tariffs

Because of Canadian customs valuations of Japanese goods, followed by prohibitive dumping and ad valorem duties, Japanese exports to Canada were seriously damaged. The prices of major Japanese goods in the Canadian market were raised extraordinarily, as shown in table 4.1.

Table 4.1 Ratios of after-duty prices of Japanese products in Canada to their original transaction prices, the first half-year average in 1935

	(percent)
Cotton rugs	1,000
Cotton socks	600
Sneakers with rubber soles	400
Rayon products	370
Lampshades	280
Silk fabrics	270
Electric bulbs	240

Source: The Vancouver Sun, April 27, 1935, in the Japan Academy of Science, Tsusho Joyaku to Tsusho Seisaku no Hensen (The Evolution of Commercial Treaties and Foreign Trade Policies), A Supplement to Diplomatic Documents related to Reforms of Commercial Treaties, ed., Ministry of Foreign Affairs (Tokyo: The Research Institute for the World Economy, 1951), 962.

Comparisons between the prices of "identical" Japanese products after tariffs and the factory prices of Canadian products were also recorded. The prices of Japanese cotton socks and rayon and silk fabrics were at least 100 percent higher than the prices of "identical" Canadian products in 1936, according to a Canadian source.[17]

Table 4.2　The decline of Japanese exports to Canada

(1931 = 100 in value terms)

Item	1932	1933	1934
Cotton knitted articles	61	35	1
Silk shoulder covers	15	3	2
Silk fabrics	13	5	6
Rayon fabrics	20	11	12
Raw silk	45	19	16
Artificial panama hats	85	13	6
Electric bulbs	210	219	71

Source:　Japan Academy of Science, *Tsusho Joyaku to Tsusho Seisaku no Hensen* (The Evolution of Commercial Treaties and Foreign Trade Policies), *A Supplement to Diplomatic Documents related to Reforms of Commercial Treaties*, ed., Ministry of Foreign Affairs (Tokyo: The Research Institute for the World Economy, 1951), 962.

In the next year, 1932, Japanese exports to Canada precipitately fell because of this high tariff wall. Most important exports tapered off by 1934, as shown in table 4.2, above.

Thus the total value of Japanese exports to Canada was sharply reduced. Since Japan imported an increasing quantity of industrial materials from Canada, the value of imports did not decline proportionally to the decline in exports during the 1932–36 period. The adverse trade balance against Japan worsened, as shown in table 4.3. The ratio of Japanese exports to imports with Canada was only 39 percent in 1929 (a tremendous imbalance), which rapidly dropped to 16 percent in 1934 (revealed in the bottom line of the table). These figures show that a constant and sizable trade deficit for the Japanese side was aggravated. Note that not only the ratios, but also the absolute export values in 1932–36 fell to a fifth of the 1929 level.

Table 4.3 The Japan-Canada trade imbalance

					(millions of U.S. dollars)
	1929	1932	1934	1936	1937
Exports	12.4	2.4	2.5	4.2	5.7
Imports	31.7	11.1	15.3	21.1	30.1
Balance	19.2	8.6	13.4	16.9	24.3
Exports/Imports (%)	39.1	21.6	16.3	19.9	18.9

Source: Statistical table 1, appendix I.

The Japan-Canada trade war

Frequent negotiations in Ottawa and Tokyo failed to persuade the Canadian government to relax these trade barriers, and on July 8, 1935, the Japanese government announced application of the Trade Protection Act (1934) to Canadian products. The Canadian government repeatedly stated that its tariff system was designed only to protect domestic industries from foreign products that invaded the Canadian market via the strong devaluation of foreign currencies, and that Canada was not targeting Japan. It also explained that Canada was buying enough Japanese silk at that time in its imports of U.S. silk products made from Japanese raw silk.[18]

By Imperial Ordinance No. 208, Japan implemented the 1934 Trade Protection Act on July 17, 1935, as a countervailing measure against the Canadian tariff policy for Japanese products. The Imperial edict did not specify the name of the country as Canada, to avoid any contradiction with the MFN clause of the Japan-Canada Commercial Treaty. The edict simply declared that Japan would levy additional 50 percent ad valorem duties to the ordinal tariffs on the products of countries that exercised unreasonably high customs values on Japanese products for duty purposes. But Notification No. 168 of the Ministry of Finance was included at the end of the edict, and it clearly stated that the country in question was Canada.[19] Thus Japan levied a 50 percent additional duty on major Canadian imports: wheat, flour, starch, pulp, paper for matchboxes, felt as material for paper, and lumber.

In response to this, the Canadian government slightly yielded by lowering the tariffs on Japanese products; it lowered the official conversion rate for the yen to C$41.51, from the long-standing C$49.85. It also claimed that the Japanese Trade Protection Act did conflict with the MFN clause in the Japan-United Kingdom Commerce and Navigation Treaty. On August 5, 1935, Canada took a countermeasure by adding a 33-1/3 ad valorem duty to already-increased duties on all Japanese goods, regardless of whether they were dutiable or nondutiable goods.[20]

During the August-November period, the value of Canadian exports to Japan sharply fell to only half the average figure of the preceding four-month period, while Japanese exports expanded an average of 35.5 percent during the same period.[21] Before the coming Canadian general election, in the summer of 1935, the *Ottawa Journal* argued the trade issue as follows:

> Canadian exports to Japan annually averaged C$17 million for recent years while imports from Japan averaged 4 million. Considering these figures, the Japanese request to relax Canadian dumping duties sounded reasonable, since the present Canadian tariff system is apparently discouraging further our already small purchases from Japan in comparison with our exports. The recent trade frictions revealed the failure of the present Conservative government's economic policies: They encouraged protection for production of too many various kinds of products that could have been more gainfully obtained by imports.[22]

New trade agreements in November 1935
In October 1935, the Liberals triumphed over the Conservatives in the Canadian general election. On the day following the establishment of the new cabinet, the prime minister of Canada (William Lyon Mackenzie) visited the Japanese Consulate in Ottawa and broached gestures to terminate the tariff war between the two countries. On November 1, 1935, favorable new trade agreements were concluded between Japan and Canada, and they become effective on the first day of the following year.

In the reforms of the Canadian tariff regulations, major points relevant to Japan's trade can be summarized as follows:

1. *The official Canadian price for the yen:* The value of the yen at C$49.85 was lowered in two ways according to categories of goods. First, the exchange rate for Japanese goods not "identical" to those produced or manufactured in Canada was at the current market price of the yen. Second, the exchange rate for "identical" products should be at the average of the previous five years and revised every year, the revision being based on the preceding five-year average of the actual value of the Japanese currency.

The Canadian official price: Twenty of 35 official Canadian prices for Japanese goods were abolished. Some major Japanese manufactured exports—cotton textiles, rayon fabrics, electric appliances, canned salmon, cotton rugs, umbrellas, pencils, and cotton knitting—were exempted from the official Canadian pricing. Furthermore, the Japanese were accorded the right to appeal to the Canadian authorities if Japanese goods were unreasonably priced at Canadian customs.

The term "identical" products: The Canadian definition of "identical," or "similar," or "same like," or "like" products became more clarified than before. To point to a Japanese product as "identical" to a Canadian product, the latter had to be domestically produced for more than 10 percent of consumption in Canada. Thus with the meaning of "identical" products being specified, major Japanese products were also dropped from official pricing. Consequently, they were no longer the target of the extravagant effective rates of ad valorem and the two kinds of special dumping duties.

2. *Abolition and limitation of dumping duties:* The scope of foreign exchange duty became narrowed for two reasons. First, the official exchange rate for the yen was lowered as mentioned above. Customs values for Japanese goods themselves fell a great deal because of the fall in the officially applied value of the yen. Second, "identical" products became limited in number as the

term was defined above. Both factors contributed to reduce the numbers of Japanese products subject to customs valuation.

The scope of applying special official price-dumping duties also became extremely narrow because of very reduced numbers of products to which official pricing applied. Numbers of "identical" products were greatly reduced, and because of the lower value for the yen, official Canadian prices on many Japanese goods became low. These improvements narrowed the margin between official Canadian prices and Japanese export prices. Thus the situations for applying official price-dumping duties were sizably reduced.

3. The Canadian government discarded the additional 33-1/3 percent ad valorem duty, which was a retaliation to Japan's adoption of the 1934 Trade Protection Act, imposed on every Japanese product.

As a result of these improvements, the Canadian average effective tariffs for major Japanese goods were lowered by half from the previous levels.[23] Furthermore, the Japanese side stopped the application of the 1934 Trade Protection Act. Japanese imports from Canada reexpanded quickly after a five-month interval. By the end of 1936, the value of imports had recovered to the 1930 level and in 1937 reached nearly the same level as in 1929. Canada's share in Japanese imports was 3.29 percent in 1929 and in 1937.

This quick recovery was largely attributable to the growth in imported industrial materials, such as lead, zinc, and aluminum. The value of these three metals in 1937 climbed to 420 percent of the level in 1929. The imports of foodstuffs, however, greatly declined. In particular, imports of wheat in 1937 were reduced to only 20 percent of the 1929 level.[24]

Concluding remarks on Japan-Canada trade

One important area remained untouched. Japan failed to conclude an *unconditional* most-favored-nation clause with Canada. The 1935 agreement was only able to stop the strong Canadian tariff discrimination, as detailed above. Canada concluded agreements covering sizable tariff concessions on a reciprocal basis with other nations after 1935; typical was the one with the United States. Beneficial tariff reductions stemming from these new Canadian agreements, however, had never been passed on to Japanese products because of the nature of the conditional most-favored-nation clause of the 1935 Japan-Canada agreement.

Japanese exports to Canada were recovering from the bottom level, but at a very sluggish pace. Export performance in the following years of 1936 and 1937 was at only 33.8 percent and 45.9 percent of the 1929 level. Thus Canada's share in Japanese exports shrank to only 0.6 percent in 1937, compared with 1.2 percent in 1929. But even this small recovery contributed to redressing Japan's heavy trade deficit with Canada: The ratio of exports to imports improved to about a fifth (20%) in 1937, from a seventh in the 1933–34 period. The continuing Japanese deficit, however, was doomed to widen because imports tended to expand due to industrial requirements, and exports tended to be curtailed further because of unrecoverable losses incurred in the major Canadian import market. Since Japanese exports were mainly consumption goods, they faced domestic and foreign competitors alike in the Canadian market.

The effects of five years of prohibitive tariffs and the following calamity of the Japan-Canada tariff war were too long and severe to permit any Japanese hopes of major progress in exports. During those years, domestic and foreign competitors had gained bases and assumed positions for expansion in the Canadian market as they replaced Japanese goods. The consumer side of benefits arising from freer trade had long been forgotten with the imposition of prohibitive tariffs. (Canadian consumer losses were partially made up for by the expansion of trade in the British Empire and in the United States after 1935.) Reflections on the excellent Japan-Canada trade relations until 1929, and Japan's trade performance elsewhere during the period, show that Japanese trade with Canada after 1930 was a missed opportunity for the two trading partners.

Another point to be noted before ending this section was the significant influence of the U.S. Hawley-Smoot Tariff on Canadian imports, since it worked to encourage strict Canadian tariff policies for non-British trade partners. Among the countries involved, Japan chiefly was victimized. Until 1929, Canada had increasingly depended on U.S. trade; it was 60 percent of the total in that year. Because the 1929 U.S. Trade Act did tremendous damage to Canada's trade and economy, Canada was pushed to move further away from freer trade. After this, Canada inclined more toward achieving closer ties with Britain and the British Empire by enlarging the Imperial preferential privileges. Canada had to find a path to avoid difficulties in trade and in international political relationships, under increasing pressures from the mother country to strengthen the Imperial tie since the late 1920s. Japan's suffering of Canadian customs valuations and consequential prohibitive ad valorem and dumping duties should be understood as just one issue of overall Canadian trade policy of the time.

After everything is considered, however, one question remains. Was the Canadian customs valuation at official exchange rates for the products of relevant countries discriminatory? The answer has to be yes, as this was applied selectively to only 6 countries, as against 12 others whose currencies fell in the same criteria asserted by the Canadian government. A further question now arises in this respect: Was Japan more discriminated against among these few selected countries, as mentioned frequently in Japanese official documents, statements that have been blindly accepted in scholarly works?

Two points provide evidence for a reply in the affirmative:

1. The application of the official exchange rate for the yen was one of the limited cases for 6 countries out of the 18 in which the value of the currency had dropped more than 5 percent of the fall of the Canadian dollar versus gold. Among these 6, Japan's total value of exports in 1933 exceeded the aggregate value of exports of the other 5 countries. Consequently, the customs duty valuation of Japanese goods fell heavily and more frequently on a greater number of Japanese exports than on those from the other 5 countries.

2. Until 1929, Canada's largest trade partner was the United States. The Canadian imposition of prohibitive tariffs on American products in 1930 was a retaliatory measure against the U.S. Hawley-Smoot Tariff; the prohibitive tariffs were initiated by the United States. Canada, however, succeeded in concluding general tariff concessions with the United States under the reciprocal U.S. Trade Agreements Act of 1934. After this, Canada's trade with the United States recovered immensely, to 60.1 percent of Canadian total imports by 1937, reducing the share of the total British Empire to 28 percent.[25]

This imposition of the customs valuation and the ensuing extreme dumping duties on Japanese products was started by Canada. The initiation of the Japan-Canada tariff war was by Canada. Thus the question becomes: Was Canadian discrimination targeting Japan?

The answer is uncertain from the viewpoint of (1) above. Japan happened to be the largest exporter to Canada among the 6 countries that became subject to official Canadian foreign exchange rates. Among the other 5, Canada lowered the official rates in a few in consideration of inflationary trends. No such consideration was given to Japan, however, although the cost of production and the price index of Japan increased greatly during the 1931–36 period, as demonstrated earlier.

In considering this question of discrimination against Japan, though, an ambiguity arises from specific Canadian customs procedures. Canada legally enforced antidumping provisions at the direction of the Minister of National Revenue. He issued regulations and other instructions to the collectors of customs at ports of entry, and antidumping duties were sometimes imposed by collectors when the goods entered. No decision or order from higher administrative authority was required. No notice of antidumping regulations or rules was published. The number of antidumping levies would tend to increase in the absence of accurate orders for customs officers, because officers became more uncertain without them. An American tariff specialist pointed out that under this automatic Canadian tariff system, more antidumping levies would occur than in any other country in the Atlantic area.[26] This tendency no doubt would apply to the many antidumping levies on Japanese goods because Japan exported more than any of the other 5 countries during the period of this survey. Therefore in part the nature of the Canadian tariff system was to blame: tariffs automatically fell heavier on Japanese products because their volume and values were larger than those of the other 5 countries.

If we consider Canada's domestic and international economic circumstances at that time, it is also understandable that Canada was preoccupied for its survival with problems concerning Britain and the United States, because Japan's trade represented such a small figure in Canada. We must note, however, that Japan was left with specific and exorbitant Canadian tariff barriers for nearly five years and was long left under the one-sided prohibitive tariff wall.

It seems a tragic mistake from our standpoint of the twenty-first century to believe that a developing country in the 1930s, such as Japan, which had started to achieve international competitiveness in certain economic fields and that had expanded exports in foreign markets, was assumed to be equally competent in other fields, such as international politics and diplomacy. The competence of the Japanese in this latter aspect then tended to develop too slowly to handle new trade problems as they occurred in the dynamism of the developing economies.

To cope with these problems and move them in a manageable direction, the representatives of Japan should have acquired broader practical knowledge in international economics, politics, and legal measures. They especially should have known unwritten common practices, customs, and dead issues in international treaties. These customs and practices had changed and were changing, accruing as a result of the dynamic development of world economic circumstances. Instead, the Japanese documents remained solemnly blaming and lamenting actions of the advanced country, Canada, on these issues. In parts of the documents, the editors and writers were in effect saying that the practices of the customs valuations and dumping duties definitely did not fit the

Most Favored Nation (MFN) clause of the 1911 Japan-United Kingdom Commerce and Navigation Treaty. These people generally reflected the inexperienced young country itself, regardless of their personal ability and chronological age.

To quote one example among many, official Japanese documents stated that the Japanese were totally bewildered by Canada's application of the MFN treatment for Japanese goods. In 1922, Canada had applied the MFN clause on Japanese products as being outside Imperial preferential treatment. This favorable interpretation of the MFN clause for Japan was discontinued in 1930, when the Canadian government applied the discriminatory customs valuation and prohibitive tariffs under Imperial preferential privileges. These were two contradictory interpretations. The official Canadian statement was made repeatedly that the application of the customs valuation and discriminatory tariffs was compatible with the most-favored-nation clause. The Japanese could not understand such completely reversed practices—tariff concessions in 1922 and prohibitive Imperial preferential tariffs after 1930—based on the same most-favored-nation clause between Japan and Canada. Neither could they determine whether the Imperial preference was inconsistent with the MFN clause, and if it was, why it was; they merely wondered, as quoted earlier, and only discussed seriously the fundamental principle of the MFN clause.[27] According to J. Viner, the application of Imperial privileges was generally consistent with the most-favored-nation treatment already in effect in the 1920s. The instance of applying Imperial privileges regardless of the existence of the most-favored-nation clause became increasingly common in the 1930s.[28] Apparently the Japanese did not know this and adhered to the original understanding of the clause in the treaty.

Another point to consider is that Japan had no fellow countries which were also catching up with the West, as today's developing nations do, to form a group to acquire and to share missing trade knowledge and to find further strength in numbers. Japan was alone. But this can be interpreted as the price to be paid for being the pioneer of non-Western nations to catch up with the West at that time.

Later, the customs valuation of imported goods for duty purposes was ruled out at the Tokyo Round of GATT (General Agreements on Tariffs and Trade) in 1976: The customs value of imported goods should be the transaction value. But even in 1986, a few instances of the practice of customs valuation were known, for example in Korea.[29] Today, whenever dumping is found, the amount of the dumping duty is the margin of dumping, but it should not exceed 50 percent of the transaction price. It was in 1969 when the Canadian government for the first time in its history was required by GATT to prove that there had been some material "injury" or threat caused by imports before definitively applying protective duties for the sake of domestic industries.[30]

3. Japanese Trade Conflict with British India

Japan's exports to India had expanded, reaching 13.6 percent of Japan's total exports in 1932 (see table 1.3 in chapter one), but that was the peak, after which they declined. The decline worsened after 1934, the reasons for which we will investigate here.

During the period of this survey, India's trade reliance on Great Britain had been declining. Its country distribution of trade was shifting from Britain to others, such as Japan and other Asian countries, the United States, and more areas in the British Commonwealth. The main reasons were two: Newcomers, such as Japan, entered and assumed a growing presence in the Indian market. Secondly, India's domestic industries, especially cotton textiles, were growing to reduce the size of its import market. Meanwhile, Japan's trade expansion in this market was marked, in contrast to the decline of British trade and to the shrinking size of the Indian import market.

Japan's total trade value, however, was still well below that of Britain's. The value of Japanese exports was about a quarter of Britain's in 1929, a third in 1933, and down a quarter again in 1937. Table 4.4, below, presents the percentage distribution of Japan, Britain, and the United States in Indian trade during the 1926–37 period.

The table shows that Japan's shares in Indian imports increased rapidly until 1932. They still grew, though at a lower rate, even after 1932 when the Indian and British governments imposed trade restrictions on Japan. The table demonstrates that Japan's trade expansion in the Indian import market was highly related to the decline of Britain's.

The Indian trade network of the period had three features:

1. India enjoyed an annual global trade surplus that more than counterbalanced a constant trade deficit with Great Britain.

Table 4.4 The shares of three major countries in Indian trade

(percent)

	Imports			Exports		
	Japan	Britain	U.S.	Japan	Britain	U.S.
1926	6.0	49.5	7.3	13.2	25.2	10.8
1929	9.2	42.4	7.3	10.6	21.2	12.0
1932	14.4	35.4	8.5	8.7	27.5	7.5
1934	15.6	41.2	6.7	14.7	33.2	8.5
1937	14.0	31.5	6.4	12.4	32.6	10.3

Sources: The League of Nations, *International Trade Statistics 1930*, (Geneva: League of Nations, 1932), 315, 337; *(1938)*, 288; *(1939)*, 310. See endnote no. 1 in chapter four, section three.

2. About 70 percent of this trade surplus was annually spent to maintain the British colonial system in India as expenses, salaries, and wages for British bureaucrats and military men and as payments of amortization and interest for British investment.
3. The purchase of gold and silver coins on the capital account exceeded the trade surplus, making India's overall balance of payments register an annual deficit.

During 1926 and 1928, India's trade surplus amounted to an annual average of $133.477 million, but the balance on the capital account was a deficit of $63.283 million. Both figures for 1929 were much improved: $292.496 million for the trade surplus and $42.716 million as the deficit on the capital account. Then, after 1930, India's trade balance became less favorable and registered a much smaller surplus. This surplus fell precipitously in 1932, recording only $11.330 million. India's net foreign exchange outflow was $163.820 million worth of gold to make up deficits on the balance of payments during the five-year period from 1930 to 1934.[1]

Japan's imports from India
Japan's imports from British India were primarily in the form of three chief commodities: raw cotton, pig iron, and natural rubber.

Raw cotton occupied a crucial position, accounting for 83.7 percent of the total value in Japan's imports from India in 1926.[2] In this respect, Japan purchased about 73 percent of India's raw cotton exports that year. Most Japanese raw and ginned cotton imports before 1925 were from India, and the lesser quantities were from the United States. Imports of Indian raw cotton reached a peak that year and declined thereafter because Japanese cotton textile industrialists tried to upgrade the quality of products by importing finer and long-fiber U.S. raw cotton. The ratio of raw cotton (quantity) between the United States and India in Japanese imports was nearly fifty-fifty in 1926. After 1927, this became weighted toward the United States.

With the decline of raw cotton imports, India's relative importance in the total value of Japan's imports became lower and lower, dropping to 15.3 percent in 1929 and to only 8.2 percent in 1932, from 23.7 percent in 1913.[3] The trends of growing exports with declining imports made Japan's trade balance with India swing from a large annual deficit to a small surplus in 1932 and 1933, as presented in table 1 of statistical appendix I.

Japanese-British competition in Indian textile imports

India's share of Japanese exports was 7.6 percent in 1926 and 6.0 percent in 1929, growing to 13.6 percent by 1932. But because of trade restrictions, it declined from 1934 (10.9 percent) onward, dropping to 9.4 percent by 1937.

Textiles earned the largest value among Japanese exports to India. Their aggregate value reached 76 percent and 79 percent of Japan's total exports to India in 1926 and 1929, but they declined to 44.5 percent by 1937. Table 4.5 shows the distribution of leading Japanese textile products to India.

Cotton cloth contributed the most as a single product, accounting for 45 percent in 1926 and 55 percent in 1929 of Japan's total earnings from India. But after 1932, its contribution declined. By 1937, it was only 21 percent, as shown in table 4.5.

Table 4.5 Japan's textile exports to British India, 1926–37

(percentage of total exports in value terms)

	Total Textiles	Cotton			Silk/Rayon Products
		Yarn	Knitting	Cloth	
1926	75.8	17.9	5.6	45.3	7.0
1929	78.9	6.7	5.0	55.1	12.1
1932	69.8	7.4	3.4	41.9	17.1
1934	53.7	4.6	3.4	28.0	17.7
1937	44.5	4.3	3.8	21.0	15.4

Source: Toyo Keizai Shinposha, *Nihon Boeki Seiran* (Foreign Trade of Japan: A Statistical Survey) (Tokyo: Toyo Keizai Shinposha, 1975, rev. ed.), *The Supplement*, 24–28.

Japan's cotton cloth exports, among other textiles, to British India increasingly created problems during the period under this survey, though Japanese competitive strength in this area had started to grow earlier. The volume of Japan's cotton cloth exports to India reached a peak in 1932, registering 644 million square yards. This figure accounted for 31.7 percent that year of Japanese total cotton cloth exports to the world.[4]

The growth of Japanese cotton cloth imports in the Indian market is comparable with the decline of Great Britain's, as can be seen in table 4.6. There was a rapid growth of Japanese products to 43.6 percent in the 1931–32 period, from 13.6 percent in the 1925–26 period, versus a decline of Great Britain's to 49.3 percent in 1931–32, from 82.0 percent in 1925–26.

Table 4.6 Comparison of India's cotton cloth imports from Japan and Britain

(percentage of the total)

	Britain	Japan	Other Countries
1925–26	82.0	13 .6	4.4
1928–29	75.0	18.4	6.6
1931–32	49.3	43.6	7.1
1933–34	54.5	44.8	0.7
1936–37	46.4	52.4	1.2

Source: Japan Academy of Science, *Tsusho Joyaku*, 895.

In addition, the size of the Indian import market was becoming smaller. The volume of India's cotton cloth imports fell to 776 million square yards in 1931–32, from 1,937 million in 1928–29, a reduction of 60 percent. This was due to the development of the Indian cotton textile industry. The output of cotton cloth in India grew 47 percent over the same period.[5] Japan and Britain competed to expand their shares in this shrinking Indian cotton cloth import market.

Indian tariffs on Japanese products

The Indian government had "financial autonomy" as a British colony and established the Indian Tariff Act in 1927 to levy a 5 percent ad valorem duty on imports of cotton yarn to protect its industry. The government then enacted the Indian Cotton Industry Protection Bill in 1930 for an extension of the 1927 act and a revision of tariffs upward on cotton yarn.

The following chart presents the margin of the Imperial preferential tariffs for cotton cloth, one of the most discriminatory tariffs in the early 1930s. The margin of preference was 5 percent to begin with. The tariff rate on "plain gray cotton goods" from Japan became 15 percent, including a 5 percent additional duty applied in 1927. But the rate on British products did not include this additional duty; the tariffs were 5 percent lower for Britain. In April 1930, the tariffs were raised to 15 percent for Britain and to 20 percent for other countries, including Japan. Plain gray cloth, the object of the new additional discriminatory duty, was the main item of Japanese cloth exported to India, bitterly competing with the cloth from Britain. The greatest sufferer of this Imperial privilege was Japan.

The Imperial preferential treatment was extended to cover all cotton cloth imports. The Indian authorities again raised tariffs in March 1931, to 20 percent for products sent from Britain, and to 25 percent for those from other countries. This time the higher rate of 25 percent was applied not only to "plain gray cloth," but to all Japanese cotton cloth.

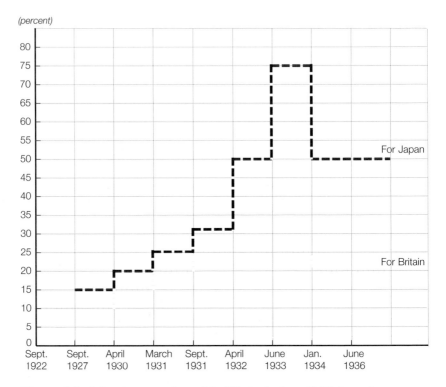

**Figure 4.1 Ad valorem rates of tariffs levied on British and
Japanese cotton cloth in the British Indian market,
1922–1937**

Source: Japan Academy of Science, *Tsusho Joyaku*, 894.

Soon after, in September 1931, the Indian government raised the tariffs further, to 25 percent for British goods and to 31.25 percent (which included an emergency duty) for goods from other countries. The margin of the Imperial preference now became 6.25 percent. These revisions in tariff rates were announced as being necessary to obtain additional revenues to meet the Indian budgetary deficit.

India was asked to widen the margin of the Imperial privilege in an agreement after the Ottawa Conference in 1932. After this conference, the application was expanded to cover not only cotton and artificial textiles, but many other items, in all a total of 160, including iron and steel, machinery, boxes of matches, and other miscellaneous goods.[6] Both the 1927 Indian Tariff Act and the 1930 Indian Cotton Industry Protection Bill had also been working to support a high tariff wall, but they were to terminate by autumn 1932.

The Japanese process of catching up with Britain in cotton cloth imports in the Indian market was accelerating during the 1928–32 period. Japan's share reached 44 percent versus Britain's 49 percent by 1932, as shown in table 4.6.

The tariffs were revised again by the Indian Governmental Notice of August 1932. The rates of preferential tariffs levied by India on the products of the mother country became generally about 10 percent lower than for non-British products. The margin of the preferential rates on cotton cloth, however, was widened more, to 25 percent, after the implementation of the 1932 notice. The tariff rate remained 25 percent for Britain, but it increased this time to 50 percent for cotton cloth from other countries. The 25 percent margin of the Imperial privilege for cotton textiles, Japan's most competitive products, worked in favor of Britain in the Indian market.

One interesting fact in regard to this tariff revision is that the Indian Tariff Committee recommended that all newly created protective tariffs should be applied to all countries, including Great Britain. The recommendation was rejected by Britain.[7]

After the 1932 Indian tariff revision, accelerated growth in Japanese cotton cloth imports stopped: Japan's relative share expanded insignificantly (0.8 percent) in 1933–34 over the level of the preceding year, and the British share was restored to 54.5 percent, from 49.3 percent, during the same period, as shown in table 4.6. Japan was the country most adversely affected by India's discriminatory tariffs in cotton textiles.

The Indian government extended the termination of the notice of August 1932 to the following year. The exercise of this 25 percent margin as the Imperial preference created two problems for the Indian government.

First, the 50 percent ad valorem duty that applied to goods of all non-British countries in 1932 was high, but not high enough to damage Japanese competition in the Indian textile import market. The tariffs were effective only to stop acceleration in the growth of Japanese cotton cloth imports, but the growth did not decline to the pre-1929 level, with imports still occupying 44 percent of the market share.

Second, it was dangerous for the Indian government to further intensify the discrimination by extending the act, bill, and notice because all other non-British trading partners might have misunderstood the intensified tariffs, as if India were discriminating against them in favor of Great Britain alone. The true objective of the tariff revision was to oppress imports, if possible, of only Japanese products. To meet this objective and to avoid any problems with non-British trading partners, the best policy for the Indian government was to establish antidumping duties that would effectively prevent the competitiveness of Japanese cotton textiles.

Employing the mother country's privilege to conclude treaties for the colonies, Great Britain notified Japan in April 1933 of the termination of the Japan-India Commercial Treaty of 1904. India had been unable to apply an antidumping duty on Japanese goods, since it was inconsistent with the most-favored-nation clause in the 1904 Treaty. The termination was therefore designed to allow India's application of the antidumping duty for Japanese products. (The Indian government had only fiscal autonomy, including tariff revisions and revenues; it had no authority to conclude treaties.) Six months later, the 1904 treaty became void.

The Indian government legislated the bill of "Safeguarding Industries" and increased the governor's right to levy antidumping duties as "countervailing" measures on the products of countries that depreciated the value of their currencies. In June of 1933 the Indian government again raised the rate of tariffs, to 75 percent, on all cotton textiles made outside Great Britain. The tariffs for British products remained at 25 percent. This procedure was a temporary measure until the application of the Antidumping Bill, which became effective in October of the same year. The margin of the Imperial privilege became 50 percent for competitive Japanese cotton cloth.

The Japan Spinners' Association—the first and largest cartel in Japan—immediately retaliated against the Indian pressure by boycotting Indian raw cotton. The boycott lasted seven months, until January 1934, when Japan-British India trade negotiations were concluded.

Earlier, in April 1933, the British government had given notice to Japan of the partial revocation of the British-Japan Commercial Treaty. By this notice, West African countries, which did not grant the most-favored-nation privilege to Britain, were excluded. Japan thereby lost its commercial treaty with them. The British government also suggested to Japan a division of world market shares of cotton textiles between the British and Japanese cotton industries, taking the Indian market as the starting case.[8] This suggestion was accompanied by a threatening implication that if it were not accepted by the Japanese, the British government was ready to adopt further discriminatory procedures against Japanese products.[9]

Meanwhile, trade negotiations on miscellaneous products had been progressing between Japan and India since September 1933.

Indian quotas and the link system

After extended negotiations, the Japan–India Commercial Conference concerning India's discriminatory tariffs on Japanese cotton cloth came to a conclusion in January 1934. Here are the main points of agreement:

1. The most-favored-nation treatment was to be accorded on a reciprocal basis for each side.
2. Indian tariffs would not exceed a 50 percent ad valorem level for all Japanese cotton cloth, including plain gray cloth.[10]
3. The total quota applied to Japanese cotton cloth was to be 400 million square yards per annum and would be linked to 1.5 million bales of Indian raw cotton exports to Japan.

The total quota for Japan was prorated among different kinds of cloth. The procedure to distribute this quota among different kinds of Japanese cotton products was the most difficult part of the negotiations among India, Britain, and Japan. The final figures: plain gray cotton cloth, 45 percent of the total quota; plain cloth with trim, 13 percent; coarse gray cloth, 8 percent; and dyed and other cloths, 34 percent. Two-thirds of the total negotiations were spent disputing the distribution within the quota.

Japan negotiated on cotton cloth exports to the Indian market not with the Indians, but with the British government. During the negotiation process, the British government strongly rejected an Indian proposal of a 10 percent quota for coarse gray Japanese cloth and insisted on the application of a smaller 8 percent quota instead, which was adopted as the final figure listed above. This coarse gray cloth, the subject of disagreement between Britain and India, was Britain's leading export product to the Indian market.[11] In the process, the British gave up the plan of sharing the Indian market with the Japanese cotton industry. It was reported that Britain feared a boycotting of British products by the Indian people.[12]

The British government recommended that the Indian government accept a Japanese proposal calling for India's reciprocal recognition of the most-favored-nation treatment clause concluded between Japan and Manchukuo. Reciprocal here meant that India's recognition was conditional on Japan's recognition of the Imperial Preferential Agreements between India and Britain. But the Indian government refused this British recommendation. If it had not, India would have faced a loss of competitiveness in pig iron exports to Japan because Manchukuo would then have tariff privileges under the MFN clause concluded with Japan.

With every clause concerning the reciprocal recognition of privileges for the two negotiating countries deleted, the new Japan-India Commercial Treaty was ratified in London in September 1934.

Results of the trade turmoil
Table 4.7 presents the fall in the volume of Japanese cotton cloth exports to India from 1933; this volume sharply declined after the

implementation of first a 50 percent, then a 75 percent, ad valorem duty in 1933. The drop was to 70 percent in 1933 and to 63.6 percent in 1934, from the 1932 peak level of 100 percent.

Table 4.7 Japanese cotton cloth exports to India

(1932 = 100)

	Million sq. yds.	Index
1929	581.1	90.2
1931	404.1	62.7
1932	644.6	100.0
1933	451.8	70.0
1934	410.5	63.6
1935	556.2	86.3
1936	479.6	74.3
1937	331.1	51.3

Source: Toyo Keizai Shinposha, *Nihon Boeki Seiran* (Foreign Trade of Japan: A Statistical Survey) (Tokyo: Toyo Keizai Shinposha, 1975 rev. ed.), *The Supplement,* 24–28.

Under the new 1934 agreement, the Indian link system was established to join values of Japanese imports of Indian raw cotton with Japanese exports of cotton products to India. After this, Indian raw cotton surged into the Japanese market. Its volume increased 45 percent in 1933, 110 percent in 1934, and more than 150 percent in 1935 over the 1932 level.[13] These increases, however, inevitably lowered the quality of Japanese cotton products because of their short, coarse fibers compared with the long-staple U.S. raw cotton, as mentioned earlier (in section 4 of the previous chapter).

Japan's pig iron imports from India also rose 55 percent and 25 percent in 1934 and 1935 respectively over the 1932 level. The reasons for the increases were twofold: to encourage India's diversified purchases of nontextile Japanese products and to alleviate Indian pressures to correct trade imbalances of the time.[14]

Thus Japan started to reincur a sizable trade deficit with India after 1935. This was mostly due to the large increase of Indian raw cotton imports required by the link system. Japan could maintain a favorable trade balance with India only in 1932 and 1933. After 1934, the aggregate earnings of textile exports in Japan's total Indian trade also declined, to 44.5 percent of the total in 1937, from 79 percent in 1929, as shown in table 4.5. This decline was unavoidable because of the large reduction in earnings of the most competitive exports of cotton textiles, despite an increase in earnings of silk and rayon exports to 15.4 percent, from 7.0 percent in 1926. Japan's powerful leading export products to India were no longer cotton textiles; they now represented only 21 percent of total Japanese exports in 1937, in comparison with more than 55 percent in 1929 as shown in table 4.5.

Exports of glass goods/chinaware, machinery, and iron products expanded. Their sales grew remarkably, but even with this growth, in 1937, their peak year of performance, they represented only 3.1, 2.8, and 2.7 percent, respectively, of Japan's total export value to India.[15] The sales of miscellaneous goods also grew from 1932 to 1937. All these increases were achieved even though they also were subject to the Imperial preferential tariffs that covered all Japanese goods in India, mentioned in the earlier part of this section. The outstanding expansion of these export goods, even though their contribution to Japan's trade balance was small, was attributable to a lesser degree of discrimination against them, compared with the weight of discrimination against Japanese cotton cloth and other cotton textiles. India's relative position in Japan's total exports dropped to 9.4 percent in 1937, compared with 13.6 percent in 1932.

4. The Australian Quota System

Australia's share in world imports was 2 percent from 1926 to 1937. In world exports, its contribution ranged from 1.5 to 2.3 percent over the same period.[1] The Australian government reformed the tariff system in 1921 to sustain the domestic postwar boom. Major reforms in tariffs relevant to Japan's trade centered on two points: First, a dual tariff system was started by applying the Imperial preferential tariffs for Britain to discriminate against other nations. This measure was to encourage continued British investment in Australia, investment that had started during World War I. This investment rose to large sums, reaching 4.37 billion to 5.84 billion U.S. gold dollars annually, which contributed to nearly doubling Australian trade from 1918 to 1929.[2] The second measure was an upward revision of tariff rates for competitive foreign products to protect domestic infant industries, although in conjunction with the first, this measure provided less protection against Britain.

Thus the application of Australian tariffs followed the three categories listed here in order of descending rates:

1. Common tariffs, generally applied to foreign products.
2. Medium tariffs, applied to products of the British dominions and colonies and to countries that held trade agreements with Australia.
3. Preferential tariffs, applied as privileges to certain products from Britain and from other areas of the British Empire.

Therefore almost all foreign products, except those from the Empire, were subject to common tariffs. Margins of common and medium tariffs ranged from 5 to 15 percent ad valorem. Another equivalent margin was set between medium and preferential rates; thus the preferential margin between common and preferential tariffs ranged from 10 to 30 percent.

Negotiating tariff agreements with Australia was extremely difficult for Japan because of Australia's strong protectionism. Australian tariffs on Japanese products were in general higher than those imposed by Canada, which levied medium tariffs on Japanese products by adopting the most-favored-nation clause from 1922 to 1930.[3]

The Australian government lowered tariffs on 80 items for non-Commonwealth countries in 1926 and again on 52 items in 1929 as a result of recommendations by the Tariff Deliberation Council, which was based on the Tariff Board Act. However, no tariffs on major Japanese products were lowered throughout the same period.

Japan's balance of trade with Australia

Australia's share in Japanese total exports was 2.5 percent in 1926, reaching a peak of 9 percent in 1934. Because of Australian protectionism, however, it declined to 4.4 percent by 1937, as shown in statistical table 1 in appendix I. In Australian statistics, Japan's share in imports was small: 3.5 percent in 1929, 4.4 percent in 1932, and 3.0 percent in 1935. In exports, Japan's share was larger and more rapidly expanding, to 12.2 percent in 1933, from 8.4 percent in 1929, but it declined to 6.6 percent in 1937.[4]

Australia's trade balance with Japan had always favored Australia. Even with its exports expanding every year until 1935, Japan saw its trade deficit with Australia steadily mounting: $36 million in 1926, $40 million in 1929, $46 million in 1931, and $45 million in 1935. Japan failed to reduce its large deficit. The value of imports reached three times the level of exports in 1935, a year before the outbreak of the Japanese-Australian tariff war.

The first causal factor of Japan's trade imbalance with Australia was the nature of the commodities being traded. Year by year, Japan imported an increasingly immense amount of raw materials (wool and scrap iron) necessary to expand its export industries, in addition to food products. Meanwhile, Japan's chief exports to Australia were textiles. The second cause of the trade imbalance was the imposition of severe Australian trade restrictions resulting from budgetary and current account deficits. The Japanese trade deficit further worsened because of British Imperial privileges exercised after 1932, although the restrictions were said to be on an egalitarian basis for every country except for those in the British Commonwealth.

Australian tariffs

Since Australia suffered from heavy deficits in budget and trade, the Australian government (controlled by the Labour Party) again proposed an upward revision of tariffs, this time in August 1929, to mitigate the deficit. But the government was dissolved before the proposal was passed. In 1930, Australia incurred a deficit of 98.2 million U.S. gold dollars in the current account alone. The Australian terms of trade constantly deteriorated, and by 1932 an increase in the volume of wool shipments did not make up the decline of the price of wool, which slid to a third of its 1929 level. Furthermore, the total value of wheat exports, among others, declined to 40 percent, with a 50 percent increase in volume, during 1931–32. The Australian economy was in the Great Depression.[5]

In May 1931, the Australian government embarked on the following policy mix: It cut salaries and wages 20 to 22 percent, increased taxes for revenue, lowered interest rates, and granted subsidies and relief for debtors. Besides having internal contradictions, these policies were too late to cope with the plight of the economy. The government was again dissolved in January 1932, when unemployment reached 29 percent, the highest there in 40 years.[6] The new Australian government (controlled by the Liberal Party) immediately adopted a new trade policy that focused on three objectives: to increase Imperial privileges, to protect domestic industries, and to smoothly reform the tariffs. This policy followed the advice of the Tariff Committee.

The strengthening of the mother country's privileges was a result of the Ottawa Agreement concluded with Britain on a reciprocal basis, and was in effect for five years after 1932. The renewed emphasis on Imperial preferential privileges intensified every year and had a significant impact on Japan's trade. Here are the main provisions of the 1932 British-Australian Ottawa Agreement as relevant to Japan.

1. Britain guaranteed (a) that the current state of free imports of Australian goods would continue; (b) that tariffs on products of other foreign countries would remain as they were; and (c) that the present 10 percent ad valorem level of tariffs on other foreign goods would not be lowered without Australia's agreement.
2. Australia guaranteed to reform the tariff system so that the Imperial privilege would cover a broader category of British products.
3. Australia's minimum *margin* of Imperial preferential tariffs took a progressive form, according to the rates of the original tariffs: 15 percent ad valorem for any products previously free of duty and for products with previous levels of tariffs under 19 percent; 17.5 percent for products with previous tariffs from 19 to 29 percent; and 20 percent for products with previous tariffs of more than 29 percent. (The highest new tariff was not to exceed 75 percent.)
4. Australia agreed to set protective tariffs against British products only for industries of good prospect. Australian tariffs for British products would be set to allow competition for the latter. Any tariff reforms would be communicated beforehand to the relevant British producers.

In accordance with this agreement, the Australian government in 1933 drastically reformed the tariff system. The main changes were a few reductions and a great many upward tariff revisions. The new government relaxed the severe protectionism of the former one, largely for British products that were under the pledges of the agreement. Imperial tariff levels were lowered for 20 items, and general tariffs became lower for 8. In contrast, the general tariffs for 440 items were revised upward. (Although in the following March the government modified the tariffs: It lowered general tariffs for 51 items, raised them for 8, and abolished additional tariffs for 13.)

Another important issue was that Australia extended the Imperial preferential tariffs for Canada, New Zealand, New Guinea (Papua), Norfolk, the British colonies, and other regions under British control (Tanganyika, for example) from November onward. Before implementation of the expanded Imperial preferential tariffs, the Australian government stated that it would favor good customers (Britain and its Empire). The Imperial preferential treatment meant that the favoring of the mother country and its empire would be exercised at the expense of others; Japan could be a good customer because Australia had a chronic trade surplus with Japan. The consequence of the measure, however, was restrictive to the entry of Japanese and American goods to the Australian market.[7]

In November 1934, Australia enacted the Exchange Adjustment Act to favor Britain in mitigating the protective tariff wall against the mother country. Most of the Australian high tariff wall was attributable to a fall in the value of its currency vis-à-vis the British pound.[8]

The margin of Imperial preference

Japan had fairly well caught up with Britain in cotton textile world markets by 1931. In that year, Japanese cotton textile exports surpassed Britain's. The competition between the two countries, especially in the Commonwealth markets, was becoming keener. Already in the 1920s, the Lancashire area in western England—where the cotton textile industry had formerly led the Industrial Revolution—had long been suffering from a serious, prolonged depression and high unemployment. Japanese competition in cotton textiles in Commonwealth markets was thus interfered with by a series of British proposals to strengthen the Imperial tie.[9]

The central issue in Japanese-British competition in the Australian import market was textiles, especially cotton and synthetic products. Table 4.8 presents the tariffs for Japan and the Imperial preferential ones applied to textiles.

Table 4.8 Australian tariff levels for textiles

(percent)

	Cotton cloth		Synthetic cloth	
	Japan	Britain	Japan	Britain
1929	15	free	30	25
1932	25	5	30	25
July 1930–July 1933	25	5	35	25
July 1933–Feb. 1936	25	5	35	20
Mar. 1936	VER (Quota)	5	35	20
May 1936	100–140	5	100–400	20
July 1936	Import permission system			

Source: Japan Academy of Science, *Tsusho Joyaku*, 983–84.

The margins of Imperial preferential tariffs between Japanese textiles and British ones for cotton fabrics were 15 percent through 1931 and 20 percent from 1932 to February 1936. From March 1936, for Japanese ones quotas in the form of voluntary export restrictions (VERs) were applied; then from May, new 100 to 140 percent tariffs were applied, pushing the Imperial preferential margins to extraordinary levels. These prohibitive tariffs and quotas applied only to Japanese products because of Japan's competition with Britain.

The margin of Imperial preference for synthetic fabrics was 5 percent in 1929; it was 10 percent from July 1930 to July 1933 and 15 percent after that until May 1936. Extraordinary margins of tariffs of 65 to 365 percent (as rates of incidence) were then applied as additions to the original 35 percent tariffs for Japan.

Table 4.9 shows why in 1936 Australian prohibitive tariffs were applied to Japanese textiles. From 1933 through 1935, before the prohibitive quotas and tariffs were applied, the widened margin of the Imperial privileges of up to 20 percent for British cotton textiles apparently failed to stop Japanese growth. Japanese cotton textiles were still strongly competitive versus Britain's in the Australian market, even in 1935. Japanese cotton cloth exports expanded to 157 percent by 1935 over the 1933 level, and those from Britain declined to 76 percent, even under the protection of a 20 percent Imperial margin during the same period, though Britain still had an edge over Japan in the absolute amount of cotton cloth exports.

Table 4.9   Australia's textile imports from Japan and Britain, 1933–35

				(thousands of sq. yds.)	
	Cotton cloth		Synthetic cloth		
	Japan	Britain	Japan	Britain	
1933	54,910	154,742	21,151	1,497	
1934	74,499	141,593	43,938	2,632	
1935	86,634	118,348	65,801	2,840	

Source: Japan Academy of Science, *Tsusho Joyaku,* 1003.

In synthetic textiles, Japan far surpassed Britain in total exports and growth rate throughout the 1933–35 period. The Japanese expansion in products was already predominant by 1933; the volume of Japanese exports in synthetic cloth had tripled by 1935 even under a margin of 15 percent Imperial privilege for Britain. This privilege could not succeed in discouraging the rapid growth of Japanese artificial textiles until prohibitive actions were taken in the following spring.

In brief, for the three-year term until 1935, under the Imperial preferential tariffs (ranging from 15 to 20 percent) for Britain, Japan still kept cost advantages in cotton and synthetic textiles versus Britain in the Australian market. It is against that background that the series of actions in quotas (VERs) and the 100 to 400 percent tariffs on Japanese textiles came in the spring of 1936.

Trade negotiations

Japan started negotiating with Australia to reduce the tariff barriers to mitigate its steadily worsening trade deficit. It even hoped to partially make up lost surpluses in markets in China, the United States, and British India.

In early March 1935, a trade mission led by Sir A. Thomson was sent to Australia from Britain. This visit had an obvious influence on Australian government policy that became clear to the Japanese side in autumn. As a Manchester businessman, Sir Thomson provided these points to support Australian prohibitive tariffs against Japan:

1. If Japan decided to control Australian wool imports, a huge surplus of wool could be expected in Australia. Should this happen, Great Britain would purchase this surplus directly (not through intermediate merchants), granted that, in return, Australia would buy Manchester products.
2. Japan would never reciprocally boycott Australian wool; it had learned that any British Commonwealth country providing it with raw materials might resort to retaliation.
3. Therefore, Australia need not worry about the possible excess of Australian wool, considering the ever-increasing Japanese demand for Indian raw cotton after the 1932 Japan-India Trade Agreement.

According to Japanese documents, the tariff negotiations seemed to be making progress for cotton and silk until October 1935, but they were then disrupted when the Australian Trade Minister abruptly left for London. On his return, he informed Japanese Consul-General Kuramatsu Murai that tariff rates for Japanese cotton and synthetic textiles should be raised, not lowered. An upward revision was explained as being necessitated by a reduction in tariff revenues brought on by the cheap prices of Japanese products. Japanese cotton cloth prices "did not fall" during 1933–35. However, prices of Japanese cotton cloth were lower than similar British products during the same period, thus the rapid growth of Japanese cotton cloth exports as shown in table 4.9.

Australian negotiators requested in March 1936 that Japan exercise voluntary export restrictions (VERs), namely, 50 million square yards of cotton cloth and 25 million square yards of synthetic cloth, instead of forcing Australia to levy higher levels of ad valorem duties. The VERs were in effect quotas, which held Japanese textile exports at approximately their 1933 levels. In other words, Japanese exports were expected to decrease in 1936 to 57 percent of the 1935 level for cotton and to 38 percent for synthetic textiles.

The Japanese government, in response, raised the export price of synthetic textiles by applying a high level of export control commissions and refused to accept further Australian requests. These Japanese procedures were said to be temporary, but their duration was not clear. The Australian side, though, disrupted by the Japanese move, threatened to apply high tariffs unless Japan kept within the newly proposed quotas. Japanese representatives aggressively countered this ultimatum by branding the quotas absurd in consideration of Japan's constant trade deficit and suggested the compromise of an upward revision of synthetic cloth prices. Australia kept to its ultimatum and shunned the Japanese proposal. As a result, a tariff revision for cotton and synthetic cloth was proposed in the Australian Parliament on May 22 and implemented the very next day.

The levels of the new prohibitive tariffs of May 1936 varied from 100 percent to 140 percent for cotton cloth and from 100 percent to 400 percent for synthetic cloth, and tariffs for Imperial-privileged British products were about 5 percent for cotton cloth and 20 percent for synthetic cloth (table 4.8).

The Japan-Australia trade war

The Australian government showed interest in continuing trade negotiations "provided that Japan would not apply the Trade Defense Bill."[10] Meanwhile, the May 1936 tariffs and quotas set by the Australians remained in effect.

Japan, after 77 years of free trade since opening its ports in 1858, yielded to a reciprocal policy of protectionism, finally applying the 1934 Trade Defense Act in June 1936 under Imperial Order 124 (Article 1). The act prohibited any Australian wheat, flour, or wool to be imported into Japan without the permission of the Ministry of Commerce and Trade. Furthermore, additional ad valorem duties of 50 percent were applied on Australian beef, butter, condensed milk, leather, and lard from the next day for the following year. Neither were Japanese export goods associated with imports from Australia to be sold domestically during that year. This regulation included wool, lamb wool, and wool fibers. Manchukuo also banned the importation of Australian wheat and flour. Until that day, the Japanese wool industry had relied on Australia for 90 percent of its wool input. The Japanese purchases constituted about 21 percent of total Australian wool exports during 1933–35. Moreover, Japan purchased an average of 21 to 22 percent of Australian wheat exports during the same period.[11]

Australia countered Japan by implementing the special permission system on July 10, 1936, for 86 Japanese items, including cotton and synthetic cloth. On that day, the Australian Minister of Commerce stated, "The policy stance of the Australian government is to issue no permission for Japanese cotton cloth and other Japanese products. Only synthetic and silk products are allowed to be imported up to the levels of the quotas."[12]

Despite condemnation by Japan, the Australian side insisted that this permission system was necessary to begin the Australian-Japanese negotiations on an egalitarian basis. The Australians further promised that if Japan abandoned the Trade Defense Act, the permission system would be abolished and they could again walk to the negotiation table. In September, the Australian side proposed reopening the negotiations, but Japan rejected this. And although they did resume in November, no progress was made.

Reconsidering its external financial position, Japan finally compromised and agreed to the Australian quota system for exports of cotton and synthetic fabrics on condition that the Australian government would agree to quantity-control of imports of Australian wool. After 10 months of negotiations, both sides signed an agreement that included quotas at the end of 1936. It became effective on the first day of the following year.[13]

The Quota System

The central idea of the quota system on both sides was a barter trade between Australian wool and Japanese textiles. At the end of 1936, both countries agreed that

1. Japan would import 400,000 *hyo* of Australian wool per season (800,000 *hyo* by the end of June 1937).[14] Australia would import a total of 102.5 million square yards of cotton and synthetic fabrics per year.
2. Japan would abandon a 50 percent additional ad valorem duty under the Trade Defense Act, and Australia would abolish the permission system in imports and reduce the general level of tariffs for Japanese goods to 40 percent, from 50.
3. The Australian government would permit imports of Japanese cotton and synthetic fabrics up to 76.8 million square yards of each, from January 1, 1937 to June 30, 1938, an 18-month period.

The Japanese government first insisted on the total quota for textiles to be 150 million square yards for one year, but it then compromised. (Japanese calico, though, fell outside the applied quotas because it was used to make Australian wheat flour bags, and wheat was the primary Australian export. But the amount of calico exported to Australia was only about 2,000 square yards annually.)

Trade after March 1936

Japan exported 52 million square yards of cotton cloth in 1936 and 63 million in 1937. Exports of synthetic fabrics were up to 42 million and 58 million square yards in 1936 and 1937. The export quotas were approximately secured. Japan imported 316,000 *hyo* and 255,000 *hyo* of Australian wool in 1936 and 1937. This was short of what was agreed to as the quotas, but in the amounts that Australia could offer. Australia was changing its policy stance to control the exports of wool.

The quotas and broadly widened preferential margins resulted in depressing Australian imports from Japan and encouraging trade with Britain. The contrasts are shown in table 4.10 over the periods before (1931–32) and after (1936–37) the application of trade restrictions.

As seen in the table, Australia succeeded in curbing its imports from Japan. They declined by 0.9 percent in 1936–37 from the 1931–32 level. In contrast, imports from Britain grew to 43.7 percent, from 39.5 percent, over the same period. The expansion in the British share was especially at the cost of Japan when we recall the decline in Japanese textile exports to the Australian market during that period.

More pronounced were Australian exports. The British share, which was already reaching 50 percent in 1931–32, gained no more during the 1936–37 period over the previous level. That was probably the maximum of Australian goods Britain could then absorb. Australian exports to Japan declined by 5.6 percent during the same period, as shown in table 4.10. Because of these Imperial preferential tariffs, the relative Australian position in British imports also increased, to 7.8 percent in 1938, from 4.1 percent in 1929.[15]

Table 4.10 Australian trade with Japan and Britain, 1928–37

| | Imports | | Exports | |
	Japan	Britain	Japan	Britain
1928–29	3.3	39.8	8.4	39.8
1931–32	5.4	39.5	12.2	49.5
1936–37	4.5	43.7	6.6	49.5

(percentage of the total)

Source: Japan Academy of Science, *Tsusho Joyaku,* 938, 991–92.

Japan's substitutions of countries and products

The effect of the 1936 Australian restrictions was immense. They brought major changes in the distribution of country and commodity in Japan's trade. The 1936 agreement required Japan's counterpurchases in quantity of Australian wool, but it did not specifically link values between Australian wool and Japanese textiles. Confined within the pledges of the agreement, purchases by Japanese importers of Australian wool declined greatly, and those from South Africa, New Zealand, Uruguay, and Argentina increased. This development was to be expected for two reasons. First, the price of Australian wool was increased because a trade war was expected. Second, the wool-exporting countries mentioned above, mostly developing countries, demanded that Japan balance trade on a bilateral basis or they would purchase much less from Japan than they had been. In demanding this, they also offered lower prices for wool than Australia did. The development of Japan's country substitutions in imports of wool is shown in table 4.11.

Table 4.11 Country substitutions in Japanese wool imports

					(thousands of kin)[a]
	Australia	New Zealand	South Africa	Argentina	Total[b]
1929	78.2	-	2.6	0.5	81.5
1933	170.6	5.5	2.9	3.1	182.5
1936	116.9	17.9	14.1	5.7	164.1
1937	73.7	29.6	55.9	12.7	195.4

Source: Toyo Keizai Shinposha, *Nihon Boeki Seiran* (Foreign Trade of Japan: A Statistical Survey), (Tokyo: Toyo Keizai Shinposha, 1975 rev. ed.), *The Supplement*, 32–35.

Note: a. One *kin*, a Japanese unit of weight, equals 600.2 grams.
b. The total figures include others.

In a second trade agreement, dated June 1938, the quota for wool was lowered from the Australian side to two-thirds of the 1936 level for the coming one-year period. When a reprise of the British-German war was expected, Japanese wool dealers also found increasing difficulty in importing Australian wool because Britain had made an agreement to purchase all wool exports from Australia and New Zealand for the double purposes of reexportation and war preparation.

The Japanese government wanted a shift in imports to iron from wool. The bureaucrats preferred iron to wool when Japan should buy something from Australia so that it would not again be the target of severe discrimination. Thus Japan imported an increasing amount of scrap iron from Australia, instead of wool. (Japan had no technology to fabricate iron and steel at an internationally competitive low cost until 1960.) It also substituted other commodities imported from Australia.

In exercising these quotas, Japan saw its visible trade balance improve, though still showing a deficit. The amount of trade between the two countries, however, shrank because of Australian import restrictions, the trade war, long negotiations, and the final quota system. The rapid growth of Japanese exports to Australia in the late 1920s and the first half of the 1930s was halted and reversed. As stated above, Australia's share in Japanese total exports fell to 4.4 percent in 1937, from 9.0 percent at the 1934 peak. In Australian markets, Japan yielded, opening a path for the recovery of British exports, which increased 4.2 percent after the spring of 1936. Most of the reduction in Japan's exports after that year was attributed to much smaller shipments of textiles.[16]

5. Egypt and Middle Eastern Countries

I. Egypt: Protectionism-cum-nationalism against Japan or Britain?

Egypt became independent of Britain in 1924, but Japanese trade was in a difficult position because of the lack of any treaty with Egypt. For example, Egypt concluded a treaty with Greece and levied low tariffs on Greek products. Japanese tobacco exports to Egypt were levied higher tariffs than imports from Greece were, and these exports tapered off because of this differential stemming from the lack of any commercial treaties.

First, Japan hoped to conclude a treaty that would include the most-favored-nation (MFN) clause concerning consulate judicial rights and commercial rights. After negotiations, however, this turned out to be difficult because Japanese exports came across tariff discrimination, and exports declined. Thus Japan concluded a temporary agreement to obtain the reciprocal MFN clause only on a commercial basis in March 1930.[1]

Table 4.12 presents the contributions of selected countries to Egyptian imports. Japan's share in Egyptian imports in 1926 was small, 1.6 percent of the total, compared with Britain's share (21.8 percent) and the shares of other countries, which included Germany, Italy, the United States, Belgium, France, and Romania. The Japanese share increased to 4 percent in 1937. Germany, Italy, and the United States expanded their shares to 11 percent, 8.6 percent, and 5.6 percent, respectively, keeping the British at 21.2 percent. Yet a significant British influence was a constant in the Egyptian economy.

Japanese imports from Egypt were also small, 3.8 percent of total Egyptian exports in 1926, as shown in table 4.13. Although Japanese imports grew to 6.1 percent, they still could not compare with the British purchases, 30.9 percent of the total Egyptian exports in 1937.

Table 4.12 Shares in Egyptian imports of major trading partners

(percent)

	Japan	U.K.	Germany	Italy	U.S.A.	Belgium	France
1926	1.6	21.8	7.2	8.6	4.7	4.2	11.2
1937	4.0	21.2	11.0	8.6	5.6	6.0	4.5

Source: League of Nations, *International Trade Statistics 1930* (Geneva: League of Nations, 1932), 319; (1938), 291.

Table 4.13 Shares in total Egyptian exports of major trading partners

(percent)

	Japan	U.K.	Germany	Italy	U.S.A.	Belgium	France
1926	3.8	44.6	4.5	5.7	13.0	0.5	11.7
1937	6.1	30.9	8.3	6.0	6.5	2.1	10.6

Source: League of Nations, *International Trade Statistics 1930* (Geneva: League of Nations, 1932), 341; (1938), 313.

Abrogation of the Egyptian commercial treaty with Japan

The Egyptian government, after sending a commercial mission to England to study commercial relations between the two countries, on July 18, 1935, repudiated the commercial treaty with Japan stipulating reciprocity on an MFN basis. The effect of the repudiation was to impose a 100 percent increase of customs tariffs on imports from Japan after the three-month notice provided for in the treaty.

This situation resulted in a protest from the Egyptian weaving industry. The Egyptians understood that the strong competitiveness of Japanese cotton goods with Egyptian products was due to two privileges, by which the Japanese were benefited: (a) the free selection of cotton worldwide; (b) the marked devaluation of the yen.

The reasons advanced by the Egyptian Minister of Finance in support of the abrogation of the treaty were that the yen's decrease in value on international exchanges had permitted the sales of Japanese products in Egypt at extremely low prices, despite the customs duties levied thereon. Moreover, whereas Egyptian law compelled Egyptian industry to only use expensive Egyptian raw cotton, the Japanese textile industry used inexpensive Indian cotton.[2]

Egypt was scarcely harmed by any retaliation from Japan because the balance of trade was favorable for Japan until 1935, as shown in the following table:

Table 4.14 Japan's trade balance with Egypt

(millions of U.S. dollars)

	Exports	Imports	Balance
1934	21.5	13.6	7.9
1935	15.3	14.6	0.7
1936	11.8	13.2	−1.4
1937	9.4	21.3	−11.9

Source: See statistical table 1, appendix I.

It is interesting to find that Egyptian domestic opinion was divided: On one side was the major part of the Egyptian press and most of the national press, which were immensely attached to the expansion of domestic manufacturers and devoted to the principle of the revision of the abrogated convention. They argued, "Egypt suffered in recent years from foreign competition and more especially from the method used by Japanese manufacturers."[3] The measures were expected to provide a distinct benefit to domestic textile manufacturers and to the improved competitive position of foreign countries against Japan, notably Great Britain. The older textile merchants, most of whom had business connections with England, supported the repudiation and wanted to protect the domestic cotton textile industry.

On the other hand, however, the Egyptian nationalists, the more advanced elements, inspired first of all by political emancipation, claimed the irrelevancy of this repudiation and the orientation of the economic policy of the present government as a direct intervention by

England. They protested that the government favored Britain instead of Egypt and asked for the protection of local raw cotton producers, as below.[4]

1. The present Nessim Pasha Cabinet had granted a new concession, without political equivalent, to the British exigencies for monopolizing the Egyptian (cotton textile) market for the interest of Great Britain, which was the most formidable Egyptian rival.

2. This interpretation was confirmed because the Lancashire manufacturers had recently refused, in manufacturing British cotton products, to pledge themselves to increase their purchases of Egyptian cotton which was produced in great quantities in the Valley of the Nile. The British remained free to use Sudanese and American cotton.

3. It was unquestionably necessary to implement an immediate and adequate protection and certain commercial accords to new economic conditions for the future of Egyptian cotton producers. The Egyptian economy, which had relied greatly on raw cotton production and exports, was threatened by foreign competition, especially by the extension of cotton plantations in Asia and Africa.

Criticism of the abrogation of the commercial treaty with Japan was also found in the press. A letter to the *Times* (London) from the former Egyptian prime minister noted that the measure was more in the interest of England than of Egypt, which was benefited greatly by the purchase of Japanese products at low prices.[5] Some Egyptian leaders had even declared their opposition to the surtax on the grounds that it was designed to assist British textile manufacturers at the expense of Egyptian consumers, who were deprived of the opportunity to purchase cheap Japanese textiles without compensating benefits.

The Japanese negotiators had voiced sympathy with Egypt's desire to balance trade between Egypt and Japan, but had pointed out that it was difficult for Japan to purchase a large quantity of Egyptian cotton because of its high prices. Japan did soon increase purchases of other Egyptian products, however, principally gypsum, salt, and phosphates.[6] At about the same time in Japan, spinning manufacturers had proposed a reprisal boycott on imports of Egyptian cotton. But it was not carried out.

The Egyptian government, which wanted to preserve friendly relations with Japan, especially hoped to limit as far as possible the inevitable consequences of the treaty's recent repudiation. It yielded to the antigovernment opinion in Egypt, and declared its intention to negotiate another convention to serve as a new and lasting basis for future transactions in Egypt on the expiration of the three-month limit imposed by the abrogation. The Egyptian government further decided to permit imports from Japan during only the grace period and on the basis of average imports for the past three years. Other imports were forbidden unless merchants paid increased customs duties, to prevent a large influx of Japanese commodities. Egyptian officials had announced that their primary aims were to equilibrate the trade balance between Egypt and Japan and to protect Egyptian textile manufacturers.

Sizable progress for Egypt in balancing trade

The imposition by Egypt, on September 19, 1935, of a surtax on articles originating from Japan restricted excessive inroads in textiles during the few years following the devaluation of the yen. This indicated the effectiveness of a surtax because imports into Egypt from Japan declined after the imposition.

After a few months of sporadic discussions, Egypt-Japan negotiations to try to reach a new commercial agreement were brought into active life. To protect local industries, the Egyptian government laid down to the Japanese delegation on March 10, 1936, an outline of these two conditions: (1) the establishment of a differential tariff on Japanese cotton textiles of cheaper varieties and other goods that competed with locally produced products. This tariff, they argued, was necessary under the depreciation of the Japanese currency, which permitted Japanese goods to undersell Egyptian products. And (2) the establishment of a net balance of trade between the two countries.[7]

The first proposal was less difficult for Japan to fulfill than the second. No indication of the nature of new Japanese proposals has been found, but because of the serious difficulties Japanese trade suffered as a result of the 40 percent surtax on Japanese goods at that time, it was understandable that the Japanese were very eager to reach an understanding with Egypt.

The balance of trade between Egypt and Japan now reversed to be favorable for Egypt by the imposition of the surtax and by an increase of Japanese purchases from Egypt in 1936 and 1937.

Egyptian textile manufacturers, however, were not experiencing the benefits expected from the surtax. The Egyptian customs statistics for 1936 indicate that imports of Japanese textiles had been largely replaced by those from Czechoslovakia, Belgium, and England.

In 1937 and afterward, Japan's trade balance with Egypt, a remote and relatively small trading partner, registered a substantial deficit, as indicated in table 4.14, above.

II. PALESTINE, SYRIA, AND IRAQ

Japanese trade with Palestine and Syria exhibited numerous analogies with the Egyptian situation. Discriminatory measures to limit the growth of Japanese exports became possible because Japan had withdrawn from the League of Nations. This excessive action moved Japan from an egalitarian international status to the position of being discriminated against, juridically and in practice, in trade and other areas, as pointed out in the following description:

> That is why the Syrian and Palestinian merchants in Beirut and Jerusalem have just appealed to the respective High Commissioners of mandate powers. In Syria and Lebanon, where the French representatives just decided to lower the customs tariffs very considerably, the maintenance of the minimum tariff granted to Japanese products provoked the greatest fears to the Syrian textile industries. The same fears and reactions are to be found in Jerusalem.[8]

The situation in Iraq was very similar. Important negotiations had taken place between the Baghdad government and the Japanese attaché in Turkey concerning a commercial treaty between the two countries. Being rich in financial resources from the petroleum concessions made for foreigners, Iraq was rapidly awakening to the potential for progress while the market possibilities of its needs were increasing. Japan was one of the first countries to understand this and to multiply its imports into that country. The Iraqi government intended to defend itself by arguing that Japan bought only a few cereals in Iraq, and it wanted more purchases by Japan to balance trade. Another source reveals similar situations:

> In the countries of the Near East as a whole, a series of measures that tended to limit Japan's liberty of expansion had by this time risen against Japanese activity for protecting the nascent industries of the interested state against Japan. Japanese competition had been considered unacceptable there.[9]

Conclusion

Nations in the Middle East and in Africa stood up together against Japan's trade, openly protecting their infant industries with discriminatory measures because Japan had left the League of Nations. One description of this is found in the following memorandum quoted from reports sent from the American Embassy in Paris.

> As long as Japan formed a part of the League of Nations, the fundamental clause inscribed in the Pact and conferring equality of customs and commercial treatment on all the mandate States rendered impossibility or inoperative of any discriminatory measures of defense. At the present time such is no longer the situation, juridical or in practice.[10]

A narrow gap in technological standards and a wider gap in productive capacity and economies of scale existed between cotton textile industries in Japan and in relatively more backward countries than Japan. This created fears in local nascent industries and provided ammunition to these countries in their hostilities against Japan. Nationalism, awakened in part by Japan's invasion of their markets, was a backdrop of this.

Chapter 5

JAPAN-NETHERLANDS
TRADE SQUABBLES

"More I say, this is a free country I know, but I 'm not going to have your stalls right in front of my shop.", says John Bull in a British poster circa 1900.

Japan also experienced friction in its trade with the Dutch East Indies, which we will consider amid the dynamically changing world markets.

From 1928 to 1937, 72 percent of Japanese exports were shipped to Asia. More significantly, 88.5 percent of those shipped to Asian regions were manufactured products, markedly higher than the 36 percent of manufactured exports shipped to the rest of the world in the same period.[1] Manufactured exports were a key factor for the continuing progress of Japan as a newly industrialized country with scarce natural resources, especially after the fall in raw-silk exports. The Dutch East Indies market played a sizable role in Japanese manufactured exports then, following China (before 1931) and British India, in 1929–37.

Japan and Dutch East Indies trade

Japan had started trading with the Dutch East Indies (the present-day Indonesia) at the conclusion of the Japan-Netherlands Trade Agreement in 1912. Privileges of the Britain-Netherlands "Sumatra" Treaty of 1872 were extended to Japanese goods, according to the most-favored-nation clause of the 1912 treaty. The Netherlands held no privileges over Japan's exports to the colony: Tariffs on Japanese goods were levied the same rates as those on Dutch products at 5 percent ad valorem until 1924.[2]

Four points can be cited in regard to trade between Japan and the Dutch East Indies:

1. Japanese exports grew rapidly, especially in manufactured products.
2. At the same time, the volume of Japanese imports was small; thus from 1926 to 1937 trade almost always favored Japan.
3. The Dutch colony started to severely discriminate against Japan in 1933.
4. One causal factor for this was that the Netherlands held the gold standard even after the British had abandoned it and had overvalued the Dutch and colonial currencies.

Japanese Exports

A rapid expansion in Japanese *exports* is revealed in table 5.1. The figures shown are for the import market of the Dutch East Indies, since these are clearer than Japanese export statistics because of the relatively small share of the Dutch East Indies in Japanese trade. In exports, it was 3.7 percent in 1928, but it grew to a peak of 8.5 percent in 1933 in Japanese statistics.

Table 5.1 Shares of major countries in imports to the Dutch East Indies

(percent)

	Netherlands	Japan	Britain	U.S.	Germany
1913	33.3	1.6	17.5	2.1	6.6
1929	19.7	10.6	10.8	12.1	10.7
1932	15.8	21.3	9.6	9.6	7.7
1937	19.1	25.4	10.3	10.2	8.5

Source: Japan Academy of Science, *Tsusho Joyaku,* 1039–40.

The Japanese export growth in the Dutch East Indies started during World War I, when shipments from Europe were reduced. Rapid growth continued. In the two decades after the opening of the trade relationship, Japan's relative position in imports of the Dutch East Indies rose enormously to 21.3 percent in 1932, from 1.6 percent in 1913, making it the most active competitor against the Netherlands.

Imports from the mother country declined to 15.8 percent in 1929, from 33.3 percent in 1913. By 1932, Japan had claimed the position of leading exporter to the colony.

During the free-trade period, in 1924, the Netherlands government revised this colony's tariffs. Most imports were levied 12 percent unitary tariffs and the rest 10 percent. But these rates were not high. Regardless of this change, Japanese exports grew as shown in table 5.1 above. The growth of Japanese exports to the Dutch East Indies until 1932 was made at the expense of other trading partners, especially the Netherlands and Britain. The rising position of Japan against the decline of the Netherlands and Britain over the period of this survey is clear from the table. Despite its small size, the Dutch East Indies market was particularly important for Japan because Japan enjoyed a trade surplus every year.

An expansion in Japanese *manufactured products* took place with the growth of exports to this Dutch colony. The leading components of Japanese exports shifted from primary goods to semimanufactured and manufactured goods, and Japanese export growth was also accelerated by such progressive changes in the exports.[3] Manufactured goods accounted for 76 to 80 percent of the total Japanese exports to the Dutch colony from 1929 to 1933. This extraordinarily high ratio of manufactured products to total shipments to the colony demonstrated how important this market was for Japan for its continuing industrialization. All manufactured goods—cotton products, synthetic textiles, bicycles, toys, and lamps—made remarkable progress. The development in distributive shares of manufactured exports during the 1929–37 period is presented in table 5.2.

i. *Textiles:* All textile exports to this colony contributed greatly to the Japanese expansion of the industry. In a listing by product base, those shipped to the Dutch colony accounted for 17.7 percent of Japan's total cotton textile exports, 14.4 percent of the total synthetic textiles, and 9 percent of the total knitted cotton clothing in 1932.[4] Cotton cloth and knitted cotton products contributed more than half the total exports from Japan from 1929 to 1933. Shipments of cotton cloth alone more than doubled in these four years to 423 million square yards, from 193 million.

Table 5.2 Japanese manufactured exports to the Dutch East Indies

(percentage of the total in 1933 value terms)

	1929	1933	1937
Cotton cloth	48.8	49.7	42.8
Knitted cotton products	2.9	2.4	1.7
Silk textiles	6.9*	0.7	0.2
Synthetic textiles		9.5	2.9
Bicycles and parts	4.1	3.7	3.0
China and porcelain	5.7	2.4	1.0
Glass and glass products	2.2	1.7	0.7
Tires	2.8	1.6	1.3
Toys	0.6	1.2	0.3
Lamps and parts	1.3	1.1	1.0
Cement	4.0	0.9	0.5
Subtotal	79.3	76.1	57.1

Source: Ministry of Finance, *Nihon Gaikoku Boeki Geppo* (Monthly Returns of Foreign Trade) (Tokyo: Ministry of Finance, December 1928, 1931, 1934, 1936, 1938).

* Silk and synthetic textiles are classified together until 1932.

A decline in the growth of knitted cotton underwear after 1933 was due to Dutch import restrictions. In silk and staple fiber textiles, only the latter made rapid progress, approaching 9.6 percent of total Japanese exports by 1933. (In Japanese official statistics, silk and synthetic textiles are separately classified only from 1933.) These textiles altogether contributed from 58.6 to 62.4 percent of all Japanese exports to the Dutch East Indies from 1929 to 1933.

  ii. Beer: 21 percent of all Japanese beer exports in 1933 went to the Dutch East Indies.

  iii. Cement: Cement shipments to this colony represented 30.4 percent of all Japanese cement exports in 1932.

The following figures in Japanese shipments to the Dutch East Indies were recorded in 1932 as peak levels.

iv. Glass and glass products: 12.5 percent of all such exports.

v. China and porcelain: 10.5 percent.

vi. Tires: 27.9 percent.

vii. Electric light bulbs: 6 percent.

viii. Toys: 5.3 percent.

ix. Iron products: The shipment of bicycles with parts, and nails grew rapidly, accounting for 14.3 percent of all Japanese iron product exports in 1934.

Japanese imports

Japanese imports from the Dutch East Indies were small in amount. Japan started at a 6.8 percent share in 1913, a share that continually declined, reaching 3.3 percent in 1929. Japanese imports registered only 4.5 percent in 1937, when Dutch discrimination against Japan's exports was in full swing. Discussions on major imports relevant to our subject are as follows:

i. Sugar: Japan purchased a large quantity of crude sugar from the Dutch East Indies for consumption and reexport during their first decade of trade. These purchases declined, and by 1919 the value of imports from the Dutch East Indies was reduced to 35 percent of the 1914 level. Sugar imports to Japan steadily declined because of successful sugar production in Taiwan. The imports were further reduced to 120 thousand tons in 1933, from 220 thousand in 1929. The price of sugar in the world market also fell sharply during that period.

The Dutch East Indies was the second leading sugar producer and exporter in the world before 1930. But after the Great Depression, the former recipients of Dutch East Indies sugar, notably, among others, British India, started domestic sugar production for self-sufficiency. In 1933 the value of Dutch East Indies sugar exports fell to only 25 percent of their 1932 level (volume down to 61 percent). Increased Japanese sugar exports to China were also responsible for this decline. Thus from 1933 the colony suffered a heavy accumulation of surplus stocks. Its total area of sugar plantations was reduced in 1934 to only a quarter of the 1930 level. By then sugar production in the Dutch East Indies had declined to the position of ninth in the world because it had become utterly dependent on foreign demand. (British India became the second largest producer in that year.) It took until 1937 for the colony to regain its initial position, second to Cuba, in the world sugar market.

ii. *Petroleum:* The United States and the Dutch East Indies were competing for exports of petroleum to Japan. In 1929, the Dutch East Indies supplied 30 percent of all Japanese petroleum imports. In 1937, petroleum, as a strategic import, suddenly increased, accounting for 49 percent of all Japanese imports from the Dutch East Indies, because of the beginning of the Sino-Japanese War.

iii. Imports of *rubber, paraffin, and wax* also increased. Yet these increases altogether, including petroleum, did not compensate for the decline in sugar imports in the 1926–37 period.[5]

Table 5.3 presents Japanese imports from the Dutch East Indies (the last column).

Table 5.3 Share of exports from the Dutch East Indies, main trading partners

(percent)

	Netherlands	Malaya	U.S.	Britain	Japan
1913	28.8	21.5	2.2	3.9	5.8
1929	16.1	22.2	11.5	8.8	3.3
1932	19.1	18.3	12.1	8.9	4.4
1937	20.1	20.6	18.7	5.3	4.5

Source: Japan Academy of Science, *Tsusho Joyaku,* 1039–41.

Japan's relative position in Dutch East Indies exports was a low 3.3 percent in 1929 because Japan replaced imports in sugar from the Dutch colony with sugar from Taiwan (a Japanese colony). Even after the 1933 Japan-Dutch East Indies Commercial Conference took place to promote Japanese imports, its share was only 4.5 percent in 1937.[6]

Exports to the Netherlands from the colony in 1929 declined to some 16 percent of total exports, from 28.8 percent in 1913. These figures reveal the same downward trend shown in imports from the Netherlands to the Dutch East Indies. In this sense, the tie between the mother country and this colony became loose. A small recovery (4 percent) of the colony's shipments to the mother country in 1937 was a reciprocal part of preferential privileges to promote purchases of Dutch products.

The increases of other main importers from the Dutch East Indies are in contrast with the Japanese experience. Exports to the United States developed very rapidly, and the relative position of the United States in Dutch East Indies total exports had climbed powerfully to 18.7 percent by 1937, from 2.2 percent in 1913. Shipments to Singapore during most of the period registered the second largest value after the Netherlands, but Malaya became the leading purchaser from the Dutch East Indies in 1937.

The final point is that the Netherlands remained under the *gold standard system,* even after Britain gave it up in 1931. The U.S. Congress decided to devalue the dollar in June and the Economic Conference in London was broken off in July 1933, while the Dutch government declared it would continue as a member of the gold bloc with France, Switzerland, Belgium, Italy, and Poland. The Dutch guilder became overvalued, and the prices of the main exports from the Dutch East Indies—sugar, petroleum, zinc, and rubber—became high internationally as a result of this strong appreciation of the Dutch guilder. This made it difficult for Japan to import from there because these imported products had high price elasticities in Japan, and thus they were substituted with products from other nations.[7] Later the Dutch government realized that holding to the gold standard only aggravated its external financial position.

The value of 100 yen for the Dutch guilder ranged from 114.4 to 122.3 during the 1929–31 period, when both countries remained under the gold standard system. After Japan left it, the value of the yen fell sharply: 100 yen equaled 69.7 guilders in 1932 and 49.6 guilders in 1933.[8] As the value of the yen dropped, Japan's surplus on the visible trade account (transactions of physical goods) rose to 16.59 million U.S. dollars in 1932 and to 26.16 million in 1933, from 2.96 million in 1930. In Japanese statistics, the Dutch East Indies share in total exports rose to 6.5 percent in 1933, the peak in the interwar period, and the Dutch share in imports fell to 2 percent.[9]

The Dutch government had to give up free trade to prevent a draining of its foreign exchange reserves; otherwise, its continuance with the gold standard system would be precarious. The government thus enacted a series of acts and orders to restrict imports.[10]

Revision of the tariff system in the Dutch East Indies

The first restrictive measure took place in 1931 and was caused by the twin Dutch deficits in trade and finance. The government created new additional 10 percent unitary tariffs, which were soon raised to 20 percent.

Although Japanese exports expanded rapidly in 1931, rumors spread in the Dutch East Indies that Japan had territorial ambitions there. Thus Japan concluded a treaty with the Netherlands in 1933 to quell these rumors. The treaty was based on a modern concept that if any territorial problems arose, they should be solved peacefully by an international judicial committee in The Hague. An international committee concerning international law and political issues was newly established for this purpose.[11] Also in 1933, Japan and the Netherlands concluded an agreement not to levy double income taxes on navigation businesses in both countries. The conclusion of these two agreements demonstrated the Japanese intention of avoiding economic problems with the Dutch colony.

The Dutch government proposed another revision, for additional tariffs of 50 percent, in the Dutch Parliament in March 1933. It was soon approved and was implemented in April, but the market response to this announcement was to increase imports from Japan in expectations of a future rise in the prices of Japanese goods. This increase in demand counterbalanced the decline in imports from Japan caused by the Manchurian Incident.[12]

The Dutch government then changed the general tariff system in September 1933. The explanation given was to make up for the lowered national revenues caused by falls in the world price of sugar. As a result, the tariffs were raised in January 1934 to 20 percent ad valorem for luxury goods from 12 percent, and to 12 percent from 6 percent for materials of luxury goods and for a small number of other goods.

Among leading Japanese exports, silk and synthetic textiles, silk thread, knitted cotton underwear, socks, men's shirts, porcelain, enameled pans, cosmetics, window glass, glassware, and automobile parts fell into the category of luxury goods and were levied 20 percent ad valorem tariffs. Japanese cotton thread, and bleached and unbleached and dyed cotton cloth, were levied 12 percent ad valorem tariffs. It is noteworthy that knitted cotton underwear cloth was classified as a material for luxury goods.

Dutch import restrictions on Japanese products

Direct import restrictions of the Dutch East Indies were started by enactment of the Emergency Import Control Act in June 1933 to increase privileges for products from the Netherlands. This act, quickly implemented in September, gave the Dutch government the right to forbid imports by means of governmental order if the imported goods exceeded a prescribed level in either value or quantity. The measure was defended as protecting domestic industries from damages incurred by the depreciation of foreign currencies.

Restrictive orders were issued for three products—cement, beer, and textiles—under the 1933 act, and a series of restrictive orders for other products soon followed.

> *i. Cement:* The Order to Control Imports of Cement was issued in September. Within the same month, Japanese and Australian producers concluded a private reciprocal agreement, as in the VERs of today, to apply quotas by themselves in exports of cement.
>
> *ii. Beer:* The Emergency Order to Control Imports of Beer was issued next, in December, to form quotas to protect domestic

brewers. The quotas were proportional to the 1932 levels of
beer imports from each country as a standard. The Japanese
suffered a low quota because Japan's beer exports grew rapidly in 1933, not in 1932.[13]

iii. Textiles: The Emergency Imports Restrictions of Textiles
and the Emergency Imports Restrictions for Unbleached
Cotton Cloth were issued in February 1934.

The Netherlands acquired special privileges of large quotas for
textiles. The Dutch authorities explained that the quota of textiles established for each country was on an egalitarian basis, but
importers were under the license system, which granted licenses to
trading companies holding memberships in European commerce
associations. The last condition confirmed only three qualified
Japanese importers, headed by Mitsui. The amount of the quota
given to the licensee was decided by the levels of import performance during 1930. Japanese exports of textiles to the Dutch East
Indies, like those of beer, grew strongly after 1930 (as shown in
table 5.2) but this year was chosen as the base. Thus the license
system effectively worked as a low upper ceiling for imports from
Japan.

Japanese companies appealed this problem to the Dutch authorities. In responding, they changed the regulation in a few minor
points: "An adequate quota could be given to those foreigners who
lived long enough in the Dutch East Indies, but they would be subject to the following conditions. First, the authority would consult
with the members of a special committee. Second, if the members
recognized the applicants as importers of the goods in subject, the
committee would submit the application to the Director General
of Economic Affairs for an approval. Third, the present importers' interests would be considered before applying new adequate
quotas to them. Fourth, the total quota for Japanese dealers was
limited at 25 percent of the total imports of the goods in subject
from Japan in each year." Furthermore: "However, fifth, the new
importers of the restricted goods were confined to members of
associations in commerce and industry in Europe."[14]

Thus the strong restrictive conditions remained fundamentally unchanged. As a result, the low quotas for Japanese dealers led to reduced imports of Japanese goods in the Dutch East Indies market. For the most part it was Dutch trading companies who gained.

Japan-Netherlands trade negotiations

Representatives of Japanese and Dutch cotton textile industries met at a privately based conference in December 1933, but this was fruitless. In January 1934, the Dutch government proposed a conference on a governmental basis. Japan agreed if a prerequisite was honored that the Dutch would not proceed with any new unfavorable measures against Japanese trading positions. Both sides agreed on a reciprocal basis. Japan sent a group of specialists led by an ambassador, although it had no effective instructions for carrying out the negotiations favorably because of the following factors:

1. Japan could not boycott trade with the Dutch East Indies, since it offered excellent markets always resulting in surpluses in the trade balance for Japanese manufactures, especially for textiles.
2. Neither could Japan increase purchases of sugar from the Dutch East Indies, since the sugar would be reexported after refining, thus further reducing sugar sales by the Dutch East Indies in China.
3. Japan already had such a huge trade surplus with the Dutch East Indies that it could not use a boycott of crude sugar purchases as a weapon in the negotiations. Moreover, Japan could not boycott petroleum, rubber, zinc, or corn from the Dutch colony because it needed such food and industrial materials.

Japan's Ambassador Harukazu Nagaoka arrived at Batavia in June 1934 and appealed to the local people that the Dutch prohibitive restrictions on imports of inexpensive Japanese products would have enormous disadvantages for them. But his statement was ineffective because the local people were unorganized. Contrary to the Japanese intention, the appeal induced unwanted repercussions from the Dutch authorities at the negotiating table.[15]

During negotiations, the Japanese asked that the discriminatory import restrictions against Japan be mitigated on the basis of the Japan-Netherlands Commercial Treaty. The Dutch defended their policy, saying it was their right to take suitable actions against the devaluation of the yen, and therefore their actions only responded to what had been done by other nations. Debates on conflicting positions of both sides were difficult to solve. The Dutch side continued to issue orders of import restrictions on major Japanese exports as follows. (This section should be read as a continuation of the description of the previous three restrictive orders.)

> iv. *China and porcelain:* When the negotiations got into trouble, the Dutch government issued another new order, in July 1934, to restrict imports of china and porcelain from Japan. "The Dutch side broke the pledge that they would not put any further offensive measures on Japanese trade during the negotiation period," the Japanese side wrote.[16]
>
> v. *Shipping:* The Dutch government applied another new order for quotas on shipment values between Japanese and Dutch shipping companies. The negotiations became more difficult.
>
> vi. *Kitchenware:* The Dutch side further imposed a new import restriction on frying pans in October 1934.
>
> vii. *Other products:* The Dutch went on establishing a series of acts to restrict more imports from Japan. Unbleached coarse cotton cloth, glassware, porcelain-coated kitchenware, and bicycles and bicycle parts were to be severely restricted starting in January 1935.
>
> viii. *Phosphoric and other fertilizers* were to be restricted from March 1935.

These strict restrictions covered 56 Japanese products in all, including almost all manufactured Japanese exports. According to a Japanese document of that period, the Dutch intended to make use of their authority for issuing these new restrictive acts as a weapon in the negotiations.[17]

The Japanese asked for alleviation at each issuance of new restrictive measures. In responding to new Dutch restrictions, the Japanese government organized export activities in each relevant industry, intending to make negotiations easier for the Japanese representatives. The newly created organizations were the Japanese China and Porcelain Export Association, the Japanese Cotton Textile Export Association, and the Japanese Silk Export Association. The South Pacific Miscellaneous Product Export Association was established for the rest of the exporters. Meanwhile trade negotiations continued, but made no progress.

The dispute over cotton textiles

Japanese exports accounted for nearly 80 percent of all cotton cloth imports in this colonial market in 1933. More importantly, cotton cloth contributed 49.7 percent of the total value of Japan's exports to this market that year, as shown in table 5.2. The next table (5.4) presents the development of imports in cotton cloth in the Dutch East Indies from Japan and other countries.

Table 5.4 Country distribution of cotton cloth imports to the Dutch East Indies

(thousands of tons)

	Japan	Netherlands	Britain	Others	Total
1929	30.9	20.8	14.3	16.0	82.3
1933	66.7	3.7	3.5	8.9	83.9
1934	63.1	5.5	2.3	6.9	78.0
1935	52.1	6.7	1.9	4.3	65.0
1936	33.8	11.4	5.5	11.8	61.9

Source: Ministry of Finance, *Nihon Gaikoku Boeki Geppo* (Monthly Returns of Foreign Trade) (Tokyo: Ministry of Finance, December 1928, 1931, 1934, 1936, 1938).

The volume of Japanese exports in cotton cloth peaked at 66,700 tons in 1933, an amount double the 1929 level; imports from the Netherlands bottomed out at 3,700 tons in 1933, only

17 percent of the 1929 level. After the application of the quota, the volume imported from Japan sharply declined to 52,000 tons in 1935 and to 33,800 tons in 1936.

Table 5.4 reveals two shifts in consumer preferences in this product market.

1. A shift to Japan: The first shift in consumer demand was from Dutch and British products to Japanese products. In a comparison of volumes in 1929 with the volumes of 1933, in 1929 Japan exported 30,900 tons, the Netherlands 20,800, and Britain 14,300. In 1933, imports from Japan totaled 66,700 tons, and imports from the Netherlands and Britain were drastically reduced to only 3,700 tons and 3,500 tons respectively. In that year the Dutch government decided to take protectionist actions.

2. A shift back to Dutch products: This shift from Japanese products occurred in the 1934–36 period as a result of Dutch restrictions. But it was only half the amount that had shifted to Japanese products from Dutch and British products in the 1929–33 period. The total volume of cotton cloth imports from all countries was reduced in 1936 by more than 25 percent of the 1933 level, and no shift back to British products occurred after 1934.

The total volume of cotton cloth imports to the Dutch colony fell as their shipments from Japan declined: The total imports to this colony peaked at 83,900 tons in 1933 and declined to 61,900 tons in 1936. Japan's volume of exports primarily declined because of more severe restrictions after 1934. It further deteriorated in 1936 to half the 1933 level after the breaking off of the Japan-Netherlands Batavia Negotiation. Meanwhile, imports from the mother country recovered to 11,400 tons in 1936.

Smaller total imports in 1936, totaling 74 percent of the 1933 level, show that reduced imports from Japan were not quite completely substituted for by an increase in imports from the Netherlands or any other country. This would imply that Japanese cotton cloth and Dutch products did not belong to the same price range. In short, Japanese goods were offered at lower prices for purchase by the local people. In comparison with the 1929, 1933, and 1936 levels of Japan versus the Netherlands and the total import levels, nearly 50 percent of local consumer demand in 1933 for Japanese products was not replaced by imports of products from the Netherlands in 1936. (The Dutch East Indies did not produce cotton cloth locally.) This implies that in the 1930–33 period, imports of cheap Japanese cotton cloth opened a new market in the Dutch East Indies of local sonsumers, who previously could not have afforded to buy cotton cloth imports.

Therefore we might ask, was it the reduced cost of production or the cheaper yen that drove exports in Japanese cotton textiles in the Dutch East Indies? Concerning the expansion of Japanese sales in 1933, the average price of Japanese cotton cloth fell to 12.5 percent of the 1929 level in terms of the old gold value. The value of the yen fell to 43.34 percent in 1933, vis-à-vis the 1929 Dutch gold guilder. The rest of the fall in the price was attributable to reduced production cost stemming from technological improvements in the Japanese cotton textile industry, in which increased efficiency had become apparent by 1929.[18]

But the Dutch misunderstood the situation, believing that the sales expansion in Japanese cotton cloth in the Dutch East Indies was due to Japanese dumping. Other prevailing misunderstandings in the colonial market: The Japanese industries were "subsidized," and their activities were "nefarious." In fact, I recently discovered letters concerning Japanese competition in the Dutch East Indies market sent to London in 1934 by a British diplomat serving in Batavia via the British Embassy in Tokyo. He reported that "the Japanese are dumping" in the Dutch colonial market; "their activities are nefarious" to gain a share in the market; and "the Japanese government is subsidizing the Japanese competition in textile exports."

But soon after separate letters sent by the British Embassy in Tokyo on 11 April strongly refuted the above report from Batavia, stating that the British Embassy had never found any illegal subsidies in Japan by the Japanese government for any export purposes.

The writers of these letters in Tokyo stressed that "Britain could have forgotten about Japan's competitive capability, if the growth of Japanese exports in textiles had been attributable to only the Japanese dumping, the Japanese government's subsidies, or even to the Japanese aggressiveness. We worry as Japan acquired real competitiveness."[19] The British Embassy people in Tokyo clearly recognised the fundamental strength of Japanese competition in the exports of textiles because they had keenly observed this matter for a long period.

Japan's defeat in the Batavia negotiations

Seeing the continuing issuance of new Dutch orders to intensify restrictions against Japan during the prolonged negotiations, Japanese exporters finally proceeded in July 1934 to put into effect an export boycott of china and porcelain, and nonbleached coarse cotton cloth to the Dutch colony. This merchandise was demanded by the local people and supplied at that time only by Japan. (The Netherlands and other countries did not export them to this colony.) The Dutch accused Japan of breaking the pledge of the starting basis for negotiations that Japan would not apply any new measures to Dutch East Indies trade. Japan stopped the export boycott of china and porcelain at the end of August, but continued to boycott other products. The Dutch continued to enact restrictive measures, and the negotiations thus became stalemated.

While the negotiations were in trouble, both nations were becoming nervous. One Japanese newspaper in Tokyo published a report asserting in effect that "England and Holland have come to a secret agreement whereby the British Navy will protect Java and the Dutch East Indies, and the Netherlands will assist British imports into the Dutch East Indies to keep out Japanese goods."[20]

British official letters from Tokyo stated that this news had been officially denied at The Hague. But the diplomatic reports confirmed that "however, such were the suspicions of the Japanese side. Rather many of the Japanese believed it."[21] The attitude of the Japanese government hardened.

Both sides persevered. Eventually the gap between the contradictory demands was narrowed, and both sides finally agreed on these two points:

1. They would hold a private trade conference in Kobe, Japan. Both sides expected little from this arrangement and just hoped to avert a complete breakoff of talks. (The previous private conference had already proved fruitless.)
2. The restrictions on Japanese products would be mitigated by an increase in Japan's purchases of Dutch East Indies sugar. The conditions were that Japan would import 90 million tons of sugar and after refining it would not reexport it to China; instead, Japan would sell it in markets where it would never compete with Dutch sugar. The Japanese insisted on a lower level of sugar purchases, at the 1933 level of 50 million tons instead of the 1926 level of 90 million, for purchases during the initial three years. The Dutch rejected this.

The conference was ultimately dissolved on December 21, 1934, and resulted in a complete defeat for Japan after one year of negotiations. Leaving a Japanese consul-general in Batavia to be alert for possibilities to rebuild the trade relationship, the Japanese ambassador and the negotiation group departed Batavia for Tokyo. The only merit of the one-year negotiation for Japan was that it helped to postpone the implementation of most new restrictions until 1935. Japan's exports to the Dutch East Indies during 1934 fell, but slightly.

After the Batavia negotiations

Now being able to ignore the Japanese response, the Dutch government put forward its restrictions on Japanese trade. Nearly all principal imports of Japanese goods were restricted at the 1933 levels. Japanese dealers who had long lived in the Dutch East Indies were allowed to transact only a quarter of the total imports from Japan. If transactions of the imports in question by these dealers did not reach 25 percent of the 1933 total imports of the goods, the quota for the Japanese importers would be set at that lower level. Thus the possibilities of growth for Japanese exports in the Dutch East Indies were strictly curtailed.

And so after 1935, the imports of Japanese goods fell greatly in the Dutch East Indies. Those restricted in August 1937 were all manufactured goods: cement, beer, calico and other cotton and synthetic textiles, bleached and unbleached coarse cotton cloth, bath towels, cotton blankets, various kinds of textiles, readymade clothes, cotton thread, enameled pans, glass and glassware, enameled ironware, bicycles and bicycle parts, chemical fertilizers, electric bulbs, toothbrushes, cutlery, petroleum, lamps, sanitary chinaware, china and porcelain, metal products, soaps, wrapping paper, auto tires and tubes, and iron sulfate.

These severe restrictions on imports from Japan worked favorably for the Netherlands, although one repercussion of the restrictive policies aimed at favoring the Netherlands was that it pushed up prices of consumer goods to the detriment of the local people. This result became clear when the Dutch East Indies suffered a series of large falls in the value of its sugar exports to the world market. Dutch protectionist policies and the holding to the gold standard jointly served in this way to deepen the economic recession in the Dutch East Indies. The Dutch government enacted the Dutch East Indies Trade Revenue Countervailing Act in May 1936 to make up losses caused by its holding of the gold standard, and it left the gold standard system in September 1937, following France.[22]

Table 5.5 presents the falls until 1937 (except for iron products and electric lamps) in Japanese principal manufactured exports to the Dutch East Indies, from their 1929 levels. By 1935, the exports of china and porcelain, cement, and beer were already nearly a quarter of their 1929 levels. The restrictions were fully satisfying their intentions. These falls—in exports of cotton and synthetic textiles, china and porcelain, cement, tires, glass products, and beer—were unrecoverable for Japan. All exports to this colony further declined from 1938 onward.[23]

In October 1937, after a lapse of nearly three years, the once-abandoned trade negotiations were reopened between the

Table 5.5 Index of Japanese manufactured exports to the Dutch
East Indies

(U.S. dollars 1929 = 100)

	1926	1929	1930	1931	1932	1933	1934	1935	1936	1937
Cotton cloth	93	100	71	70	73	141	99	97	89	97
Knitted cotton	61	100	69	20	58	89	106	98	106	89
Silk textiles & synthetic textiles	39	100	147	147	135	137	141	132	120	60
China & porcelain	57	100	43	30	29	41	30	24	20	21
Cement	41	100	101	65	46	21	10	8	10	5
Tires	63	100	84	52	35	54	89	75	36	18
Glass products	41	100	56	60	32	57	64	62	72	42
Beer	88	100	94	50	77	227	27	27	22	11
Iron products	46	100	62	50	89	141	189	135	151	180
Electric lamps	86	100	17	230	852	186	165	134	134	108
Toys	52	100	126	147	973	208	126	95	113	60

Source: Ministry of Finance, *Nihon Gaikoku Boeki Geppo* (Monthly Returns of Foreign Trade) (Tokyo: Ministry
of Finance, December 1928, 1931, 1934, 1936, 1939).

Netherlands and the Japanese consulate. Japan, however, sent no
representative group from Tokyo.

A new Japan-Netherlands trade agreement was concluded in
April 1938 as follows:

1. Quotas for Japanese dealers were raised to be at a minimum
   of 25 percent of the 1933 imports of items from Japan.
2. Japanese dealers in the Dutch East Indies were not obliged
   to join one of the commercial associations in Europe to be
   qualified as importers.
3. The Japanese purchase of the Dutch colony's sugar was defined
   to be "as much as possible." This improvement implied that
   Japan was no longer forced to import sugar at the level proposed by the Netherlands at the Batavia negotiations.

These were improvements in minor points, but not in essential
ones. The so-called improvements in the 1938 agreement imply
that the Dutch authorities saw that the restrictions had already

been working fully. The further drops in Japanese exports shown in governmental statistics prove this.[24]

We can make several conclusions about Japan's trade with the Dutch East Indies during this period.

1. Discrimination against Japanese products in the Dutch East Indies market after 1933 was mainly caused by strong Japanese competition in certain manufactured products: cotton and synthetic textiles, china and porcelain, cement, tires, glass products, and beer. The main cause of discrimination was the rapid growth of manufactured exports that had become marked by 1929.

2. The overvalued Dutch guilder under the gold standard system was a strong factor supporting the discrimination because it further aggravated the deterioration of the Netherlands Commonwealth trade balances.

3. There was no allied discrimination against Japanese products, especially in cotton textiles, by the Netherlands and the United Kingdom, as we noted in an earlier section.

4. The only greatly influential British factor relevant to Japan's trade with the Dutch East Indies was that Britain had imposed stringent discriminatory measures against Japan within the British Empire, measures that in a couple of years had become a historical precedent: The protectionism exercised in British India, Australia, and Canada became a normative model followed by other countries internationally for protecting their domestic industries by excessively counteracting the devaluation of the Japanese yen. Thus discrimination against Japan became an "internationally understood fact" and a "justified" norm, as quoted by the Dutch authorities in the 1934 Batavia negotiations.

5. The Chinese who had lived in the Dutch East Indies for several generations were concerned about the Manchurian Incident of 1931, but the decline of imports from Japan at that time was temporary. Japanese exports in this Dutch

colony followed the market price mechanisms of the time. The market mechanisms, however, were distorted by import restrictions practiced from 1933 onward.

Anti-Japanese feelings were shown in such expressions as "subsidized" and "aggressive" and those claiming that the Japanese were "dumping," as seen in the earlier cited letter sent from Batavia. Those implied unfair practices by the Japanese in overseas economic activities also seemed to reflect Japan's actions in invading China. In this aspect, the anti-Japanese boycott movement in China exerted a far greater influence on Japanese trade than the Japanese had imagined.

6. As a result of the discrimination in this market, Japan was forced to diversify its exports. This was an inescapable course for Japan, in order to develop international competitiveness in a variety of manufactured goods. Whatever drove Japan in this direction may not be utterly unfortunate for the country from a long-term historical viewpoint because Japan then strove to diversify exports and its industrial capability. But at the time, history having not yet made its judgment, little was available to soften the blow of a forced and painful economic readjustment.

Chapter 6

LATIN AMERICA:
THE NEW TRADE FRONTIER

1. The Latin American Market

Japan's export drive

The Japanese looked for a new trading world where they might face less trade friction, and they found new markets in Latin America. Japan hoped the barriers that had arisen in trade in the markets of British India and Dutch East Indies might be avoided and partially compensated for. That expectation was realized: Japanese exports were growing in a freer new Latin American market. The steady Japanese export expansion to Latin American countries was attributable first to Japanese efforts to find new markets abroad, second to improvements in Japanese productivity, and third to demand in Latin America.

The strongest factor, which well explained the demand by Latin Americans for Japanese products, was that competitive Japanese pricing fit the low per capita income in Latin America. Two contemporary witnesses back up this conclusion: A Japanese reporter strongly believed that "even if all Japanese imports were eliminated, American products would not be substituted for the Japanese products because U.S. products were much more expensive."[1] An American observer wrote that only because of competitive prices did Japanese products penetrate rapidly into Latin American markets.[2] We will examine below how Japanese pricing worked and if this indeed was the only factor in Japan's expanding exports.

The total Japanese exports shipped to this region increased rapidly after Japan had experienced bitterly sharp declines in its exports to China, the United States, and the British Empire. Japan's expansion in exports to Latin American markets peaked in 1935, but was short-lived because of strict restrictions and discrimination imposed on its products.

As early as February 1934, Japanese exporters began to take steps to counteract the possibility that Central and South American nations would enforce restrictions on imports of Japanese commodities. Japan sponsored a goodwill group, an economic mission, to tour Latin American countries. Also in 1934, Japan's Foreign Ministry and the Ministry of Commerce and Industry met and decided to encourage imports from Latin America by offering subsidies, which were paid for from the proceeds of control fees levied on exports to those countries.[3] But the very successful drive by Japanese manufacturers to capture the lucrative South American market was suddenly curtailed by the various nations as their apprehension increased at the rapidly increasing balance of trade in Japan's favor—a balance they could ill afford. Import quotas were established, tariffs were raised, and restrictions were placed on further Japanese trade.

Restrictions on Japanese products

The total value of imported Japanese products into Latin American countries was not large. U.S. sales to Latin America increased in 1934 to $216 million, while those of Japan increased to $3 million.[4] What was feared about Japanese competition, by Western and local Latin American producers alike, was the rapidity of the increase in Japanese exports of some specific items in a short period. The products that became the object of trade friction between the Japanese and the Western-vested interests and local producers in Latin American markets were focused on a small number of categories in manufactured goods, namely, cotton and synthetic textiles, electric light bulbs, and some medical and chemical instruments such as forceps.

Developing Latin American countries went on the alert and seized the opportunity to improve trade and budgetary deficits by practicing protectionism. Chile was among the first to stem the tide of Japanese imports by ruling that the foreign exchange to pay for them must consist of yen bills arising from Chilean exports to Japan, in other words, a trade-balance equalization scheme. Peru, Colombia, and Mexico followed suit. These countries had closer ties with the United States and declined to open a new trade relationship with Japan. This was understandable because of their historical and geographical ties: The distance from Latin America to Japan was much greater than to the United States.

Reportedly, Japanese traders blamed American and European exporters for having convinced South American nations of the "menace of Japanese dumping."[5] According to an article in the *Chugai Shogyo* newspaper in Japan, a movement was astir in U.S. commercial circles aimed at preventing the entry of Japanese merchandise into Central and South America.[6] Here is the essence of the article:

1. Because of a steady increase of Japanese exports, certain U.S. businessmen and manufacturers feared that their commercial interests in Latin American states would ultimately be jeopardized. Therefore a movement to prevent Japanese goods from entering these states was started.
2. The U.S. government was said to be in favor of a proposal to convene an international conference to discuss measures to remove trade barriers, thereby stamping out economic depression throughout the world. Reciprocal agreements became effective between the United States and Latin American countries, intending to give favors to all.

Exports from Japan faced two dimensions of trade friction in Latin America: On the one hand, Japanese-manufactured products partially replaced the products of such industrialized countries as the United States, Great Britain, the Netherlands, and Germany. On the other, they competed with local manufactured products of low quality. In my analysis below, Japan's competition with local manufacturers will also be examined.

Even after restrictive practices were imposed against imports from Japan in Latin American nations, the sales of some Japanese merchandise continued to increase because of purchases by many Latin American consumers. But total shipments ultimately declined.

A difference in restrictive policy stance

The policy stance toward Japan of the Argentinean and Brazilian governments differed from that in other Latin American nations. The components of trade in Argentina and in Japan became complementary in their economic development process. Brazil had Japanese immigration. But these two countries—Argentina and Brazil—were not exceptions to the general trend in Latin America to tighten restrictions on imports from Japan after they saw a dangerous Japanese trade expansion.

2. Chile and Colombia: The Trade-Balancing System and Treaty Abrogation

I. The trade-balancing system in Chile

Japan's export drive

Japan did not openly make a determined drive to penetrate the Chilean textile market until the arrival of a special Japanese trade mission in Chile in January 1934. Apparently to prepare the ground before its arrival, Japan had resumed purchasing Chilean nitrate in late 1933. During the October–December 1933 period, Japan purchased 22,500 metric tons of Chilean nitrate valued at $390,000 and washed wool valued at $125,000. These large purchases gave the trade mission an excellent bargaining position with the Chilean government when it arrived in Chile, since Japan's imports from Chile exceeded its total sales of $298,900 by $238,700.

The Japanese trade mission was composed of representatives of the largest Japanese cotton textile manufacturers, and its object was to consolidate and to expand the existing Japanese market in Chile. The mission brought 17 metric tons of cotton textile samples and a complete assortment of Japanese cotton yarn and textiles, with comprehensive descriptions, advertisements, and price lists; it was prepared to answer all inquiries and thus to come into sharp competition with the United States and Britain in the Chilean market.[1] Within eight months following this January 1934 trade mission, Japanese competition in the Chilean textile market had assumed alarming proportions. From the point of view of American observers, Japan had already penetrated the most important world textile markets in its global trade drive and was concentrating on Latin America as the final goal.[2] Japan delivered textile products to the Chilean market at prices no other country could meet, prices that even undercut the Chilean tariff wall.

The growth of the Chilean textile industry

Meanwhile, the size of the textile import market in Chile had shrunk because of two factors. One was the Great Depression; the other was the import-replacing growth of the Chilean textile industry. This growth occurred behind protective barriers: exchange control, high tariffs, and depreciation of the Chilean currency.

Formerly, Chile had imported large quantities of cotton blankets, cotton/rayon and silk underwear, silk and cotton velvet, cotton/silk and rayon hosiery, cotton bedspreads, carpets, knitted cotton cloth, and cotton toweling from the United States and Japan. Imports of these items had stopped or been greatly reduced.[3]

During the four years following 1928, Chilean imports of all classes of textiles totaled US$137 million. Imports from Japan in that period were $3 million, and those from the United States $21 million. In the 1932–33 depression period, the total Chilean imports of textiles showed a marked slump, declining to only $8 million. Textile imports from Japan in that period dwindled to $300,000, and those from the United States to $2 million. Since 1931, the United States and Japan had both lost much of their profitable textile exports to Chile because of the newly established Chilean textile industry. Largely because of a steady development of domestic cotton goods manufacturing, Chilean cotton cloth imports from all countries decreased again, to 3,352 metric tons in all of 1937, from a total of 4,086 metric tons in only the first five months of 1936.

Japanese competition

In the Chilean market, the Japanese offered cotton textiles at prices 40 percent lower than similar American products. An American observer wrote about how the Japanese competed there:

The price cutting by the Japanese was so ridiculously low that their penetration into this field appeared that the Japanese were making a deliberate effort to monopolize the Chilean market at any cost.[4] American cotton products that were sold in Chile mainly were staple lines, with little ingenuity and invention in the way of new style, therefore Japanese competition in this line was especially keen. The Japanese had copied nearly all the U.S. cotton textile products in the Chilean market. They also copied American packing methods, tickets, and labels.[5]

British cotton textiles shipped to Chile were more sophisticated and, for the Japanese, more difficult to imitate.

Another important aspect of Japanese cotton textiles in Chile was that Japan had, over a few years, improved quality and become competitive against American and British products by means of price differentials. Japanese products were no longer inferior in quality. During a short time, 1929–33, Japan's only success in exports was in unbleached cotton cloth. This sole item had then totaled 29 to 38 percent of all Japanese textile exports to Chile, and in 1934 textile exports accounted for 37 to 43 percent of Japan's total exports to this market.[6]

The details of Japanese competition in the Chilean cotton textile market in 1934 were described as follows in an official record sent from Santiago.[7]

Osnaburgs (coarse cotton cloth for bagging) had for years been the leading U.S. textile export to the Chilean market. American manufacturers in the past had a monopoly on the osnaburg market and to the end of 1933 had supplied more than 95 percent of these imports. Japanese manufacturers had been making strenuous efforts to invade this profitable U.S. market in Chile and was offering all means of inducements to gain a foothold there. Chilean importers were constantly being approached by representatives of Japanese mills who offered to undercut the best American osnaburg. Chilean importers sent samples to the Japanese mills for copying at a much lower price.

For example, quality "A" osnaburgs sold by leading importers under various trade names ran from 29.5 to 30 inches wide, measured 3.33 yards to the pound, weighed 195–200 grams per square meter, and had 12 threads per five square millimeters. The same quality produced in the United States was being quoted at 7.5 cents per square yard CIF (cost, insurance, and freight), and the Japanese offered imitations for as low as 5.5 cents CIF.

Quality "B" osnaburgs were one inch narrower and 30 grams lighter than quality "A." American mills offered them at 6.25 cents per square yard CIF, and the Japanese offered the imitation for as low as 5.0 cents.

Quality "C" osnaburgs had the same width, but were lighter. They were offered by American mills at 5 11/16 cents CIF, whereas Japanese mills offered an imitation for as low as 4.5 cents per square yard.

In other cotton clothing, the United States had formerly brought in large quantities of gray sheeting and shirting, which were now imported from Japan because of the great price differences. Japan also displaced American goods with very attractive cotton drills, covers, and cotton goods. Within a comparatively short period, Japan had effected a truly remarkable improvement with regard to designs and finish in the manufacture of printed fabrics, bringing its products nearly up to the standards of advanced manufacturing countries. This quality, combined with absurdly low quotations, had allowed Japan to gain the bulk of the market in these lines.

Great Britain (not the United States), which had been the leading supplier of most colored woven drills, denims, prints, and ginghams, suffered most from Japanese competition. The United States had been losing its textile market in specialized lines—dyed shirting, khakis, and blue drills—to the Chilean textile industry, which dyed and processed imported Japanese gray drills.

The trade-balancing system

Toward the end of 1934, Chilean textile manufacturers organized a protest against unfair Japanese competition. They stated that Japan was dumping textiles, silks, toys, novelties, and the like in the Chilean market at prices less than the cost of production. It is noteworthy that Chilean textile production expanded enormously in conjunction with Chilean protectionist measures against imports from Japan. The production volume of all Chilean cotton cloth increased from 100 (as the index base) for the three-year 1927–29 average, to 300 in May 1935, to 400 in May 1936, and to 500 in May 1937.[8]

Responding to this and other protests, the Chilean Minister of Finance on December 11, 1934, instructed the Exchange Control Commission to deny the purchase of Japanese merchandise unless the transaction was financed by foreign exchange obtained in exports to Japan, that is, the adoption of a trade-balancing system on a bilateral basis. The commission issued a circular to the Chilean Chamber of Commerce and banks entitled "Imports of Merchandise Proceeding from Japan," which read as follows:

> The International Exchange Commission has ruled that from this date it will only authorize the importation of merchandise proceeding from Japan on the basis of exchange originating Chilean exports to that country.[9]

In response, the Japanese immediately promised to purchase additional Chilean nitrates and wool, but it was too late.

After 1935

In its textile exports to Chile, Japan still had a strong competitive edge in unbleached cotton cloth: the Japanese unit value per kilogram in the first quarter of 1937 was 1.91 gold pesos, versus 4.28 gold pesos for such cloth shipped from Great Britain. Italy was another low-priced supplier and provided the product at a unit value of 2.22 gold pesos, or slightly more than the Japanese price.[10] In volume, Japan accounted for 89 percent of Chilean imports of unbleached cotton cloth. In value, Japan's share in 1937 was 80 percent: 10.4 percent was from Great Britain and 9.6 percent from the rest of the world.[11] Chile accounted for about 70 percent of Japan's unbleached cotton cloth exports; these made up 56 percent of total exports to Chile in 1937.[12] In bleached cloth that year, Britain supplied nearly 60 percent, and Japan was competing seriously.

Three-fourths of Chilean purchases from Japan in 1937 consisted of cotton yarns for looms and cotton cloth. Other minor items exported from Japan to Chile were canvas cloth and rubberized cotton cloth. In Chilean cloth imports, about two-thirds containing more than 80 percent silk and about half its cotton towels were shipped from Japan, though their values were small.

The Japanese also offered easy credit terms ranging from 30 to 90 days. Five percent was discounted for cash payments. But the great distance for each trip between Chile to Japan required some four months from the placement of an order until the goods reached the local market. Therefore, Chilean merchants preferred American goods. The 15 percent differential they had to pay for them was more than compensated for in the quick turnover of their inventories. In this respect, the following general consul's report,[13] [written by American Consul General Edward A. Dow in Santiago to Washington] summarized the American viewpoint in July 1937.

> The Chilean market is a price market and in view of the low purchasing power of at least 80 percent of the population, quality is overlooked in favor of low prices. In this respect Japan has a great advantage as its low priced products appeal to the majority of the Chilean public. There is no denying that most Japanese textiles are inferior to American, but they are on a par with domestically manufactured materials to which the Chilean has become accustomed and will sell as long as the price is advantageous.

The basis of trade between Japan and Chile was that Japan could not sell to Chile in excess of Chilean exports to Japan. The rate of the Japanese currency advanced from 30.37 Chilean pesos on average in 1935 to 33.07 pesos in 1936; then it declined to 26.27 pesos in 1937. Because of the trade-balancing system, Chilean exports to Japan gradually increased and Chile obtained a favorable balance of trade by a wide margin. The sizable surplus of Chilean trade with Japan was settled in two ways: by payments in Chilean pesos to Chilean exporters, and by the placement of dollars and other foreign exchange credits in a third country, such as the United States. Some of those dollars and credits were used to permit imports into Chile from countries like the United States.

Japanese sales efforts in Chile concentrated on textile products, which represented 93.2 percent of all exports from Japan to Chile in 1936, though they declined to 89.5 percent in 1937. Despite Japan's interest in the Chilean textile market, its share in Chilean textile imports was only 11.3 percent in 1936 and declined to 9.1 percent in 1937.[14]

Other products

Other exports from Japan include electric light bulbs imports that were in the low-priced class in Chile. Germany was the leading supplier of this commodity, shipping about half the total of 130 tons in 1936; Japan supplied 9 tons and the United States 22 tons. Other items of small value but that were increasing exports from Japan were pencils, celluloid and similar materials, toys, and cigarette paper. (The last item had been primarily supplied by Spain.) Complaints had often been made in Chile about Japanese bicycles.

The Japanese share of Chilean imports increased to 3.7 percent in 1935, from 0.6 percent in 1926 and 0.9 percent in 1929. The share then dropped to 2.6 percent in 1937 and to 2.5 percent in 1938 because of the above restrictions in the Chilean market.[15]

Japan's imports

In imports from Chile, Japan had shown special interest in wool and such mining products as the copper content of minerals. Mineral shipments to Japan had markedly increased and thus contributed more than 55 percent to the total exports to Japan in 1937.[16] In 1935, Chilean exports to Japan were chiefly 103 metric tons of silver, 10 metric tons of copper concentrates, and 260 metric tons of tin plate trimmings. In 1937, nitrate exports to Japan were officially absent from Chilean and Japanese statistics. Of the total imports from Chile to Japan, electric copper totaled 8.6 percent; wool, 28.9 percent; rawhide, 0.6 percent; barley, 5.8 percent; sodium nitrate, 16.1 percent (an unofficial estimate); and all others (chiefly mineral products) 40 percent.[17]

II. COLOMBIA: ABROGATION OF THE TRADE TREATY

In Columbia the Japan-Colombia Commercial Treaty expired on April 30, 1935. It seems that the Colombian government had been contemplating the establishment with the United States of preferential duties against Japanese goods,[18] and Japan was unable to renew the treaty before its termination. The Colombian government's guiding principle for Japan was to prohibit large imports because of the increasing trade gap between the two countries. Japanese exports to Colombia were rapidly expanding, though Japan's share of total Colombian imports was small; it increased to 5.5 percent in 1935, from 0.5 percent in 1926.[19] And Colombia had no products that Japan could profitably import. The Colombian prime export-earning commodity was coffee, for which the demand in Japan was low because of its oriental lifestyle.

Aware of the problem in trading with Colombia, the Japanese made inquiries in Atlantic coastal cities regarding imports of crude oil and bunker fuel for use by Japanese vessels. Japan failed to obtain the Colombian government's acceptance of petroleum exports for balancing trade between the two countries, for unknown reasons. In fact, not long after Italy succeeded in obtaining an acceptance for the same purpose.[20] On May 15, 1935, the Colombian government announced that it had established a new basis for its trade with Japan. Sections of the announcement pertinent to our study are as follows:

a. The government of the Republic of Colombia would not decree any provisions of a customs nature regarding Japanese merchandise imported into Colombia.
b. For six months, from May 1 to October 31, 1935, the Board for Control Exchange and Exports of Colombia would grant licenses to limit imports from Japan to a third (1,415,398 pesos) of the 1934 level (4,246,196 pesos).
c. Beyond the above annual figure of imports, or 707,696 pesos for the six-month period, imports would be restricted under a system of balancing the values of trade between Colombia and Japan.
d. The Central Board would authorize orders for Japanese merchandise up to a monthly sum of 117,950 pesos. To use a license, an importer had to register at the Central Board Office; orders would be numbered and registered and sent to the Japanese exporter to obtain a consular invoice in Japan; Colombian consuls would certify only a appropriately registered applications to the Colombian Central Board. The document then should be sent back to the Colombian government and to the importer for obtaining an import license and foreign exchange to make payment for Japanese commodities.[21]

These drastic measures were clearly aimed at curbing imports of Japanese goods. In summary, (1) the import level for the first six months was only a third of the 1934 level; (2) beyond this level, imports were restricted by a trade-balancing system and an import license system; and (3) the letters of import order for any Japanese commodity had to make a round trip between Colombia and Japan before any import license could be obtained. One can imagine how much time would be required until any imports from Japan could actually take place.

Hull's memorandum
According to U.S. legation reports, there was a suspicion in Bogota that this discriminatory limiting of imports from Japan was based on a suggestion by the U.S. government.[22] The United States stated

it was an illusion on the part of the Colombian government that its actions against Japan would please the U.S. government.[23] U.S. Secretary of State Cordell Hull sent a memorandum stating that balancing trade on a bilateral basis would be more restrictive than prohibitive tariffs because of its intensifying and prolonging effects resulting in the greatest trade contraction. He further claimed that the policy tended to divert purchases from the best markets and forced the importation of goods that were less urgently required. Thus Hull officially refused any preferential treatment.

"My government does not ask reductions in duties by foreign countries of any products under such [preferential] agreements because the application would be confined to products of the United States," he said.[24] He instructed that this view of the U.S. government must be presented in a way that would not be misunderstood by the Colombian government as a criticism of Colombian commercial policy. And when a private representative of the U.S. textile industry made contacts with Latin-American governments to get preferential treatment, the U.S. government formally declared that this representative's behavior was independent of the government.[25]

The abolition of tariffs with the United States

Meanwhile, a new U.S.-Colombia agreement was under progress since May 27, 1935, between the Colombian Minister in Washington and the U.S. government. In July, a new U.S.-Colombia Commercial Agreement was ratified. National treatment on internal taxes were accorded reciprocally, as seen in Article IV of the agreement:

> All articles, products, or manufactureds of the United States or the Republic of Colombia shall, after importation into the territory of the other country, be exempt from any national or federal internal taxes or charges other than or higher than those payable on like articles of national origin.[26]

The Colombian government was negotiating on conclusion of trade agreements similar to the U.S.-Colombia Commercial Agreement with France and Chile in May 1936.[27]

The tariff concessions of the U.S.-Colombia Commercial Agreement were not extended to Japanese goods since Japan had no *un*conditional most-favored-nation clause with the United States. Nor did Japan succeed in concluding a new commercial treaty with Colombia, even though the Japanese government offered a future basis of a "greater proportion of Colombian sales" to Japan.[28]

For Japan, at the termination of the Colombian license system against Japanese commodities on November 1, 1935, the Colombian government adopted a strict trade-balancing system on a reciprocal basis. Under this new system, Japan-Colombia trade was almost completely suspended. The Japanese share in Columbian imports dropped precipitately to 0.1 percent in 1936 and to 0.3 percent in 1937, from 5.5 percent in 1935.[29]

3. PERU AND MEXICO: TREATY ABROGATION AND VOLUNTARY EXPORT RESTRAINTS

I. MANUFACTURER PROTEST AND TREATY ABROGATION IN PERU

Japan enjoyed a trade surplus with Peru each year from 1916 to 1934, though the amount of the surplus was small, that is, no more than $1.5 million, which it reached in 1934. Even the invisible trade balance for the same period decidedly favored Japan, since all merchandise was moved in Japanese cargo ships and also handled chiefly by Japanese commercial interests.[1] Japanese-manufactured goods of all types had been flooding the local market since 1933 at prices far below those at which competition might take place.

Japanese exports were largely cotton textiles, which constituted more than 50 percent of total Japanese imports into Peru during the 1929–37 period; Peruvian exports to Japan consisted almost exclusively of a small quantity of raw cotton (1.44 percent of all Peruvian raw cotton exports) in 1933. An exception was in 1934 when Peru exported an abnormal value of minerals to Japan; Peru shipped large quantities of gasoline as payment for guns and ammunition supplied by Japan related with the Leticia Conflict in Peru.[2]

The Peruvians protest
The increasing competition facing Peruvian manufacturers from Japanese cotton goods caused widespread protest among domestic

218

manufacturers. The Peruvian press continued its bitter attacks on the Japanese, especially with regard to the rapid increases of textile imports from Japan. Finally, the Peruvian government abrogated the Peru-Japan Commercial Treaty in 1934.

The textile industry which constituted the principal branch of Peruvian industry was affected by Japanese competition. Those engaged in this industry were the most active in distributing propaganda and appealing to the Peruvian government to curb this real threat to their economic welfare and existence.[3] The Sociedad Nacional de Industrieas del Peru had distributed a circular to the public, illustrated by statistics and graphically showing the rapid rise in Japanese cotton good imports into Peru during the past seven years. American and British markets for manufactured goods in Peru were also seriously threatened by Japanese competition.[4]

Despite the rapid growth, Japanese textiles were not competing among themselves to the point of ruining their own business. The Cotton Manufacturers Association and the Automobile Importers Association adopted a resolution in December 1934 urging that steps be taken to prevent the "dumping" of Japanese textiles in Peru. In the Constituent Assembly, Deputy Montes of the Cotton Manufacturers Association stated that Peruvian textile manufacturers were confronted with a severe crisis because of Japanese textile competition. "The picture is even more serious and unjust if it is considered that the Japanese colony in Peru is amassing all the trade of the country without investing locally its profits and savings," he said.[5] Table 6.1 was distributed to the assembly to show the Japanese threat.

Table 6.1 Peruvian cotton textile imports from Japan

	Metric tons	Number of pieces
1932	120	48,000
1933	233	84,000
1934 First quarter	249	99,600

Source: 623.9417/4, Lima, Dec. 1934. (Washington: Diplomatic Section, National Archives), 2.

The Constituent Assembly approved a motion, submitted by Deputy Montes, that the Minister of Finance should take the most suitable measures of protection against this situation, which would seriously affect thousands of Peruvian workers employed in the cotton textile industry.

Peruvian quotas

To protect the domestic cotton textile industry, especially against Japanese competition, the Peruvian government issued the Executive Decree of May 10, 1935, sectors 1 to 167 of tariff law number 5954, providing that the total imports of cotton textiles for six months were to be limited to 2,458,209 kilograms. It became effective on the first day of the following June. An American diplomat reported the following to the Secretary of State in Washington:

> The allotment of quota for each country concerned was based on 1929 imports statistics. In thousands of kilograms, largest quota was given to Great Britain 877, followed by the United States 476, Italy 448, Japan 204, Germany 174, and Belgium 144. Domestic manufacturers were prohibited to raise prices above their levels prevailing in first quarter 1935 in the local market. This measure aimed directly against Japan.[6]

It is essential to note here that the quota was based on the 1929 import level, which was before the rapid Japanese growth had taken place—yielding a discriminatory effect.

A decree on November 30, 1935, the second decree concerning the matter, extended the quota system until December 31, 1935. And then a new decree on December 30, 1935, the third decree, abolished the quota system for all countries *except for Japan*. The entry into Peru of Japanese cotton textiles was regulated on the basis of a percentage of the 1934 entry levels at various Peruvian ports.

The quota for Japan in 1936 was increased to 612,714 kilograms.[7] In the following spring, a decree on March 28, 1936, the fourth decree, continued this quota. This time it was called a *voluntary* limitation instead of a quota. The Peruvian government explained that this change of terminology was made at the request of the Japanese government, so that it would not wound Japanese sensibilities being discriminated against alone.[8] The limitation continued to be in force until September 24, 1937.

On March 23, 1937, Japanese importers in Peru and exclusive agents had *voluntarily* agreed to limit imports of Japanese cotton manufactures into Peru to 306,357 gross kilograms for a six-month period—the same level as 1936—beginning the following day. The government of Peru approved this agreement and authorized the importation of that maximum amount.

Yet Peruvian protests against Japan continued. Several interested Peruvian manufacturers and importers presented a protest against this new agreement to the Chamber of Commerce of Lima, which in turn presented it to the government of Peru. Their complaint was directed solely against the manner of distribution prescribed by the decree that made distribution on the basis of nationality of importers. They protested that it gave the great bulk of the business to the Japanese, who had been interested in this market only during the past four years.[9]

The protesters gained a favorable result. The Minister of Foreign Affairs of Peru sent a note to the Chargé d'Affaires of Japan in Lima on September 23, 1937.

> Governments of Japan and Peru agreed that the voluntary limitation of the importation into Peru of Japanese textiles would be extended from September 24, 1937, to December 31, 1938, and the total imports for that period were fixed at 850,000 kilograms. This amount was 10 percent larger than the previous quota.

There was a modification of distribution of Japanese goods affected so that in lieu of the division of 70 percent to Japanese merchants and 30 percent to non-Japanese merchants, according to the new agreement each of these groups would handle 50 percent of the total.[10]

Besides cotton textiles, direct imports of Japanese electric light bulbs had flooded the Peruvian local market to such an extent that the bulbs had to be sold at a loss. This caused a great setback for local plants manufacturing this good, whose owners were of Japanese nationality. Japan also exported 400 to 500 automobile tire casings, increasing the competition in this field in Lima.[11]

Japanese imports
Of the total value of Japanese purchases from Peru in 1935 and 1936, more than 98 percent was accounted for by raw cotton.[12] In these two years, Japan had deliberately increased its purchases of this commodity from Peru. The American Embassy in Lima had been informed that Japan was preparing to make use of this increase for an upward change of the quota for Japanese cotton textiles. The Japanese government, through its consulate in Lima, which worked through the Asociacion Central Japonesa del Peru, in 1937 ordered Japanese cotton growers to increase the cultivation of cotton in Peru's coastal valleys.[13] But no increase, either of the quota or of the cultivation, took place.

The effect on Japan's exports
Although Japanese exports and imports with Peru had both sizably increased since 1933, Japan had not shown a remarkably enlarged participation in Peru's total import trade, as had been anticipated. Japan remained a minor trader in Peru until 1937. From 1916 to 1932, the Japanese share had averaged well under 1.7 percent. It peaked at 6 percent in 1934 before the quota system was imposed. Its share decreased to 5.2 percent in 1935 and to 4 percent in 1936 because of the quota on Japanese textile goods. Table 6.2 shows a steady decline of Japan as a Peruvian import nation, contrasted with growing exports from the United States, Germany, and Argentina to Peru after 1934.

In Peru's import trade, the United States recovered by 6.5 percent in 1935 from the 1934 level. Yet Germany gained the most during the same period. German participation had unmistakably increased since 1934, largely because of compensation trade with

Peru and the increasing sales of Peruvian cotton to Germany, which was a stronger competitor than Japan in the Peruvian market against the United States and Britain. Argentina also steadily increased its participation in Peru's import trade.

Table 6.2 Distribution of imports to Peru

(percent in value terms)

	U.S.	Germany	Britain	Argentina	Japan
1928	41.4	10.5	15.8	1.2	1.2
1929	41.8	10.0	15.0	3.3	1.2
1931	40.5	9.3	14.1	4.7	1.7
1934	26.5	9.0	17.3	4.6	6.0
1935	33.0	14.0	13.6	7.6	5.2
1936	32.1	18.6	13.6	8.8	4.0

Source: 623.9417/8, Encl. dispatch 5371. (Washington: Diplomatic Section, National Archives), 2.

Great Britain had received a greater setback in its exports to Peru than other countries had because of the Japanese and German inroads. Before World War I, the value of British exports to Peru was nearly twice what it was in this table, and at that time Britain was in the first position in the Peruvian import trade.

Why did Peru target Japan?
I must ask why Japan was the target of discrimination.

In 1935 and 1936, Japan was able to increase imports from Peru just to increase exports, but the effort was not very fruitful. The increase brought Japan only a trade deficit with Peru for these two consecutive years, although it was impossible for Japan to increase the Peruvian quota for its textile exports. The trade account was balanced in 1937. Japan's trade with Peru would not grow after that unless Japan would agree to a deficit in its trade balance—which it could no longer afford. Thus Japanese exports to Peru were effectively curbed, and trade between the two countries subsequently shrank below the 1934 level.

I repeat the question. Why did Peru target Japan? Historically we can see that Peruvian discrimination against Japan occurred when the infant Peruvian cotton textile industry was taking off backed by an abundant supply of domestic raw cotton, and thus initiating the country's industrialization. The surge in Japanese exports was due to Japan's achievement in classical comparative cost advantage, largely in textiles, at the beginning of the 1930s. A narrow technological gap existed between Japan and Peru, and perhaps Japan was ahead only by one step. But Peru was still importing textiles from Japan and other relatively advanced countries. Japan exported manufactured products to relatively backward countries, such as Peru, which were also following their own course of economic development, initiated by the cotton textile industry.

Then why did this particular industry lead a country's industrialization? The age-old cotton textile industry was labor-intensive with a narrow technological front; thus it was easy for developing countries to borrow this technology. Furthermore, its products were always in demand domestically if prices fit the consumption level, and establishing the industry required a small amount of initial investment capital funds. In these respects it was an ideal industry for developing nations to begin their industrialization and replace imports.

In this sense, Japan was doomed to be discriminated against in the Peruvian market. Peru strongly wanted to protect its own growing cotton textile industry because its products were roughly competitive with Japanese products in terms of quality; the only difference was the higher cost of production in Peru. In addition, when Japan caught up with the international standard in textiles, old hands such as Britain and the United States wanted to protect their existing shares in the shrinking Peruvian market.

II. Japanese products in Mexico

If we compare Japanese exports with Mexico's during 1932 and 1933, it is evident that Japanese commercial activity constituted a threat to Mexican industry. In 1932, Japanese exports to Mexico amounted to $2.042 million, and in 1933 their value had risen to $5.273 million, an increase of 158 percent.[14]

> Japanese exports to Mexico even reached cities in southern Sonora; they included such novelties as toothbrushes, cheap bracelets made of glass and other materials, lead cores for pencils, and cheap watches.[15]

> Those cheap commodities were sold on cash on delivery terms, and the merchandise was delivered on the spot by the Japanese salesman.[16]

Historically, Mexico had always opposed high tariffs because they tended to increase the cost of living for the Mexican people. But the Mexican government could not afford to see its textile industry destroyed by the Japanese. In May 1934, an American diplomat sent a report to Washington:

> Japan was said to be *unexpected rival* in regard to her competition against the United States and Britain in the world market, and Japan now started the competition in the Mexican market. It was well known that Japan was attempting to increase her manufactured products in Latin America. But it was also expected that Japan would not increase her exports of textiles to Mexico to such a degree that the Mexican textile industry would be threatened.[17]

How Americans and Mexicans felt about Japanese competition there was described in this way: "The Japanese were able to produce the manufactured articles more cheaply due to their lower standard of living."[18] Japanese competitiveness, according to the report, stemmed not from any technological improvement, but from Japan's low standard of living, which connoted the *exploitation* of laborers by the manufacturers; therefore the competition was unfair.

Concerning the quality of these Japanese products, the American Consulate informant stated that Japanese brushes looked cheap, but they gave good service. The brushes sold were conventional, old-type brushes, with apparently no intention of closely imitating modern American brushes of special designs. These brushes were made with no indication as to the country of origin and had trade names similar to Mexican products, for example, *Promex*, which hinted at the phrase "Pro-Mexico."[19]

The following three points may prove interesting. They are quoted from other reports by the American diplomat to the Secretary of State in Washington. First, he looked at Japanese efforts to compete with the Americans and concluded that the Japanese and the Germans appeared to make a greater effort to cater to the desires and whims of Latin American buyers than the Americans did. They placed more emphasis on using desired colors and markers, as an example, for indicators on cash registers.[20]

Second, most Mexicans were anti-Japanese (according to his report), but the vast difference in the prices of Japanese and other foreign articles in the Mexican market overbalanced their prejudice from an economic point of view. To quote one example, Japanese medical and chemical instruments were quoted at extremely low prices. The Japanese priced their forceps at US$2.75 per dozen; similar forceps made in the United States would normally cost a Mexican doctor $1.75 to $2.00 each. This difference, which amounted to 632 to 772 percent, was maintained throughout. But Japanese trade in surgical instruments was still insignificant in 1935.

Third, the Japanese regarded profits from a long-term viewpoint. The diplomat said another interesting feature the Japanese offered was to make medical instruments in any size, shape, or type the Mexican doctor desired. This offer undoubtedly was intended not only to get business—as a rule this practice unfavorably affects profits by increasing production costs—but also to obtain new ideas worldwide to attain a supremacy in design and manufacture, a policy that beyond doubt played an important part in helping the Japanese reach such an outstanding position in the industrial and commercial world in a short time.[21] This is an excellent observation, applicable even today to Japanese investment decisions based on long-term profits compared with the decisions U.S. companies make on a short-term profit basis. The latter often must consider the yearly profit-to-capital ratio that influences the value of the company's stock, and thus the popularity of the stock among investors. The manager of an American company could be fired if the annual profit rate dropped. This acts to prevent managers from making decisions on a long-term basis.

The total of Japanese exports to Mexico was very small in relation to U.S. exports, and even a tenfold increase over a few years signified an increase of only several thousand dollars, constituting a small portion of U.S. exports to Mexico. It nevertheless exhibited a trend that seemed certain to ultimately prove embarrassing to American exporters in this field.

This diplomat also made another important point: A comparison between American and Japanese exports to Mexico made in terms of U.S. dollars might be highly misleading because of the vast difference between U.S. and Japanese prices on nearly every commodity, that is $1.00 worth of Japanese goods did not replace $1.00 worth of American merchandise, but rather displaced from $5.00 to $15.00 worth.

In 1935, Japanese exports to Mexico increased very little, but it was feared that they would greatly increase thereafter with no advertising by the Japanese, all because of the extremely low prices coupled with the quality of Japanese merchandise. Older Mexican merchants and leading exporters to Mexico, the Americans, were opposed to the Japanese and their commercial methods, low pay, and sales policies. Mexican merchants could not, for business reasons, forgo purchasing Japanese merchandise at the extremely low prices prevailing in the market.[22] For example, a Mexican merchant who had returned from California told an American consul that Mexican merchants had to follow the example of American merchants in regard to the flood of Japanese merchandise. The 5- and 10-cent stores in California literally sold nothing but Japanese merchandise.[23]

Sales in June 1935 were still increasing several times over because Japanese prices were so low that Mexican merchants could not fail to take advantage of Japanese products. One strong reason was that the bulk of Mexico's population earned low wages, which meant a demand for extremely low-priced merchandise regardless of quality. In 1935 the Japanese sold knives, forks, and spoons in the Mexican market. Japanese bicycles were quoted CIF Guaymas at only about a third of the price of regular American bicycles. A Mexican merchant paid 4 pesos to have each of the large Japanese bicycles assembled in Mexico, and 3 pesos for the small ones. He was selling the large bicycle locally for 75 pesos, for a sizable profit.[24]

Anticipating anti-Japanese import restrictions, Japanese merchants and industrialists in Yokohama started a lobbying campaign in the Mexico City newspaper, *Excelsior*, on June 15, 1935.[25]

Japanese sales usually were in yen payable at prevailing bank rates in pesos, although customs declarations and entry manifests in most instances showed values in U.S. dollars.

The Mexicans and the Americans in Mexico thought that the sizable increase in Japanese merchandise would be for a short time only and that the competing American lines would regain full control of the Mexican market. This view was based on two assumptions: (1) The inferiority of Japanese workmanship would be proven and Mexican consumers consequently would turn away from these purchases, and (2) the small local market soon would be saturated with Japanese goods. But both postulates had proved faulty by mid-1935. Thus the Mexican government instituted strict import controls.

Weak Japanese competition

Table 6.3 presents the development of each major country's exports to Mexico. During the first half of 1937, the figures show an increase in all countries—except for Japan, which slightly decreased—over the same period in 1936. The relative position of the United States in Mexican imports was strengthened the most.[26]

By 1937, none of Japan's principal imports into Mexico were competing with the principal imports from other countries. Although the principal Japanese export to Latin America was cotton cloth, it did not even figure among the principal Japanese exports to Mexico. Cotton thread and cotton cloth were first in importance among the exports from Great Britain to Mexico.

Table 6.3 Imports into Mexico from the United States, Germany, Britain, and Japan, first six months

(thousands of pesos)

		1935	A: 1936	B: 1937	Change: B − A / A x 100
U.S.	Total	24,143	34,887	59,064	
	Automobiles	23,628	25,101	35,989	43.4%
Germany	Total	5,703	5,607	8,361	
	Colors & varnishes	1,699	1,485	1,727	16.4%
Britain	Total	4,875	4,645	4,962	
	Cotton threads	2,061	1,880	2,358	25.4%
	Cotton cloth	0,930	987	940	− 4.8%
Japan	Total	1,262	1,533	1,462	
	Rayon yarns	880	1,216	1,139	− 6.3%
	Brushes	58	55	26	− 52.7%
	Sockets*	36	41	16	− 60.6%
	Electric wires[†]	13	8	2	− 75.0%

Source: 621.9417/13, American Consul General, Oct. 26, 1937. (Washington: Diplomatic Section, National Archives), Enclosures. Original figures were from Mexican government statistics.
* Fuses & outlets for electric installations.
† Wire & cable.

Japanese exports to the United States via Mexico

It was estimated in August 1936 that at that time about 25 percent of the Japanese merchandise imported into Tijuana, Mexico, ultimately was consumed in the United States. Japanese merchandise was sent to the United States from Mexico via free zones in Tijuana and Ensenada.[27] This estimation was made by the president of a company named Nelson, S. A., of Tijuana, which in its stores in Tijuana and Ensenada sold fully 95 percent of all Japanese merchandise sold within the district. This was possibly another reason the United States and Mexican governments strictly tightened imports from Japan.

4. ARGENTINA AND BRAZIL: COUNTRY SUBSTITUTION UNDER STRICT IMPORT RESTRICTIONS

I. ARGENTINA: FRIENDLY BUT DISCRIMINATORY

The Japanese made significant inroads in the Argentine market after 1932. One factor in this was U.S. import restrictions from 1930, including restrictions on Argentine commodities. This policy led Argentina to increase its purchases from oriental countries, including Japan.[1]

Two favorable characteristics stood out for Japanese and Argentine trade: Japan exported manufactured goods, especially textiles and cheap electric lamps, and imported an increasing diversity and quantity of raw materials—wool, foodstuffs, and minerals. Argentine and Japanese trade became potentially complementary.

Japanese exports to Argentina grew rapidly and peaked in 1935, constituting 4.1 percent of total Argentine imports. They soon declined to 3.4 percent in 1936. The following eight issues were significant, from the viewpoint of our study, in the fall in Japanese exports to the Argentine market.

1. Battles over imports of electric lamps
An international cartel—Phillips, Edison, and Osram lamps—initiated a prolonged price war that targeted Japanese electric lamps.

Imports of Japanese incandescent lamps had attained a predominant share in the Argentine market, growing from 69,000 pesos in 1931 to 850,000 pesos in 1932 and to 1,002,952 pesos in 1933.[2]

a. The cartel, named the Overseas Lamp Company, embarked on a strong advertising campaign, for moderately successful results in 1934. Determined to fight Japanese competition on a price basis by importing cheap household lamps, they imported some 500,000 Chinese lamps, which had been manufactured by affiliated interests, and placed them on the market at prices consistently lower than Japanese quotations. On November 1, 1934, the lowest price was reached when Chinese lamps were offered to dealers at 20 centavos (about 5 cents in U.S. dollars), while the Japanese price quotation was 21 or 22 centavos. Six months later, the supply of Chinese lamps had been practically exhausted, and Japanese prices had risen slightly.[3]

b. A large quantity of Set brand incandescent lamps was imported from Russia by an old and well-known Argentine company in the latter part of 1934 for distribution throughout Argentina. This plan was somewhat successful because of an advertisement that referred to the lamps as being the best European lamps, without any mention of their Russian origin. The Russian lamp was offered at the advertised retail price of 40 centavos each, the same price being asked for the Japanese product. (These Japanese lamps were different in size from the lamps described in the previous paragraph.) An informal inquiry, however, found that at one dealer's shop the Russian lamps could be purchased at retail for 27 centavos each; in the same store the lowest price for a Japanese lamp was 35 centavos.[4]

c. To continue the price war against Japanese lamps, the Overseas Lamp Company ordered from European-associated interests another very cheap 500,000 incandescent lamps of household sizes to be placed on the market at prices lower than Japanese quotations. This was said to be merely one more step in the price war initiated by Overseas Lamp against Japanese lamps because they would need to sell the cheap lamps at a slight loss to undercut Japanese prices.[5]

   d. Imports of incandescent lamps from Japan in 1934 therefore declined to half the volume of the 1933 level and were
   further curtailed.[6]

   The Japanese lamps exported to Argentina were manufactured
by small Japanese plants unrelated to the highly organized industries that produced incandescent lamps for domestic use.

2. Argentine dual attitudes

The British textile interests announced that they expected
Argentina to protect British textiles against foreign dumping.[7]
Argentina put the shoe on the other foot and negotiated with
Japan for some kind of agreement.

3. Appeals by British importers

Discriminatory measures were expected against Japanese textiles
because of their unusual rate of growth. More than 80 percent of
imports from Japan were textiles, including rayon yarn and cot-
ton/rubber yarn; Japan's share of total Argentine textile imports
rose to 14 percent in 1935, from 5 percent in 1932. Therefore,
Japan was elevated to third place, from sixth, among exporters to
Argentina. Much of Japan's gain had been made at the expense of
British and Italian manufacturers, not American.
   U.S. textile imports to the market declined to 1 percent, from 6
percent, during the period from 1926 to 1937. Most American textiles were much more expensive than those from Japan, but they were
different in quality: Thus Japanese textile commodities were not actually competing with American products. The U.S.-Japan competition
therefore existed only in limited, unimportant lines of merchandise.
The most important single textile item in this sense was cotton-elastic
rubber woven goods, though their values were quite small.
   British importers held a conference, seeking a way to check the
seemingly limitless increase of Japanese cloth. They concluded that
they would place a limit on imports from Japan, since the Japanese
imitated British textiles; further, the restrictions should be on a
quota basis, which was similar to the quota system in force in some

British colonies. The British also sought to invoke Argentine laws against Japanese products that were exact copies of fine British printed cotton goods.[8] Should both projects fail to secure adequate protection for the British textile trade in Argentina, the British importers planned to request their embassy to take extreme measures in threatening Argentina with British reprisals in the form of future restrictions on Argentine meat imports into Britain.[9]

4. Japan's rayon and miscellaneous exports

Japanese exports in rayon yarn expanded tremendously to 8 percent of Japanese exports to Argentina in 1936, from a negligible amount in 1933. But a joint enterprise financed by Du Pont and British Imperial Chemical in Argentina formally opened in June 1937 and went on to supply the bulk of local rayon demands.

The rest (about 20 percent) of Japanese exports to Argentina consisted of crocheted goods, chinaware, incandescent lamps, buttons, toys, industrial chemicals, and miscellaneous goods of small value.[10]

The Japanese imitated old, established German crockery for a third of the German prices, which drew attention to their "unfairness in marketing."

The value of imports of Japanese rubber and rubber products soared more than tenfold from 1933 to 1935, totaling 2 percent of all Japanese shipments. Meanwhile, the value of those products shipped from the United States had fallen almost in half during the same interval.[11]

Japan was the principal supplier in the Argentine market of buttons, celluloid, celluloid toys, dolls, hats of miscellaneous fibers, mats, bicycles, tricycles, and phonographs. It was the second most important supplier of toys of all kinds (including mechanical); common pencils; bicycles; velocipedes and tricycles (smaller sizes); miscellaneous articles of paste, celluloid, ebonite, and bakelite; and imitation jewelry made of gum, paste, bone, and other materials.[12]

5. A discriminatory foreign exchange allotment for Japan

The Argentine government concluded an agreement with Japan in June 1934, which gave the Japanese some improvements in its situation. The Argentine Exchange Control Board would grant 90 pesos for importations from Japan for each Japanese purchase of 100 pesos from Argentina. Purchasing exchange on the free market was also possible at a premium of about 25 percent.[13] Nevertheless, this agreement served to stimulate trade between the two countries.

Imports of Japanese commodities were under foreign exchange control in January 1935. In the official exchange allotment, competitors were believed to get a 25 percent greater amount, an advantage over Japan; Japan's price advantage over its competition had to offset this 25 percent. On the other hand, Japan's competitors were worried that if exchange controls were abolished, Japan would greatly increase its textile exports and perhaps would become the principal supplier in the Argentine market. The so-called Roca Agreement between Great Britain and Argentina was to ensure Argentina's obligation to apply quotas on Japanese textile imports if Argentina abolished the exchange control.[14]

In Tokyo, the Japanese Association of Exports had devised an import promotion scheme for Argentina for 1935 as follows: (1) For the first 12 million yen worth of Japanese goods exported to Argentina, the Japanese government would deduct 4 percent of the value. It would then place the money into a fund for equalizing wool import price differentials between Argentina and Australia, the country with which Japan expected to undergo a bitter trade war. A potential Japanese purchaser of Australian wool at 10.5 pesos per 100 kilograms would be given a portion of the fund to enable him instead to buy Argentine wool at 11 pesos. (2) The next 6 million yen of sales would be subject to a deduction of 6 percent, and each succeeding 6 million yen, a deduction of 8 percent.[15]

The Argentine official exchange allocated to Japan in 1936 was 3,084,000 pesos, or only about 12.5 percent of the value of Japan's 1935 total shipments to Argentina.

6. Development of complementary trading

Argentina slightly relaxed exchange controls for Japan, responding to the new Japanese trade policy stance to diversify imports of resources to Latin America from seriously troubled markets.

Little by little, traded commodities became more complementary between Argentina and Japan. Japan now purchased from Argentina large quantities of several staple commodities, the most important of which were corn, wheat, linseed, quebracho bark extract, salted cattle hides, cotton fiber, casein, canned meat, scrap metal, salted horsehides, frozen beef, greasy wool, slag, and ashes of zinc, bones, and hoofs. Japanese wool-buying decreased temporarily, but Japan actively resumed its imports from Argentina in 1936, reducing purchases of wool from Australia.

7. The customs valuation system

The Argentine government practiced a customs valuation system for tariff purposes from 1935 onward.[16] The Argentine customs values were arbitrarily fixed by the Argentine authorities and had no direct relation either to local or to foreign market values. Argentine official statistics were expressed in terms of these customs values for Japanese imports.[17]

These customs figures reveal the impossibility of estimating the exact amounts of official exchange allotments to specific concerned foreign countries during any fixed period. The discrepancy between customs values and invoice values of imported Japanese goods were estimated in 1935 at 69 percent, in 1936 at 73 percent, and in the first half of 1937 at 50 percent. Table 6.4 shows the distribution of official and free exchange values according to data in the Argentine Exchange Control Office.[18]

Table 6.4 Argentine import values from Japan, 1935–37

(thousands of pesos)

	1935	1936	1937 (1st 9 months)
Official	2,337	3,084	2,562
Free	25,222	21,222	20,265
Total	27,559	24,303	22,829

Source: 635.9417/29, 1938, Buenos Aires, Argentina, 1938. 11.

Notes: 1. These were the CIF values of the Exchange Control Office, and do not show the actual pesos paid by importers. (The conversion base: 15 pesos per pound sterling).

2. It was well known that the General Statistical Bureau's "tariff values" were arbitrary and did not correspond even approximately to the actual CIF values.

8. VERs

Japan agreed in 1935 to voluntary export restraints (VERs) for competitive piece-goods to Argentina, providing a greater profit margin both to the Argentine manufacturers and to the Japanese exporters. This was in return for a promise of more Argentine exchange allotments and exclusive exchange privileges in regard to products supplied previously by the United States and some other countries.[19]

The final outcome

Argentina was anxious to sell more hides, wool, cereals, meat, and other products to Japan; Japan was willing to buy if it could obtain fairer exchange treatment in Argentina. But to allocate additional exchange to Japan required a complicated consideration by the Argentine government. Great Britain and local Argentine textile interests were most anxious to forestall any additional price advantages being granted to Japan because their situation was already precarious enough.

To look at one Japanese export to Argentina, in 1936 imports of Japanese lamps decreased to 535,515 pesos, or half of what they had been in the previous year. Four reasons accounted for the decrease. First was the price war set by an international cartel targeting Japanese electric lamps. Second, the customs valuation system brought prices of Japanese products 73 percent higher on average than their transaction values in 1936, according to the report sent by an American diplomat which was quoted earlier. To counterbalance this, Japanese producers would lower the price of the product if they could afford to in terms of the cost of production. Third was the discriminatory foreign exchange allotment. And fourth, the total Argentine imports of the lamps also declined approximately 15 percent in value from 1935 to 1936.[20] In 1937, Japanese lamps were priced at 18 centavos wholesale. Retailers sold them profitably for 30 centavos. American and European licensed lamps were sold for 80 to 85 centavos, regardless of whether they were imported or manufactured locally.

According to an official Argentine announcement, quoted in a U.S. diplomatic report, the Japanese share in Argentine imports was 3.6 percent in both 1936 and 1937, an eighth of the share held by the principal exporters. But Argentine customs estimates overvalued Japanese goods and therefore should be reduced by approximately 49 percent to arrive at a reasonably close estimate of the actual CIF value.[21]

Because of this, Argentina's import figures after 1935 in the statistics of the League of Nations were inaccurate. The Japanese shares in Argentine imports, 0.5 percent in 1926 and 0.6 percent in 1929, were correct, but their changes to 5.1 percent in 1935 and to 3.7 percent in 1937 in the League statistics need to be lowered to about 2.8 percent and 1.98 percent when we calculate based on this report, as in table 6.4.[22]

In Japanese export data, the Argentine share was 0.3 percent in 1926. This increased to 3.9 percent in 1929, peaked at 8.1 percent in 1935, declined to 6 percent in 1937, and dropped to 5.5 percent in 1938.[23]

In Argentine exports, Japan's relative position was twelfth, its share being 1.2 percent in 1937. The reason for low purchases by Japan was that Japanese industries had been unable to adjust satisfactorily to the Argentine government's drastic curtailing of Japanese imports. Japanese purchases, however, were steadily catching up. The Japanese commercial mission that quietly visited Argentina in 1937 failed to obtain more favorable exchange treatment, even though it offered to increase fixed-quantity purchases of Argentine products.[24]

II. INCREASING JAPANESE RAW COTTON PURCHASES FROM BRAZIL

Exports to Japan

The developing trade between Japan and Brazil created unfavorable U.S. feelings against Japan, and reports of a U.S. diplomat revealed the U.S. government's increasing concerns over the growth of this trade.

Finding it difficult to get good quality raw cotton from British India, Japan since 1933 had endeavored to arrange for the acquisition of that commodity from Brazil.[25] In early April 1935, a Japanese trade mission visited Brazil for two purposes: to increase purchases of Brazilian raw cotton to amend a one-sided trade that favored Japan, and to settle issues concerning the emigration problem. Japanese businessmen sent an industrial and economic mission to Brazil not only to explain to hostile interests there the present state of Japanese industry, but also to convince these interests that the Japanese were not dumping. On the contrary, they were selling at a profit, and they hoped to be able to increase imports of various Brazilian products to Japan.

One mission objective was to substitute purchases of raw cotton from the United States with purchases from Brazil. Increased Japanese exports to Brazil would adversely affect U.S. manufacturing exports and thus would aggravate the unfavorable U.S. trade balance with Brazil, which had already been in deficit. Unable to export more to the United States because of restrictions with high tariffs, Japan could neatly equalize its trade deficit with the United States by shifting some of its cotton purchases to Brazil. Brazilian exports of raw cotton to Japan would thus greatly assist Japan in selling more general merchandise to Brazil, whereupon Japanese exporters believed they could increase their sales to Brazil. But raw cotton from Brazil was lower in quality than the U.S. product. Therefore, Japanese textile producers had offered a low quotation that failed to induce Brazilian cotton producers to shift their production from other attractive crops to cotton.

Japan also had the hope of sending further thousands of people each year to Brazil, since Manchuria by this time had not provided an adequate outlet for Japan's acute population pressures. Japanese emigrants preferred Brazil to other Latin American countries for various reasons: mild climate, tropical abundance, less political unrest, better economic performance, and fewer restrictions.

An American diplomat reported that if Japan succeeded in preparing the ground for compensatory trade with Brazil, "It will not only contribute greatly towards promoting the settlement of the immigration problem and advancing diplomatic relations between the two countries, but will also favorably influence Japan's relations with Latin American countries, though in varying degrees."[26]

Imports from Japan

Brazilian imports from Japan still did not amount to much, but they continued to increase steadily, though slowly; therefore, Japan remained an unimportant supplier to the Brazilian market in the first half of the 1930s. Its share in total Brazilian imports increased to only 1.2 percent in 1936 and to 1.6 percent in 1937, from 0.2 percent in 1926.[27] Relevant statistics do not show imports from Japan displacing the products normally imported from other countries. The characteristic feature of Japanese exports to Brazil was a multitude of products of relatively low value, which caused Japan to make no serious threat in competing against any other Brazilian trade partners in any specific line.

In Japanese exports to Brazil, woolen yarn, silk yarn, and electric lamps stood out as relatively high export earners.

a. Imports of *woolen yarn* from Japan increased to 265 metric tons in 1937, from 5 in 1926. This was one of the few commodities in which Japan displaced imports from other countries, notably from France and Great Britain. However, Germany was also responsible for this replacement, even to a greater extent than Japan was.[28]

b. Imports of *silk yarn* from Japan increased to 103 metric tons in 1936, from 6 in 1934, and imports decreased from all other sources, such as Italy, Switzerland, France, and the United States. Thus Brazil imported more silk products directly from Japan, in contrast to Canada, which imported U.S. silk products made of Japanese raw silk.

c. *Bicycle* imports from Japan and Great Britain decreased, and imports from Germany increased to displace the Japanese and British products.

d. Japan competed chiefly with the domestic Brazilian industry in *electric lamps*, but made little headway; imports from Japan showed only yearly fluctuations.

e. Japan increased exports in *wooden accessories* for textile machinery and *rubber tires* for automobiles toward 1937, though their values represented only 1.9 percent and 3.2 percent, respectively, of the total Japanese exports to Brazil that year.

Japan had few imports from Brazil in these years: 97 percent consisted of raw cotton, and most of the rest was coffee.

In 1936, its imports from Brazil increased enormously, to 10 times the level of 1935.[29] Thus for the first time in many years, Brazil had a favorable trade balance with Japan. Most of the increase was due to voluminous raw cotton purchases, revealing that Japan had exhausted years of cotton stock. It also revealed Japan's determined will to replace raw cotton imports from the U.S. market even partially, a market where Japan suffered a heavy deficit. In this sense, improved trade with Brazil brought with it increased unfavorable feeling about the Japanese in the United States.

PART II

THE POSTWAR PERIOD, 1948–85

Chapter 7

The inaugural session of the preparatory committee for the ITO held at Church House, London, in 1946. GATT was born out of ITO Charter.

JAPAN'S ACCESSION
TO GATT

Foreseeing the end of World War II, leaders of the United States and the United Kingdom spearheaded a plan to firmly establish peace and to improve worldwide living standards. They held an international conference in Bretton Woods, New Hampshire, in July 1944, including John M. Keynes, the British economist, and Harry D. White, former Treasurer of the United States. The Bretton Woods group consisted of minds generally recognized to represent the wisdom of the world. In consideration of the plight of people who had suffered the tragedies of war, in reflection on the causes of the war and on each nation's collective suffering of it, and in looking forward to the hopes of establishing a new world order, the Bretton Woods representatives set up the International Monetary Fund (IMF) and the International Bank for Reconstruction and Development (IBRD), commonly known as the World Bank. These two international institutions started the following year. The IMF worked as a stabilizer of the world monetary system. The World Bank was initially concerned with post-war reconstruction in Europe, but after the European Recovery Programme in 1948, its main objective has been to assist the economic development of member countries. Only one institution was still to be established to promote international trade for supporting a steady development of the world economy.

Earlier in November 1945, the United States made a proposal to promote international trade and to bolster employment throughout the world. Under this proposal, the first preparatory conference was held in London in June 1946 as the United Nations Conference on Employment and Trade.[1] The second preparatory conference was held in Geneva in August 1947. Both conferences contributed to the drafting of international regulations on world trade agreements and to the creation of an international trade organization. Resulting in many cooperative efforts, another international conference for trade and employment was held in Havana from November 1947 to March 1948. On March 24 its members decided to adopt a Decree of an International Trade Organization. This charter stated that it would implement perfect employment policies, adopt policies for economic development and rehabilitation, create international commerce treaties, prohibit restrictive customs on trade, and build up international agreements on commodity trading. It covered all fields related to international trade in deciding principles as a base of policy making—customs tariffs, trade regulations, subsidies, and employment. To reaffirm the implementation of these policies, they declared the establishment of the International Trade Organization (the ITO or, because of where the conference was held, the Havana Charter) to regulate international consultation conferences and judgments.

While progress was being made to set up an international trading system, the cold war began between the United States and the Soviet Union. The cold war created tension that weakened the newly enhanced spirit of resentment over the past and World War II and discouraged hopes of building a new world system.

THE ITO CHARTER

In the United States, a deep-rooted protectionism and separation from world matters gradually regained strength. The U.S. Congress denounced ITO codes as having priorities that were unacceptable: The Havana Charter forced each member country to follow ITO rules before domestic policies and to allow it to judge international economic frictions. Thus the ITO agricultural issues were dropped because they predictably presented the most difficult problems in getting the approval of Congress. President Harry S. Truman felt he could not submit the ITO draft to Congress for ratification even excluding agricultural issues.

The United Kingdom wanted to retain the favorable Imperial privileges and restrictions in imports that still prevailed in British possessions worldwide, and it failed to follow the ideas and leadership of the ITO. Other winning nations (the Allied powers) of World War II in Europe were absorbed in domestic recovery from the war's devastating results. They also claimed they could not bind their countries to the idealistic trade policies of the ITO and therefore refused to ratify the ITO draft.

Besides the Allied powers, other industrialized countries also refused to accept the ITO because restoring their economies had the first priority. The developing countries did not agree to the ITO because they needed to protect their infant industries in contradiction of the ITO regulations. The ITO Charter draft that was signed by 23 countries when it was first introduced ended with ratification by only 2: The ITO was not born.

The General Agreement on Tariffs and Trade (GATT) was born out of this buried ITO Charter. Before drafting the charter, the United States had proposed mutual tariff reductions and the abolition of tariff privileges among the countries of the ITO. The ITO charter preparing committee members of 19 countries, led by the United States, had agreed with the proposals at the first London conference. They decided to hold the second conference in Geneva to negotiate the lowering of tariffs and to abolish privileges in tariffs. As mentioned above, it was held there in August 1947. These 19 countries and 4 new participating countries multi-laterally negotiated tariff reductions from April to October in 1947.[2]

To recognize the fruits of the negotiations as great accomplishments and furthermore to secure the effectiveness of the tariff concessions by each country, the main principles and common international rules in international trade and commerce were extracted from the ITO Charter. The result was GATT, born in 1947. The Tables of Concessions, which were lists of each country's promises to lower tariffs or to not raise them, were annexed to the rules of GATT.

THE ESTABLISHMENT OF GATT

Since the ITO Charter itself turned out to be ineffective, the GATT rules that were at first considered to be provisional measures came to be treated as having nearly a permanent nature. Twenty-three countries signed GATT in 1947 when it started, but only 8—Australia, Belgium, Canada, France, Luxembourg, the Netherlands, the United Kingdom, and the United States—became members of GATT on the first day of January 1948. These 8 countries started GATT by signing a Temporary Application (a draft protocol) of GATT until GATT's rules became effective.

Thirteen countries (Brazil, Burma, Ceylon, China [Chiang Kai-shek's government], Cuba, Czechoslovakia, India, New Zealand, Norway, Pakistan, Southern Rhodesia, the Republic of South Africa, and Syria) joined GATT in June 1948, and Chile joined it in 1949.[3] The second GATT tariff negotiation conference was held in 1949 with 9 newly joined members—Denmark, the Dominican Republic, Finland, Greece, Haiti, Italy, Liberia, Nicaragua, and Sweden. The Third Tariff Negotiation followed in 1951 with new member countries: Austria, West Germany, Peru, and Turkey. Indonesia, after becoming independent of the Netherlands, joined too.

China (Taiwan) quit the membership in 1950 by raising tariffs to finance its preparations for war against the People's Republic of China. Lebanon and Syria quit the agreement in 1951 by raising tariffs to finance budgets, and Liberia followed them in 1953. Thus 4 countries had given up membership by 1953.

I have named the initiative member countries because the original 23 GATT members included not only advanced countries, but also developing countries. Among the latter, some remain as Less Developed Countries (LDCs) even today. Most member countries were principally based on the free market economic system, but some were under Communist regimes. By the end of the 1990s, what had happened to the countries that had resigned their memberships?

Except for Taiwan, which became one of the Newly Industrialized Economies (NIEs), their economies regressed for a long time.

WHAT IS GATT?

GATT means, directly, the GATT Secretariat, but it also means the GATT Contracting Parties (CP). The CP distinguishes a group of countries that have contracted agreements with GATT. Furthermore, GATT means the international commercial contracts that the GATT Secretariat and the CP have made.

GATT agreements have been improved and added to through various GATT negotiations since the founding of GATT. GATT was promoted to be included in the World Trade Organization (WTO) in the beginning of 1996.

Nondiscrimination (fairness with imports from every nation), the mutual granting of the Most-Favored-Nation (MFN) clause, and domestic citizenship treatment (the equal treatment of imported products with domestic products) to each member country have been the main principles of GATT from its establishment. Japan's very difficult historical experience in the interwar period (as seen in the previous six chapters) would not have been possible if GATT had existed then. MFN is always unconditional in GATT. Now we will examine what happened to Japan under the GATT system.

FIRST EFFORTS FOR JAPAN'S ENTRANCE TO GATT

It was difficult for Japan to become a GATT member. When GATT started, Japan was under U.S. military occupation; it lacked international autonomy as an independent country to conclude treaties and change tariff rates.

Japan applied specific duties [on the volume] on imports as a major source of government revenue, but they had became meaningless because of hyperinflation (on average 300 times the rates) after Japan's defeat in World War II. Before the war, for example, Japan levied a specific duty of 3 yen per ton on imports; with hyperinflation, the value of 3 yen was reduced in purchasing power to 1 *sen*, a hundredth of 1 yen, and Japan's tariff revenues approached virtually zero. Japan was unable to apply to GATT to negotiate tariff reductions because the nominal tariff rates were in effect nearly zero. A U.S. civil officer in Tokyo was sent to the first Contracting Party (CP) meeting of GATT in 1947 to request MFN treatment for Japan, but this request was rejected.[4]

THE GRANTING OF MFN STATUS TO WEST GERMANY

The United States led member countries in granting MFN status to West Germany and invited it to the Torquay tariff negotiation conference in 1948. Except for the politically sensitive issue of the division of Germany, no important objection existed for granting membership to West Germany. Except for covert conversations on that issue, most countries expressed fear only that the treatment of West Germany would become a precedent for the future treatment of Japan.

DISCUSSIONS ON THE FUTURE TREATMENT OF JAPAN

At the twelfth meeting of the United Nations in Geneva to sign the final document for granting MFN status to West Germany, the United States submitted Annex I, dated August 25, 1948, to GATT. The following are heated discussions on the applicability of the agreement to areas under military occupation:

> Mr. Coullard (Canada) said that his government has sympathetic consideration . . . bearing in mind the interests of Canada in the trade of Western Germany, the importance attached to it by the United States and the relations of such an investment to the GATT.[5]

> Mr. Tonkin (Australia) said he has not received instruction from his government, pending which he opposed the proposal to extend most-favored-nation treatment to militarily occupied areas. . . . "The avowed intention of the United States government to bring up at a later date a similar proposal in

relation to Japan was the point that caused embarrassment to the Australian government."[6]

Mr. Nicol (New Zealand) found himself in exactly the same position as Mr. Tonkin, to which he wished to support . . . .

Mr. Wunsz King (China [Taiwan]) said, "The proposal before the meeting caused him anxiety and alarm because the United States delegates had let it be known that they had in mind to present at a later stage a similar proposal relating to Japan. From a legal point of view he saw considerable force in the agreement of one delegation that the Agreement, as it was, could only be applied between the Contracting Parties."[7]

Mr. Shackle (United Kingdom) said that regarding Germany, the United Kingdom had already exchanged notes with the United States on this point, but that the Exchange of the Notes was an independent bilateral agreement with no reference to the GATT. Although it was practically identical with the present United States draft . . . . As to Japan, the United Kingdom had not signed and did not at present propose to sign any instrument in relation to Japan analogous to the Exchange of Notes already mentioned regarding Germany.

Mr. Philip (France) said that his country was in a similar position to the United Kingdom. . . .

Mr. Lamsvelt (Netherlands) said his country was in the same position as the United Kingdom and France . . . . He said that in his opinion it was not necessary to discuss Japan, but Germany was a neighbour of Benelux which had a great interest in its economic recovery. He did not agree that other countries should necessarily have to come into the Agreement before most-favored-nation is applied to this occupied territory.

Mr. Cassiers (Belgium) said he had not much to add after what had been said by the representative of the Netherlands.[8]

The chairman saw that a number of countries appeared to oppose the U.S. proposal and suggested setting up a working party to examine further questions. These member countries decided to have a Working Party (WP No. 6), consisting of Australia, Canada, China (Taiwan), Cuba, France, the Netherlands, Pakistan, the United Kingdom, and the United States, before granting membership to West Germany. The latter did became a GATT member in June 1951.

It is noteworthy that even in 1948, GATT members, except for the United States and Canada, were already objecting to the extension of MFN to Japan in the future, while they had extended it to West Germany. These objections began to turn up again as these opposing members implemented the discriminatory measure, GATT Article XXXV, in regard to Japan later when Japan became a GATT member in 1955.

U.S. recommendations

When West Germany became a GATT member, the United States recommended that Japan also become a member. The United States appealed to member countries to abolish discrimination against imports from Japan that had been carried over from the prewar period to postwar days. It tried to persuade member countries that they should grant MFN treatment to Japan as they had done earlier for West Germany. One reason for these persuasions was that the United States had a special responsibility for Japan, and if any obstacles arose against imports from Japan, they would ultimately fall on U.S. shoulders. From the viewpoint of this study, however, this seems to be only part of the reasoning.

The United States argued as follows: Some GATT members were imposing restrictions against Japan's trade beyond GATT's recognized reasons. This led to an accrual of a deficit in the international accounts of the exporting country. The more countries that restricted imports from Japan, the more new trade frictions that would arise between those discriminatory countries and Japan. If treated equally with other countries, Japan psychologically would feel important and would continue to cooperate with the West.

Furthermore, another issue was involved that was difficult to mention openly. If countries continued to discriminate against imports from Japan, when the U.S. military occupation of Japan ended, Japan might revoke its policy of limiting trade with the People's Republic of China and with North Korea. These two countries represented more than 30 percent of Japan's trade from 1934 to 1936. It was desirable to prevent Japan from reopening these prewar trade routes. The cold war and a fear of Japan going communist were underlying concerns.

U.S. representatives ultimately tried to persuade members by saying that if Japan were to expand its trade through comparative advantages, it would contribute to world trade expansion and ultimately to a better world economy. Aid from the United States would inevitably decline, and countries would no doubt be made to pay for their discriminatory behavior by a shrinkage of exports to Japan. At the end of the fourth CP meeting, the United States officially proposed discussion of granting MFN treatment to Japan at the next GATT general conference. After this met with swift objections the United States withdrew its proposal, and this issue was not on the agenda of the fifth CP meeting.

ANTI-JAPANESE FEELING

When the United States recommended Japan as a member, several major Western countries complained, influenced by thoughts of Japan's prewar dumping behavior. They complained that after gaining membership, Japan would start dumping again. They disliked being put into international cooperation with the Japanese, who were so brazen in their prewar trading policies. These harsh objections were prevalent in GATT and were expressed by many representatives. Dr. Gardner Patterson, GATT former Deputy General Director, wrote on the accession of Japan to GATT:

> Countries in Asia and Oceania said that they flinched [from accepting] because of strong anti-Japanese feeling at this U.S.

proposal, that proposing this right now is absurd, and that if we are asked strongly to recognize this, we may withdraw participation in the GATT Tariff Concession Conference.[9]

Most GATT members, except for the United States, were absorbed in expanding trade with other countries and uninterested in liberalizing trade with Japan. Discrimination against Japan by GATT members was continuing. The United Kingdom wanted to recover the prewar power that had so strongly centered there. Most countries of the former British Empire supported a rejection of Japan. They had majority power in the newly established GATT.

How much truth was there in the prewar "dumping" remarks that were often quoted to denounce Japan's behavior in international trade? How much knowledge of dumping and of the issues was held by those who mentioned them? These are dubious in terms of present-day economic and historical analyses as shown in Part I of this volume.[10]

Such opinions against Japan continued for a few years after 1949. Objections that Japan had competed unfairly in the prewar period and that it surely would do so again were loud. The major areas being denounced were dumping, exploitation of Japanese workers, ignoring of copyrights and patents, and production of fake brands. The last two points are related to intellectual property rights under WTO regulations today. Japanese methods in exporting products were also compared with torrential rainfalls and floods to destroy market competition.

If these criticisms were all true, to grant MFN status to Japan was out of the question. The United States and Japan protested and explained that a revival of these problems was impossible under Japan's new laws and systems. But for years no country believed them. At the center of objections was "dumping," which was discussed in chapter 4. The "exploitation" theory of Japanese workers was at the base of "dumping." This theory held that cheap Japanese products were based on a cheap labor force. Cheap wage rates were not a result of low productivity; they stemmed from an exploitation of laborers. Simply, Japan's international competition was unfair because it exported low-cost products based on an "exploitation" of workers. This was thought to be a solid reason to restrict imports from Japan, a belief that prevailed internationally among leaders and that dominated public opinion. This logic, however, had neither been posited nor proven by economic analyses.

FEAR OF JAPAN

Even people who did not believe in this logic feared Japan's strategy of competing internationally in exports by concentrating in a few fields—textiles, simple cloth, china, footwear, and toys. It was these fields that the advanced countries wanted to protect and also that developing countries (more backward in historical timing than Japan) wanted to promote in the beginning stages of their industrialization. These industries were ages old, inefficient, and labor-intensive in advanced countries; without Japan's competition, most of their growth rates were falling, and they held little prospect for the future. Thus their unemployment rates were on the rise, as in the cotton textile industry in Lancashire of the United Kingdom.

People related to GATT thought the following factors were the reason why Japan could export with market-destroying low prices. First, the dual structure of the Japanese economy—the coexistence of large companies and numerous small enterprises—allowed Japan to export at cutthroat low prices that were incomprehensible in ordinary economic thinking. Second, employee salaries in Japanese companies were based on commissions to encourage voluminous exports of cheap products. Beyond these reasons was the following, discussed overtly and seriously at GATT. In competing in world markets, the Japanese offered products at prices cheap enough to attract consumers abroad who hated made-in-Japan products.

These excuses to discriminate against Japanese products, however, for the most part disappeared in 1951. The discussions then boiled down to a single strong belief standing in the way of

Japan's entry to GATT. This belief was the fear that, regardless of whether Japan's competition was fair or unfair, it surely would start a cutthroat competition in fields that many countries wanted to protect and promote.

Japan reformed its tariff system and implemented it in May 1951, thus removing another big obstacle for applying to join GATT. West Germany became a GATT member in June 1951.

Many countries concluded the Treaty of Peace with Japan (generally known as the San Francisco Peace Treaty) in the autumn of 1950. This solved many legal problems that could have occurred at the time of Japan's application to GATT. The Japanese expected that its application would then be on the agenda in the general assembly. The GATT member countries, however, had already negotiated three times—in Geneva, in Annecy in France, and in Torquay in England—and the results of tariff reductions were satisfactory. These countries had no interest in Japan's application to GATT. It meant they would have to restart negotiations for tariff reductions because a new applicant should reduce many tariffs for the member countries. Japan's opportunity to apply for GATT was slipping away.

Gradually, the GATT people came to feel that these objections were ill-founded. Reflecting the spirit and pledges of GATT at its establishment, countries started to question how long they could continue to reject Japan. The trend was changing; they felt that rejecting Japan out of hand was wrong.

A BREAKTHROUGH

At the sixth GATT CP meeting in 1951, the United States proposed "a simplified tariff negotiation procedure for a country hoping to become a GATT member." This opened a new route for countries wanting to become GATT members. The proposal states that a newly applying country need not wait until the opening of the negotiation program but could simply write its name and apply for negotiations. The applying country could name countries with which it wished to negotiate. Both sides could start negotiations.

The proposal seemed to be mainly in consideration of Japan's situation, and was approved at the CP meeting of October 23, 1951.

A little earlier in the assembly, at the beginning of October, the "Recognizing Japan as Observer" issue was passed over the disagreement of the United Kingdom and Australia. For the first time, Japan attended the CP meeting as an "observer" with no right to speak. Its seat was not on the members' side. The invitation was designed to discourage Japan's application for membership by convincing it that joining GATT was not easy. The process and discussions before issuing the invitation were appended to inform Japan that a great many countries had severely disagreed with the issue and continued to disagree.

Unperturbed, however, Japan officially applied to GATT for membership nine months later, on July 18, 1952. By applying, Japan accepted the condition of the application of GATT Article XXXVIII on Japan by member countries. This article was later changed to Article XXXV. On application, Japan remarked that it was already a member of the IMF, of the World Bank (IBRD), and of the World Food Organization (FAO), and it pledged to cooperate with COCOM (Coordinating Committee for Export to Communist Areas) in the same way other GATT members did.

Japan refuted the objections to its application to join GATT: The politics, economy, and society of Japan had improved enough to wipe out fears of the recurrence of prewar "unfair" competition. Japan's labor unions enjoyed rights, and real wages had been increasing. Laborers were not exploited, and new laws had been made to control infringement of industrial and intellectual property rights concerning fake brands and copyrights.[11] No country denied this. However, deep distrust remained of Japanese methods in commercial transactions. Therefore more than three countries rejected Japan's accession to GATT. Japan's application thus became included as a preliminary agenda of the next, the seventh, GATT CP meeting. But the time and conditions for the accession of Japan to membership were not discussed in the assembly that autumn.

Over time, anti-Japanese feelings seemed to be gradually mitigated. Many GATT countries gradually started thinking about discussing more meaningful matters than discriminating against Japan in arid protectionist debates. They even decided to discuss the preconditions that would allow Japan's access to GATT. Tariff reduction meetings, however, were already over for GATT members. If Japan desired to become a full-fledged member, it needed to grant MFN status to every GATT member and thus make tariff concessions as specified by GATT regulations. The GATT members decided to set up a committee during the session to discuss the timing and preconditions for the accession of Japan. The representatives of Oceania objected that anti-Japanese feelings in their home countries were so strong that it might be difficult for them to remain as GATT members if they had to immediately implement GATT rules with Japan. They said that more time was necessary to mitigate these public opinions. Some countries demanded more time to investigate what Japan would export.

The committee for the accession of Japan met in February 1953. However, in the United States, the new Eisenhower administration could not decide on the timing for tariff negotiations, facing two domestic problems—the turmoil of the reextension of the Mutual Commercial Treaty and the enhanced protectionism for domestic industries. The problem was postponed until the next CP meeting.

A TEMPORARY ACCESSION

Eric Wyndham-White, GATT's Director-General, then thought of a measure of temporary accession for Japan. This was based on a point in GATT's Article XXXIII, a statement therein that an applying country could be treated as having the same rights as a formal GATT member. Thus Japan was now able to apply for that status.

The GATT Secretariat created and distributed "A Decision for Provisional Accession of Japan" on August 20, 1953. Japan's provisional accession would be decided by a two-thirds affirmative vote of the CP.[12] U.S. support at this time effectively blocked the disagreement of the United Kingdom, Australia, and New Zealand. The application was to be discussed at the eighth CP meeting on September 24, and a working party (WP) to inquire into Japan's accession was created.

Two principles were stated in the WP document of October 23, 1953. The first asked for the CP to participate in the meeting for the provisional accession of Japan while the second referred to applying GATT regulations to commercial relations between each CP member and Japan.[13] The reason of the separation was GATT's consideration that certain countries were agreeing to attend the meeting but rejecting the immediate application of the major GATT obligation, the nondiscrimination principle, in trade with Japan.

Japan's provisional accession was decided with 26 affirmative votes. There were seven absentees from the voting: the United Kingdom; Australia and New Zealand in Oceania; the Republic of South Africa and Rhodesia on the African continent; Czechoslovakia in the Communist bloc; and Burma (which joined the affirmative side the next day). After signing the document, the GATT Secretariat and the Japanese government announced "a declaration concerning trade regulations on Japan's application for accession" on the next day, October 24, 1953, and annexed Japan's tariff concession table.[14] This was only for temporary acceptance and not a declaration to accept Japan as a member.

Japan promised to grant MFN treatment to all GATT members including those countries that had rejected granting MFN status to Japan by applying GATT Article XXXV in No. (vi) of the declaration preface.

Here we must consider that GATT members had to grant MFN status to Japan because of GATT's nondiscriminatory principle. The existence and the application of Article XXXV seems to contradict this principle, the ideals of GATT. The article's existence was founded in the reality of its historical background. GATT does have some escape clauses, and this article is one of them. GATT is a multilateral trade agreement to provide rules of conduct for international trade relations and to provide a forum for negotiations to resolve trade problems and to eliminate tariffs and other trade barriers. This procedure has the merit of deciding not only on the result of voting and can be considered a democratic procedure. But it also has its drawbacks. For example, reaching a decision always seems to take an unusually long time. If many countries should want to do something as a result of mutual discussion and consent, there is room to create exceptions to the principle. And this happened when GATT applied Article XXXV to Japan. Some GATT members refused to treat Japan as a member even after it joined GATT, and this continued for a long time. We will discuss this in detail in chapter 8, because it needs an entire chapter for full coverage. Japan could apply for membership only by accepting the implementation of this exemption clause of Article XXXV.

Now without GATT tariff negotiations, Japan made the concession of not rising tariff rates on 860 items (equivalent to 87 percent of Japan's import value in 1952), as it had promised to do when it made application for membership. Thirty days after 24 GATT countries had signed this temporary "declaration" it came into effect on November 23, 1953, and was effective until June 30, 1955, one day before Japan supposedly became a member.

Earlier, countries that disagreed with the accession of Japan had considered various policies to prevent it from joining GATT for quite a long time. These countries convened a working party to review GATT regulations to prepare strategies against an expected rapid increase in imports from Japan after it became a member. It was found, as a result, that GATT's Article XIX, which allows measures for members to urgently limit imports against a special member country, could not be used against Japanese products because it contradicted the nondiscriminatory clause of the ITO Charter.

Vicarious concessions of the United States for Japan

Under GATT rules, Japan should offer reciprocal tariff concessions in response to those offered to Japan by GATT member countries. But Japan's economy was weak at that time. It recovered to its prewar peak level GNP of 1936–37 only in 1955; the declaration to apply for GATT membership was made in 1953. The foreign exchange necessary to rehabilitate the economy was almost always drained. Its expected export-earning commodities (iron and steel and autos) failed to penetrate international markets and were returned to Japan. The small domestic market in Japan then was unattractive to its international trading partners, and Japan was unable to satisfy their requests.

The United States then proposed a plan to promote the accession of Japan to GATT. It tried to open up negotiating opportunities for Japan by offering U.S. tariff concessions on various items as a substitution for Japan's concessions to its potential trading partners. The United States believed that the GATT multilateral negotiation system was a good one. If Japan's trading partners offered Japan tariff concessions and Japan could not fulfill the requirements, the equivalent U.S. tariff concessions would then cover Japan's responsibility. In return, Japan would grant an equivalent amount of tariff concessions to the United States.

Thus the United States encouraged the accession of Japan to GATT by granting tariff concessions to third countries. Here the GATT system gained a strong reason for existence. If it didn't exist, what could Japan do to move toward fulfilling its hope to negotiate when member countries did not desire to trade with Japan? The United States opened a new way for Japan's multilateral negotiations by substituting tariff concessional offers for third countries. Japan accepted this, and started negotiations with its trading partners that would have been very difficult without U.S. help, as seen in the examples below.[15]

Norway was not interested in Japan's offers from the beginning. Bilateral negotiations with Japan, therefore, did not go smoothly, and there was no hint of solving the problem. Realizing that it could expect U.S. tariff concessions, however, Norway participated in the tariff negotiation meeting. The United States offered tariff concessions for dried fish and smoked fish, iron and steel, and iron ore. Norway accepted them, and the United States asked Japan for tariff reductions on U.S. oil.

Japan could not accept this. Nevertheless, it continued negotiations and obtained U.S. accord to a new reduction of tariffs on liquors (excluding rum)—that had once been given up on—

and no rise in tariff rates on ceramics; furthermore, a reduction of tariffs on aluminum hydroxide was restored as repayment for the U.S. substitutional tariff concessions for Norway. But Norway was not satisfied because the U.S. offers to Norway were smaller than Norway had offered to Japan, and it withdrew its concessions on Japanese silk scarves. Japan then withdrew two offers that had been granted to Norway. Thus the negotiation was finally concluded with compromises.

Japan's bilateral negotiations with Italy and Denmark were difficult because the offers by both sides did not match. For Italy, the United States granted concessions for the U.S. market on leather purses and coin containers and sewing machines; and for Denmark concessions for the U.S. market on tiles made of cork. Japan returned equivalent concessions to the United States. In this way, the negotiations between these two countries and Japan were concluded.

After concluding concessions with Japan, Finland further offered no tariffs on Japanese buttons made of nacre (mother-of-pearl) and optical glasses. To compensate for this, Finland asked for U.S. tariff concessions for sulfite wrapping paper, and the United States agreed. In return, the United States asked Japan for concessions on asbestos cloth and canned pineapple. Japan agreed only to a concession for asbestos cloth. In this way it found another breakthrough in a deadlocked situation in foreign trade via GATT multilateral negotiations and U.S. concessions.

Similar examples occurred for Japan with Sweden and Canada. The United States granted tariff concessions in its market for products from these two countries. In this way Japan's negotiations with Sweden and Canada were settled, and mutual international trade expanded.

The United States joined hands with Japan in the international trade arena. As a result, Japan received concessions from these trading partners that as a whole exceeded all concessions it yielded to them. Japan's aggregate concessions to the United States were smaller than what Japan gained through U.S. concessions on behalf of Japan from these third countries. The total of U.S. concessions was more than $300 million in its 1955 import values. These European countries that had reopened trade with Japan through U.S. concessions later sent affirmative answers for the accession of Japan to GATT. None of them applied GATT's Article XXXV to Japan.

The request for Japan's accession

Less than one year after the "declaration," in July 1954, Japan formally requested GATT to discuss its desire for membership and to promote negotiations necessary for the accession. In response to this, the GATT Contracting Parties were again divided into two groups. This time, however, Japan's situation differed from the past. Twelve GATT members declared that they were going to prepare for negotiations with Japan by the middle of September: Burma, Ceylon, Chile, Denmark, the Dominican Republic, West Germany, Italy, Norway, Peru, Sweden, the United States, and Uruguay. Gradually, a total of 24 countries signed the declaration.[16]

The final nine nonsignatories were Austria, Australia, Belgium, France, Luxembourg, the Netherlands, New Zealand, the Republic of South Africa, and the United Kingdom. How did they refuse? Here is one example: An Australian government representative sent the GATT Secretariat a letter dated October 11, 1954, that stated, "We are preparing."[17] The next official letter, dated January 3, 1955 that the GATT Secretariat received from the Australian government read, "After considerations, the Australian government did not recognize any necessity to negotiate (with Japan)."[18]

After more than a year had passed from the effective date of the "declaration" on February 1, 1955, it was clear that the time left for the deadline of Japan's accession on July 1 was insufficient. Japan and GATT wrote a "Protocol to extend the effective date of the 1953 Declaration on regulations in trading with Japan" and requested the extension of the date until the end of 1955. By the recognition of GATT members for the accession of Japan, the terminating date was postponed further.

Japan made various efforts, negotiations, and offers of cooperation with the opposing group. Finally it negotiated with 17 member countries, including the United States, throughout the spring of 1955 and made tariff concessions on 248 items (reductions on 75 items and no changes on 173). As a result, the "Protocol for conditions on the accession of Japan and a table of concession" of GATT was written on June 7, 1955. Japan made more concessions. It formally became a member on October 10, 1955, with the approval by all members, on the condition that it accepted the application of GATT Article XXXV.

The condition of the accession was that special countries applying GATT Article XXXV to Japan could reject treating Japan as a GATT member and could deny granting it MFN treatment. This was implemented from the day of Japan's GATT membership and was still being continued in 1959 by 14 member countries, led by the United Kingdom. It continued for a long time in the GATT system, and its contents and abolition will be treated in chapter 8.

Between the ideal and reality

The road of Japan's accession to GATT was a long one, and evident throughout were power struggles and diplomatic strategies among GATT member countries focusing on Japan in the international trade arena.

In concluding, I am faced with the question of why West Germany, also on the losing side in World War II, was permitted to attend a tariff meeting in the early days of GATT, only two years after its establishment. West Germany had already been accepted into GATT as a member by 1951. I explained above that it seemed much easier for West Germany to gain acceptance into GATT, but the Japanese should consider why such a wide difference in treatment emerged. In addition to the reasons considered above I can cite the following:

1. Japan still had insufficient positive publicity, even in the postwar period, for an appeal to be understood fairly by the world's public. The German military had confronted other Western military

powers in the two world wars, but it had strong human ties with Western countries through ancestors, relatives, friends, and acquaintances. Japan does not have these ties and should therefore make greater efforts to mitigate international misunderstandings.

2. Biased images of Japan continued from the prewar period and were a root cause of misunderstandings. "Dumping," for example, is generally defined as selling a product abroad for less than its domestic price, which ultimately stems from its cost of production. One night in the arguments, I was interested to find that in Vienna even in 1998 most of the intellectuals discussed the cost of production in terms of their own country, ignoring the comparative cost of production in the exporting country. Their argument presents an estimated cost in that foreign country as if the imported goods were produced by domestic producers and unconsciously tries to deny a cheaper comparative cost. They do not want to recognize that a cheaper production cost in a foreign country will depend on two things: technological improvements and production expansion. Furthermore, they evade considering purchasing parity problems in their argument.

Worldwide cultural and social differences are always found among countries. When facing such differences, people often believe that only they are correct because they do not understand a foreign value system and they do not recognize that an imported foreign product reflects a difference in the social value system peculiar to a particular foreign country, as stated in Alexander Gerschenkron's theory of economic backwardness. Furthermore, almost always there are people wanting to protect their established interests in international trade, and they stubbornly resist imports. Although, on the other hand, people are interested in and pleased to encounter new things or new creations via imports.

3. The process of catching up with advanced countries by latecomers, which is a integral part of the development of the world economy, was clearly exhibited by Japan's accession to an international institution, GATT.

4. From a different viewpoint, one might say that the process revealed the dichotomy between the ideals in some people's minds and the hard reality stemming from historical circumstances and established interests.

5. However time passed, and the supporters for Japan's accession increased from only one, the United States, to three, Canada, West Germany, and the United States. In the process, Japan changed. The member countries' way of thinking about Japan and about world conditions also changed. Supporters of Japan gradually increased and overcame the opposition group, and Japan's formal accession was finally achieved. The historical pendulum swung from only U.S. support of Japan to a majority including countries indifferent and even hostile to Japan's position. The movement was slow, but the reversal was a dramatic milestone in history.

A second major question is why did the United States apply for Japan's accession to GATT, working tirelessly to recommend the accession and finally seeing it become a reality? Strategic factors were certainly involved: to reduce the economic costs of the U.S. military occupation of Japan, to encourage Japan's independence, to avoid Japan's inclination to trade with Communist China during the cold war and thus keep Japan inside the world's free trade zone. But were these all?

There is room to believe that in the hearts of the people there existed a profound idealism and humanistic vision. Certain people are constantly intent on pushing the world up to those ideals, even one small step at a time. The first director-general of GATT, Eric Wyndham-White of Britain, was without doubt one such person. The ideal found in GATT is that if a country understands the GATT spirit and qualifies for membership, it will be granted MFN status as a GATT member and treated in a nondiscriminatory manner in international trade. It is the will of today's modern humanity to recognize this as the base of international economic activity.

Chapter 8

Applying
GATT Article XXXV
to Japan

An Encounter

When I was a new graduate student walking toward Harvard Littauer Center one autumn morning, a gentleman on the other side of the street took off his felt hat as we passed. Another morning I met the same gentleman, who again removed his hat as we passed. Some days later, he took his hat off for the third time and waved toward me. I looked around only to find nobody else around, only me. This tall and stout gentleman, I thought from past experience, must have saluted me by taking off his hat. Rather embarrassed, I instantly waved back. I learned a year later as a second-year Ph.D. candidate that this gentleman was Professor Gottfried Haberler, of Harvard University. His international trade course was required for Ph.D. candidates. It was beyond my expectation that such a famous professor at Harvard would doff his hat for a mere new student from Tokyo.

Professor Haberler was a great teacher who touched my heart in several ways. He was famous for his penetrating insight into economics and had been invited from Vienna to teach at Harvard. He was a fair-skinned person with warm eyes. In international economics, he exhibited his creativity in the production-possibility curves of nations (aggregate) to break, for the first time, the rigidity in David Ricardo's comparative advantages in cost of production (assumed constant marginal costs) stemming from classical labor value theory. In 1958, Professor Haberler wrote the famous Haberler Report for GATT on primary products, agricultural policies, problems of developing countries, and the long-term stance of GATT as an institution.

He often went to Washington to advise President John F. Kennedy on current U.S. foreign trade policies. Once back from the capital, he would leave the textbook aside and criticize other scholars' recommendations for U.S. foreign policy. Sometimes he would even refute a Harvard teacher. We listened and felt we were directly contributing to the United States in this way. Between classes and at lunchtimes, free discussions on current U.S. economic policy measures in which fresh economic theories and facts had been applied led to heated discussions in classrooms and in the student-teachers' coffee lounge. The department's atmosphere was lively, full of vitality. Participation in these discussions would cause a young person's intellectual interest to surge, inducing more practical debates.

One day at the end of class, Professor Haberler said, "Countries applying GATT Article XXXV to Japan should stop it right now." At the edge of the classroom, I was captivated by these words. Articles on Japan seldom appeared in those days in American newspapers, maybe only once a week or less, or in a corner of the paper as a small, uninteresting item. When I asked about GATT Article XXXV, none of my classmates could answer. No wonder— at that time it was only a minority problem of GATT. Japan's per capita income then, in 1962, was some $600. I did not know how the problem was so seriously affecting my country, but at least I could comprehend that Professor Haberler deeply sympathized with Japan's status in GATT.

After I passed the Harvard qualification exams for my Ph.D. dissertation, I visited the professor to thank him and to say goodbye. With a nod, he asked, "Is that so?" Then he added, "Japan is a harsh country for women." At that time I paid but little attention to his words. I was energetic, young, and short-sighted. This word, *harsh*, though, had sunk into my heart and was often revived later in my life.

That time I was not sure about my future. How could I have comprehended then that I would later be serving in GATT and that my lifetime work would be in international economics!

WHAT DOES IT MEAN TO APPLY ARTICLE XXXV TO A GATT MEMBER?

GATT Article XXXV means not applying the GATT Agreement by particular Contracting Parties (countries) to a member country (or members). This is made possible when, as stated in Clause 1(B) of the article,

> This Agreement . . . shall not apply as between any contracting party and any other contracting party if:
>
> . . .
>
> (b) either of the contracting parties, at the time either becomes a contracting party, does not consent to such application.

This means that, under special conditions, GATT members can escape from the obligations of its rules. This is an escape clause of the GATT rules. Under this clause, if any member country by applying Article XXXV to another member declares that it will not treat it as a member, GATT agrees to authorize this declaration, thus allowing the member applying the article to escape from normal GATT rules. For example, when Japan became a GATT member in 1955, some members that declared the application of Article XXXV to it were allowed by GATT to refuse treatment of Japan as a member: Japan would be a *nominal* member for them in GATT even after having become a full-fledged member of it. In applying Article XXXV to Japan, those dissenting GATT members agreed only that Japan (nominally) had become a GATT member; they would not treat it as a member *in reality*. This would not have happened if member countries understood the GATT nondiscriminatory principle and if, only if, they kept its rules in mind. But this unthinkable fact happened in the mid-1950s: GATT approved the practice of Article XXXV.

I must say that the article is meant to contradict GATT's nondiscriminatory principle, which is to treat all member countries equally, because GATT members that applied Article XXXV to Japan needed neither to treat Japan as a member nor to grant it MFN (Most Favored Nation) benefits. Therefore the dissenting GATT members could discriminate in trade with Japan by limiting imports, levying high tariffs, applying an import licensing system, forbidding Japanese imports, or by imposing a combination of these practices.

It was an astonishingly extreme measure. Why was this article created? The reason goes back to the founding of GATT on October 30, 1947. When GATT established its rules, any country could apply for it and this article did not exist. If an unsuitable country applied to GATT and one member country refused, the applying country failed to become a member. In this way the rule rigidly limited members to only a small group. Requiring agreement from all members, this regulation made it hard for the accession of a candidate country and was a great obstacle to the expansion of GATT activities. Gradually, the representatives of GATT members came to think that this rule would ultimately contradict the ideals of the organization, which were aimed at contributing to the expansion of world trade and economic development.

Then GATT improved the situation, stipulating that if a country wished to join, it would be possible to do so with a two-thirds vote of the members, and this became Article XXXIII as it remains today. The stance of this article was to mitigate conditions for the acquisition of GATT membership, easing the process to become a member. But this change created another problem in that every member was obliged to have a good GATT relationship with the new member, regardless of its wishes. GATT therefore created Article XXXV to solve this problem and recognized the special right of original members to reject the opening of GATT relationships with a new member. The organization compromised for the sake of old members discontented with the creation of Article XXXIII and its easier access to membership (two-thirds of members agreeing will allow a new membership). GATT implemented this new Article XXXV in March 1948.

Japan was then far from meeting the conditions necessary for it to apply for GATT membership. The United States and India had their own problems, and Article XXXV was created by proposals of the United States and the United Kingdom. Nobody could then predict that so many members would later apply the article to Japan, creating a grave problem for GATT.

By the end of 1954, 24 GATT members had signed "the declaration for Japan's accession to GATT," as described in the previous chapter. When the accession of Japan became clear in March 1955, the members that did not sign the declaration officially informed GATT that they would apply Article XXXV to Japan. These 14 members—Australia, Austria, Belgium, Brazil, Cuba, France, Haiti, India, the Grand Duchy of Luxembourg, the Netherlands, New Zealand, the Federation of Rhodesia and Nyasaland, the Republic of South Africa, and the United Kingdom—applied the article to Japan on the day of its accession to GATT.[1] In May 1961, 14 members applied Article XXXV to Japan.

Some changed from the previous 14; Brazil and India ceded the application, but Cambodia, Ghana, Haiti, and Nigeria, all former colonies and now developing countries, newly applied the article to Japan because of their deficits in current accounts on trade, making a total of 16 members in August.[2] Having been subjected to Article XXXV by 16 members, Japan proposed to the 17th GATT Contracting Party (CP) meeting in August 1961 that trade relationships between Japan and these members be reviewed. GATT CP members appointed a Working Party (WP) to review the matter at the 18th annual CP meeting.

The results of the application of Article XXXV

The Belgian government applied *quota* and *import license* systems to Japanese imports.[3] It applied Article XXXV based on a Benelux (Belgium, Netherlands, and Luxembourg) protocol, which was synthesized with the Netherlands tariff system and included quotas and a licensing system for Japanese imports.

The quota was a quantitative restriction, one of the most effective import restrictions short of a complete restriction, extremely protective and beneficial only to domestic producers at the expense of domestic consumers. These applications were flagrant violations of GATT rules, the violations of which were practiced by many GATT members then against other GATT members. There is some evidence that Article XXXV being applied by members to Japan within the GATT framework later became a strong reason for the deterioration of GATT workings. GATT had no legal binding power then and was therefore later transformed into a new organization, the WTO (World Trade Organization).

The report of the 1961 Working Party

Eric Wyndham-White, the director-general of GATT, chaired the WP for six days, from August 28, 1961, to investigate how members applied Article XXXV to Japan. The WP intended to recommend improvements and to add some general considerations for the country to which it was applied.

The GATT secretariat reported on the treatment of imports from Japan by members who applied Article XXXV.[4] This is a summary of the report:

> Two members, Haiti and the Republic of South Africa, did not grant MFN treatment to Japan.

> The other 14 members that applied Article XXXV had granted Japan MFN treatment by this time through bilateral treaties concluded with Japan. One of them levied no restrictions and applied complete nondiscriminatory principles for imports from Japan. [The GATT report did not mention the country's name.] Some members continued restrictions on special important items, although as a principle, based on nondiscrimination. Some members continued considerable restrictions on Japanese imports from time to time by negotiating on a bilateral basis. The rest were not opening their markets for imports from Japan.

The application of Article XXXV by members regarding imports from Japan widely varied from nearly free trade conditions to no imports. Furthermore, if a country granted MFN treatment to Japanese products and then reported that the imports were causing serious damage to domestic industries in *either* member [stressed by the author because this "either country" would be deception/lip service by any GATT member in citing legal equality for both importing and exporting members] or that it feared they would cause serious damage, the importing country had the right to cancel the promise of granting MFN to Japan. The Working Party mentioned, "In these treaties, if trading duties were canceled, for example, to grant MFN treatment to Japan, they [Japan and the country applying Article XXXV] should discuss on a bilateral basis."

On the other hand, Japan granted MFN treatment to all 16 members that applied GATT's Article XXXV to Japan, just as it did to all other members, such as the United States, that supported Japan.

The approach to the issue from the beginning was one-sided, since Japan was almost always the exporting country. But the report states that importers (members applying Article XXXV) and *the exporter, Japan,* had equal rights to cancel MFN status to the other, if either member experienced damage to its domestic industries. The members applying Article XXXV to Japan were always fearful that an increase of Japanese imports would harm them.

The WP investigated the influence of the application of Article XXXV on Japan's foreign trade. The contents of its report, based on reports and statistics of GATT members applying Article XXXV to Japan, are as follows:[5]

> The absolute total amount of imports from Japan was increased in their markets. Furthermore, Japan's shares in these markets considerably increased. Therefore the application of Article XXXV didn't necessarily oppress bilateral trade between Japan and its trading partners. The more important thing in possibilities in foreign trade is if discriminatory import restrictive measures are implemented. If these members are discriminating against imports from Japan by restrictions that would be impossible to apply on other members' products, imports from Japan would stay at levels lower than those from other members [to which Article XXXV was not applied], or the growth rate of imports from Japan would be lower than those from other countries.

The discussion in the report, however, was neither sophisticated nor fair. Above all, it overlooked the possibility of a more rapid increase in productivity in Japan than in competing countries. In the case of improved productivity, Japanese products could grow more rapidly than the products of other countries. In this situation, imports from Japan could have grown, even in the face of the counterbalancing discriminatory measures, such as higher tariff rates. However the growth rates of Japan's products could have been much higher if they had not been discriminatorily treated, since they were able to increase even under discrimination. On the reverse side, a relative fall in productivity by countries competing in exports with Japan could induce a faster growth in imports from Japan.

Another possibility was that a relative fall in absolute aggregate export values by other countries could cause a relative increase in Japan's share in the markets of members applying Article XXXV. The report totally ignored these possibilities as if they were outside the scope of international economics. Should either occur—an increase in Japan's productivity or a decline in that of its competitors—Japan's share could increase. Even if only a small increase took place by overcoming higher tariff rates or import restrictions, the statistics would show only that those imports from Japan increased by oppressing the shares of other countries.

As a result of this shallow analysis, the WP concluded in a report issued to all GATT members that the application of Article XXXV did not cause a worsening of Japan's trade. But this observation was superficial in overlooking the changeable potentialities of productivity in dynamic multilateral world trading and viewed international trade only in the short term. It is most unfortunate that the people participating in this WP report failed to perceive the process of dynamic evolution in interdependent world trading and growth of the world economy.

A comparison of members who applied Article XXXV with members who did not

The WP members further investigated the relationships between Japan and GATT members that treated Japan as a member, such as the United States. The WP findings: Some members didn't treat

Japan on the same level that other countries did; they de facto discriminated against Japan, which sometimes conducted special negotiations with members to receive fairness in trading. Some members had no specific import regulations concerning trade with Japan except for a limited quantity of imports: Japan made VERs (Voluntary Export Restraints) with them.

The report continues on to find that imports from Japan would or could cause serious damage to domestic industries in importing member nations as the basis for the application of Article XXXV (therefore justifying its application). Some members' representatives in the WP thought that the Article XXXV system imposed an apparently severer impact (on the Japanese side) than was really incurred in damages by the members applying Article XXXV.

However, the report was imperfect in its inquiry into discriminations revealed in the application of Article XXXV. It explained that some members interpreted the situation to mean that the implementation of Article XXXV was based on the Japanese trade system and that this was satisfactory because Japan had granted nondiscriminatory treatment to products of the applies of Article XXXV to Japan as being equal to products of members that did not apply it, such as the United States. (Thus the report implied that the present status of applying Article XXXV to Japan needed no changes.)

It compared two groups of members, one that was applying Article XXXV to Japan and one that was not. The two groups exhibited a huge chasm between them, though this was somewhat blurred on the edges because of differences in practice. In the latter group, for example, if the United States imposed some import restrictions on Japanese products, GATT would examine and ask for some improvements at the request of the suffering CP member, Japan. Apparently the members of the group that did not apply Article XXXV were more loyal to the spirit and the system of GATT.

The WP thus requested the following:

> The members applying Article XXXV have a right to continue it. This application, however, is not only influencing trade between these two countries, but is also creating problems for the third

members. Import limitations, however, adversely influence trade. Trading between members that applied Article XXXV and Japan developed as a whole, but the lack of GATT relations between these members and Japan created factors of uncertainty and hampered Japan's exports. This situation is adversely influencing Japan's capability to earn foreign exchange and lowers its export potentiality. Members that consider Japan an important export market should deeply consider these facts.

Japan announced its intention of considerable withdrawal in restrictions on imports. It is afraid that broadly spread facts of the application of Article XXXV to Japan might prevent Japan's willingness to achieve this goal. Japan has no obligation to implement GATT liberalization measures to products of these members that applied Article XXXV to it. It is preferable, however, that Japan continues its liberalization measures.

The last two sentences are superfluous, because Japan equally treated products of members applying the article to it and products of members that actually treated Japan as a GATT member. The report continues.

A widely implemented Article XXXV among members becomes an obstacle to GATT, especially for tariff reductions. From this viewpoint, the lack of relationship among the members because of the application of Article XXXV is an obstacle. Particularly, we fear that this will hamper Japan's efforts to be deeply involved in the tariff negotiations. The WP recognizes that the above discussions are valid and asks the members to pay due attention to the contents of this report.

The WP ended this part by saying that it would be better to stop the application of Article XXXV. It then concluded that

Considering this, we recommend to negotiate [with Japan] either in bilateral or multilateral ways. To implement the results of the bilateral negotiations, however, it may be necessary to get a decision from the CP.

It added information about examples of Japanese exports that concentrated on a few items as one reason for making tariff reductions impossible.

> The CP members several times discussed problems of so-called market-destructive exports that often occurred in the members' markets. If we find some solutions that satisfy multilateral members, it will surely promote the solving of problems of the application of Article XXXV.

A change in the GATT stance

By the end of 1961, a stance to solve the problem of application of Article XXXV to Japan had gradually developed among GATT members. This progress was achieved by continual efforts over a long time by GATT and its relevant member countries. The concluding remarks of the report reveal that there existed fairness and people other than the Japanese who had made efforts as a backdrop of this evolution in GATT.

The economic boom that had occurred from the end of the 1950s in Japan strengthened demand for production and the economy grew, but this caused shortages in manufactured goods. The situation then saw imports continue to increase, the financial sector to tighten, and the economy to go downward. The country registered a large deficit in balance of payments at the end of 1961, at which time Japan's GNP was less than 9 percent of the U.S. GNP.

Japan had unsuccessfully been pushing to increase exports since the mid-1950s. For example, the iron and steel industries could not cope with international price competition. Therefore the steel industry tearfully junked equipment which it had only recently installed after World War II. Manufacturers borrowed huge amounts of money from banks and started again from step one to establish a big, comprehensive iron and steel factory on the seacoast. Some exports that challenged world markets finally restarted in the mid-1960s.

A good example of these efforts involves a Japanese manufacturer of automobiles. In 1955, Toyota landed one of its Japan-produced cars at a U.S. port for exhibit to the American public. (The size of the Japanese economy then had just recovered to its prewar high of 1936–37.) But the car was unable to climb an ordinary slope en route to the exhibition hall. Its Japanese escorts desperately pushed and pushed, but they couldn't get the car up the incline. Finally, unable to exhibit it, Toyota shipped it back to Japan. But two decades later, Japan was annually exporting a great many cars to the U.S. market. "Time flies quickly. It seems as if only yesterday when we were in tears over our brand-new troubled car," a Toyota executive in Washington, D.C., said in 1986.

During the five-year periods of 1959–63 and 1964–68, the average annual growth rate of total factor productivity in the United States was 2.25 percent; in Japan it was 1.66. In the periods of 1964–68 and 1969–73, the ratios were reversed: The rate in Japan became 2.59 percent, surpassing the 0.92 of the United States.[6]

New GATT members apply Article XXXV as a heritage of their mother countries

Many countries became newly independent of their mother countries after World War II. Under item 5 (c) of GATT Article XXVI (later Article XXXIII), newly independent countries became GATT members. These countries acquired freedom and autonomy in trade relations upon GATT membership. An important issue was that in becoming members, they continued the treaties of their former mother countries, including legal rights on tariffs and terms that had been implemented in their territories. If the mother countries had been applying Article XXXV to Japan, that would have continued in effect exactly as before between the new independent governments and Japan, unless they declared a stop to them. The article also states that the new governments need not declare an immediate halt to the application of Article XXXV. It is understandable that after acquiring GATT membership, the new governments were so preoccupied in establishing themselves that they had little time to reconsider the issue of an automatic application of Article XXXV to Japan. Some members even applied Article XXXV to Japan only to show off their status as GATT members.

Colonial powers such as the United Kingdom, France, and the Benelux countries that had rejected Japan's accession to GATT had also instantly applied Article XXXV to Japan when it became a member in 1955. Australia and Austria joined them on the same day. A large number of the newly independent countries, many without conscious review, automatically applied this GATT article to Japan. One after another, new members applied it to Japan, apparently just following in the footsteps of their former mother countries. Some, however, eliminated its application to Japan.

As mentioned earlier, 14 members were applying Article XXXV to Japan in 1955. It was then that GATT, at the request of Japan, called for the Working Party to inquire into the effects of the application.[7] In August 1962, the application of Article XXXV was not confined only to Japan; it was also applied to some other members. For example, Cuba applied it to 12 GATT members from Australia to Uruguay, including Japan. In the same year, however, only Japan was being subjected to Article XXXV by as many as 23 of the total of 53 GATT members, making it extremely conspicuous in the international arena.[8]

Japanese Ambassador Eiji Wazima in Brussels sent a telegram in March 1960, for preparations to the Dillon Round (the fifth GATT multilateral negotiations), about the Belgian reform of February 24, 1960, to Foreign Minister Aiichiro Fujiyama in Tokyo.[9]

1. The Belgian government has no intention to enforce again the restriction on imports from Japan but will continue the quota on Japanese imports.

2. Reciprocal Trade Clearance Agreements have been concluded with Spain and Turkey. The Belgian government will abolish the licensing system with Spain, because Spain joined the EEC last summer and the Belgian trade balance with Spain has been improving.

3. This reform accompanies only the implementation of the Protocol on Benelux New Tariffs Reform synthesized with the Netherlands old system, and de facto nothing has changed at all.

Therefore, please understand that import licenses are necessary for all Japanese imports as they were before and they have no intention to strengthen the restrictions.[10]

The United Kingdom, France, and Benelux withdraw the application of Article XXXV to Japan

The U.S. Trade Expansion Act of 1962 permitted the administration of President John F. Kennedy to negotiate a reduction of tariffs of up to 50 percent. He inspired the world to start new GATT multilateral negotiations. In preparation for the GATT Kennedy Round, GATT held the first Ministers' Meeting in 1963. The world tide had dynamically changed toward the new GATT round, though Japan, as before, was treated by many members as an outsider within GATT, even though it was earnestly struggling to improve its position. In the changing world, the United Kingdom, Australia, France, and the Netherlands had no choice but to withdraw the application of Article XXXV to Japan.

But they felt it should not be done for free. They proposed that if Japan should conclude a reciprocal commercial agreement with each of these countries, they would proceed with the withdrawal. The proposed options for Japan were either (1) to allow Article XXXV to be continuously applied, or (2) to conclude a reciprocal agreement with each of them. Japan felt it had to accept this proposal and thus concluded a reciprocal commercial agreement with each of those members: the United Kingdom, France, Belgium, the Netherlands, Luxembourg, and Australia. The contents of the agreement on a reciprocal basis were twofold: to implement (1) *transitional* import restrictions against imports from Japan and (2) selective *safeguarding* clauses. In the former, the meaning of "transitional" could be dubious, because the length of the period is not mentioned at all. The difference between the new agreements and Article XXXV is only the former being on a *reciprocal* basis.

The reciprocal agreement means, for example, that if France implements a safeguarding clause on a Japanese product, Japan is able to impose, as a countervailing measure, a safeguarding clause on imports from France. Carrying, however, a grave balance of payment problem in foreign trade, Japan's economic conditions were in a vicious circle: Whenever a rise in GNP pulled up demand for material imports, it brought on a deficit in foreign trade. After growth in its economy, Japan needed constant, long-term efforts to make up the deficit on current account in the foreign trade balance. Even if, for example, France or any of the Benelux countries implemented the safeguarding clauses for imports to segregate Japan in their domestic and colonial markets, how could Japan implement any selective reciprocal safeguarding clauses to prevent imports from them which would certainly create a new trade friction and only worsen the situation?

Safeguarding clauses are concluded with a commercial treaty with two conditions:

(1) When imports of specific items are destroying a market (markets), the exporting country has been informed, and it has not stopped the situation within 30 days after negotiations have started, the importing country can discriminate against the goods by import restrictions. When the case is urgent, the importing country can immediately restrict the imports.

(2) Against this, the exporting country can immediately implement countervailing measures.

For *sensitive items* the importing country can bilaterally impose restrictions of imports during a certain period.

These are forbidden under GATT rules.

It should be noted that while the European Economic Community (EEC) had removed within it all *quotas* in industrial goods by 1961, Japan had to accept *safeguarding clauses* and *sensitive items* to have them withdraw the application of Article XXXV. Thus Japan concluded with the **United Kingdom** the new Japan-U.K. Commercial Treaty of 1962. It was accompanied by the second protocol for commerce that decided 18 negative items and 61 VER offerings by the Japanese side. (Before this, discriminated-against imports from Japan totaled 175 items.)[11]

In the case of the three **Benelux** countries, withdrawal negotiations had made little progress because the Netherlands had posed strong objections. At last the negotiations met with success under the condition of Japanese acceptance of safeguarding clauses and negotiation of sensitive items in November 1962. The protocol which decided the two conditions was signed in April 1963. The Japanese Diet recognized it in July while Belgium and the Netherlands did so after general elections; it came into effect that autumn.

Periods and the exporting country's countervailing measures became most difficult matters for safeguarding clauses. The final conclusions were as follows: The period was tentatively set for six years, but after the expiration of the first period, agreement by both sides was necessary to terminate it; countervailing measures were decided in the way unfavorable for the exporting country, which differed from either GATT rules or the safeguarding clauses of the Japan-U.K. Commercial Treaty of 1962.

The Japanese side accepted being discriminated against for 38 sensitive items, which were the same as when Article XXXV was being applied, though Japan wanted to reduce the number of the items.

The conclusion of a new Japan-U.K. Commercial Treaty and the progress of negotiations with the Benelux countries pushed a new negotiation with **France** to start in January 1963. The Japan-France Commercial Treaty (a six-year period and MFN treatment clause), with a protocol of commerce which regulated safeguarding clauses and sensitive items, was signed in May 1963. Japan accepted safeguarding clauses (the period and countervailing measures were the same as those of the Benelux countries) as compensation for the withdrawal of Article XXXV. Japan accepted 107 sensitive items with France. The reduction of the number of sensitive items would be examined from time to time. Under the application of Article XXXV, France maintained 148 import restrictive items. When the treaty became effective in November 1963, French application of Article XXXV ended.

Earlier, in February of 1963, France recommended to six EEC countries that they include a similar safeguarding clause when they concluded a commercial treaty with Japan. The contents of these reciprocal agreements surprised the Japanese because they were the same or as harsh and bitter, in a sense, as those practiced under Article XXXV, as described above.

On conclusion of the Japan-U.K. Commercial Treaty in November 1962, the United Kingdom promised the withdrawal of application of Article XXXV to Japan and did so in April 1963. The Benelux countries followed in promising its withdrawal in April. Following their lead, France at last promised the withdrawal of Article XXXV in May. This meant that Japan now had a regular relationship with these chief European members in GATT.

Australia applied Article XXXV to Japan on the day of its accession to GATT in 1955. It partially gave Japan MFN treatment in tariffs and imports after the coming into effect of the Japan-Australia Commercial Treaty of 1957 and 1960. It promised the removal of the application of the article to Japan. Negotiations broke off, however, when Japan proposed a considerable relaxation of the import restrictions in October 1960. After a time, when the negotiations reopened, Australia promised unconditional withdrawal of the application of Article XXXV in 1962, and a new protocol accompanied the renewed Japan-Australia Commercial Treaty which was signed in August 1963. Japan offered to Australia (1) to maintain wheat imports on a stable base, (2) to import its barley at a non-discriminatory basis, and (3) to keep tariffs on sheep wool free. It should be mentioned that Australia designated no discriminatory import restrictive sensitive items against Japan.

The conclusion of the agreements broke the deadlock, as most European members started to gradually withdraw the application of Article XXXV to Japan in 1963 and 1964. Meanwhile, during these years Japan continued to appeal to GATT members to withdraw application of the article. Without these processes being undertaken, history could not have progressed as it did. Eventually many former colonial members withdrew application of the article to Japan, one by one, following in the footsteps of their former mother countries. This was a watershed issue.

Withdrawal of the Application of Article XXXV to Japan by former British colonies

Time passed. The governments of Australia, France, Belgium, Luxembourg, and the Netherlands officially declared that they had withdrawn the application of Article XXXV to Japan in January 1964. The government of the United Kingdom implemented the GATT treaty with Japan; it withdrew the application of Article XXXV to Japan in March. At that time, the U.K. government notified GATT that a total of 16 territories belonging to the United Kingdom, including Gibraltar, Bermuda, British Honduras, and Hong Kong, had immediately implemented a GATT treaty with Japan (withdrawn the application of Article XXXV to Japan).[12]

The British government in October 1966 announced that Persian Gulf territories, including Bahrain and other former British possessions, had withdrawn the application of Article XXXV to Japan. In 1967, it further announced that many territories, including the Virgin Islands, Dominica, the Fiji Islands, Abu Dhabi, and Dubai, had withdrawn application of the article to Japan and had entered normal trading relations based on the GATT treaty.[13]

By this time, Britain had thus withdrawn the application of Article XXXV to Japan in 26 colonies and territories of its possessions before World War II, except for the members that had already been independent of it before 1967. Among them, Article XXXV was in practice in 18 territories and legally implemented in the rest. When they became independent countries after November 1967, British government notices on the withdrawal of the application in 1964 and 1967 were already in effect. For example, when the United Arab Emirates became independent in December 1971, no problem existed with Japan about the application of Article XXXV; it had already been withdrawn.

The majority of the newly independent countries that had become GATT members earlier than the U.K. withdrawal halted the application following the British measures of 1964 and 1967. Malaysia in 1960 and Ghana in 1962 had become members before the British declaration of withdrawing halted the application of the article to Japan.[14] The British government registered with GATT that all territories that had been under its control had withdrawn the application to Japan by March 1970.[15] Some territories, however, remained.

In 1971, when developing countries were accorded General Special Privileges (GSP), Japan persuaded those members that had been applying Article XXXV to Japan to withdraw their applications. In October 1973, however, 22 members still continued the application to Japan. Among them, 14 were African members, including Kenya and Tanzania. They received the right to apply Article XXXV as a heritage through GATT Article XXVI (c), a result of their mother countries' legal GATT rights. For a while, developing countries on the African continent continued to newly apply the article to Japan. Some continued to do so for more than 10 years, but gradually withdrawing members increased. Other members that still practiced its application to Japan in mid-1971 were the Republic of South Africa, Haiti, Jamaica, Austria, Cyprus, Ireland, Portugal, and Spain. Spain withdrew it in December 1971. Ireland applied the article to Japan in 1967 and withdrew it in 1975. Indonesia was independent of the Netherlands in 1949 and acquired GATT membership in 1950, but it did not apply Article XXXV to Japan.

In the same period, some members that had become independent of Portugal de facto applied Article XXXV to Japan. Up to 1992 there had been no report that they had withdrawn application. About 14 former French colonies became independent in the 1960s, including Congo and the Ivory Coast. They were one step behind the global trend, but they gradually withdrew the application of Article XXXV to Japan by the mid-1970s. The Republic of Burundi and the Republic of Rwanda became independent of France in 1962 and withdrew their applications of Article XXXV to Japan in the beginning of the 1970s. Cambodia was independent in 1952, Algeria in 1962; since then they, as recorded in 1992, applied the article to Japan.

Thus many countries, one after another, withdrew the application of Article XXXV to Japan. In October 1975, however, Austria, Cyprus, Haiti, Kenya, Senegal, and the Republic of South Africa still pursued the practice.

Austria severely discriminated against Japan in its import system by application of Article XXXV from September of 1955. Japan asked many times for its withdrawal. Austria probably had not thought of such a withdrawal at all, until the withdrawal of the article by the United Kingdom, Benelux countries and France. In the belief that compensating conditions for the withdrawal of Article XXXV would become more unfavorable, Austria proposed starting negotiations in 1962. After more than a year, negotiations ended, in June 1963, and both sides exchanged a document in which Austria promised to treat Japan similarly to regular GATT members. However, its restrictions against imports from Japan increased, approaching as many as 300 sensitive items in autumn 1963. Japan hoped first to reduce the number of these items. It was in October 1976, when Austria finally announced that it would withdraw the application of Article XXXV to Japan.[16]

For quite long periods up to then, Japanese representatives had made strenuous efforts for the withdrawal of the application of the article to Japan. Some fair and internationally minded people, such as Harvard Professor Gottfried Haberler had contributed to make it happen over the long term. Joining GATT but not being treated as a member by other members was a headache for Japan, which was then a weak country. From 1955 through the 1960s, this failure to be treated as a GATT member persisted. The GATT members applying Article XXXV had changed, but Japan still suffered incessantly.

This national disgrace is comparable to that of the earlier unequal treaties concluded between Japan and Western nations. Japan, toward the end of the Tokugawa shogunate, had concluded unequal treaties with the United States, the Netherlands, Russia, the United Kingdom, and France in 1860, and with Switzerland in 1863. The concluded treaties were most often titled Friendship and Commercial Treaties. Having been essentially segregated from world free trade, Japan had suffered:

1. Lack of tariff autonomy (5 percent tariffs on imports *and exports*—tariffs on exports discourage exporters).
2. The existence of extraterritorial rights (a foreign consulate's judiciary rights).

About 55 years later, in the 1910s of the Taisho period, they were terminated, one by one, and finally all were invalidated. Until then, the elimination of the unequal treaties had been an earnest desire, and hard efforts were made by the nation in public and private sectors alike, during the 45 years of the modern Meiji period, and through the beginning decade of the Taisho period. In comparison, the efforts to have withdrawn the application of GATT Article XXXV to Japan are unknown to most Japanese today, even including international representatives and diplomats.

According to the investigations of the GATT secretariat in 1981, members that applied Article XXXV to Japan then totaled 48. The Republic of South Africa withdrew its application in 1985. Cambodia and Algeria recorded in 1992 the de facto application of GATT Article XXXV to Japan. The GATT general director, Arthur Dunkel, announced that Cyprus withdrew it at the end of April 1992, the last report of its being applied to Japan.[17] Applying members still remained, however, even though by this time Japan had become one of the financial donors, helping developing countries and others.

AFTERWORD

We live on light created through nuclear fusion within the sun. Light is further transformed into various nutrients through photosynthesis and forms the basis of life on earth. Looked at from the dynamism of the universe and earth's history, the period and the events I concentrated on in my research constitute only a short instant, a snapshot of history, though it is a record of truth in pursuing a hope in human life.

I wrote this book at two separate times: the first six chapters were submitted in connection with a Harvard Ph.D. degree in Economics in 1989 and later the last two chapters pursued the same subject, looking at the change of trend in the postwar period.

The question for economists was how Japan survived the worldwide anti-Japan trade crossfire during the1920s and 1930s. Nobody could answer since everything was unknown until an economics student asked for the declassification of the relevant documents in national archives in Tokyo, the Library of Congress in Washington, D.C., Richmond in the United Kingdom, and at the WTO (GATT).

Through this retrospective journey, some of the contents inspired me to think more deeply about trade conflicts and economic development. Such reflections, findings and implications are discussed below.

The Historical Background

Japan emerged as a quickly modernizing nation in 1868. Succeeding in industrialization, the Osaka Spinning Company's yarn, for the first time, drove out Indian yarn from the domestic market. Why Japan's cotton spinning industry had to compete in the domestic market was that the unequal treaty agreements concluded with Western countries in the Tokugawa Period deprived Japan of tariff autonomy. Tariffs were fixed at the same rates on both exports and imports. The company, nevertheless, started to export cotton yarn to China in 1891, as a successful pioneer.

Decades later, through many international conflicts in trade competition, particularly in cotton textiles, Japan awakened to realize itself as a young country that was catching up with Western countries in some industrial areas. It was a latecomer at the end of the 1920s, after the main interwar world markets had already been divided among the Western powers via imperialism-cum-colonialism.

Japan overcame difficulties to sell its products abroad but growth rates in exports declined or stagnated in the world market. The country started shifting the weight of markets, from China and the United States, to Western dominions and colonies (particularly in Asia), to South America, to the Middle East, and finally to Africa. However, towards the end of 1935, Japan's main trading partners, except for certain north China regions, forbade the importation of Japanese products. Without any route to sell its products, a feeling that the nation had no future stifled Japan, since it was an island country with scarce natural resources. In the 1930s, it was the only non-Western country to catch up with the West, and it did it from a corner of Asia. However, it was alone and remained a relatively backward country throughout the interwar period. Japan struggled, as a latecomer, to live in an already interdependent international world. The advanced countries' attitude toward this newcomer was harsh and cold beyond imagination. The only way to survive in this hardship spiral was either to endure, or to face a strong possibility of proceeding to war. The last to enter was the first one to depart from the field. In Foreign Office documents, marked as secret, Japan's "perceived enemy" shifted from its longtime enemy, Russia, to the United States in 1936.

In the midst of international trade conflicts, no ordinary Japanese citizen perceived or understood that the country would plunge into the Pacific War as a result. Researching, I came across a Japanese entrepreneur who came of a *nanushi* family, that is, an administrator of a village under the Tokugawa regime (in his case, generations had continued to carry swords and every villager had his surname). He came to town, pioneered in opening a shop as the first importer of Monopoly bicycles in his prefecture, and actively welcomed the new Taisho democracy. People elected him to chair the town council. He was pleased that the prefectural school superintendent came by train to ask him how he brought up all of his children as the top students of their classes. While he was establishing a new bus company around Lake Kasumi, northwest of Tokyo, the economy went into a severe financial crisis in 1928 due to a governmental bank failure caused by a deflationary policy aimed at reestablishing the gold standard in Japan.

How could he know that the Great Depression in the United States would follow such a financial crisis to engulf the economy? In bankruptcy, he lost almost all his possessions—a movie theater in the center of the town, rice fields bringing him seventy-seven *hyou* (4,620 kilograms) of rice rent in kind per year, and several lots with rental wooden houses around his home. In addition, he lost his second daughter, a beauty, top student and sprinter representing the prefecture in the Meiji Shrine Sports Festival, to tuberculosis in 1931. He used to calm himself by saying "she went away to get married in a faraway region," not thinking about how he could not afford to send her to a sanatorium for clean air and nourishment. The only things remaining for him were a small bicycle shop and his family. The prefectural public high schools censured his third daughter and fourth son for unpaid fees. Conscripted, his third son served as a military physician but suffered from lung disease and finally was sent back for nursing. The second son went to Singapore as a military attaché journalist and drowned in the South China Sea, of which the family was informed only after the end of the war in 1946. The family was supported by his fourth son, who was conscripted. He closed his shop by an order to mobilize all national power to the war system in 1937. He suffered a stomach disease, declined for a long time, and passed away before the war ended in defeat.

In the same town, there was a house labeled with the national notice of "Heroes' home"; only an elderly farmer lived there since their seven sons had been conscripted and one by one all killed in the Sino-Japanese War and the succeeding Pacific War. Those are snapshots of Japanese families as a backdrop of the time treated in this book. There must be millions of this sort of family history related to the Great Depression and World War II regardless of nationality in the world at large.

JAPANESE APPEALS FOR FAIR TREATMENT

When the League of Nations held a conference concerning the anti-Japanese boycotts in China in early 1932, Japan showed much backwardness by sending there only one professor from the University of Tokyo, who coolly discussed international illegal aspects of the Chinese anti-Japanese boycotts. China sent representatives including citizens who patriotically appealed in easily understandable words with a passion that was impressive to the League of Nations. The resultant stance of the latter was revealed in the *Report of the Commission of Enquiry* (the Litton Report). At the same stage, furthermore, a Czechoslovakian representative questioned directly, "Why doesn't the Japanese government appeal here as Great Britain did on the occasion of the anti-British boycotts in Hong Kong?" The Japanese did not respond to this supportive remark.

Losing in the vote in support of Manchuria in 1933, Japan withdrew from the League of Nations, an action that had a long-lasting and far-reaching negative impact on its economic development.

Chinese citizens further made persistent appeals to the American people in justifying their boycotts by connecting them to Japan's invasion of China and created a base to gain the sympathy and support of American intellectuals. The anti-Japanese movement spread further to all Asian regions and to other continents.

That may have influenced the stance of U.S. political leaders toward Japan. In its New Deal policy, the Franklin Roosevelt administration was ambivalent as to whether to embrace protectionism or liberalism in foreign trade. The policy to encourage the recovery of the domestic economy by protecting its industries and promoting agriculture contradicted the policy advocated by Cordell Hull, the Secretary of State, which was a general tariff reduction and removal of quantitative restrictions in imports. The government relaxed its foreign trade policy, but raised tariffs discriminatorily, for example, on Japan. The administration had to compromise due to strong opposition over New Deal policies since opposition existed even within the Democratic party. The government thus politically demonstrated that it would not be flatly reducing tariffs, but could take a hard stance towards certain countries like Japan.

While investigating source materials for my thesis in Washington, D.C., I met a second-generation Japanese-American. He told me that in his young days in the 1930s, when the anti-Japan movement was severe, many second-generation Japanese-Americans were worried about it. The Japanese government was also deeply concerned and sent a mission to mitigate the criticism focused in the anti-Japan movement. He willingly volunteered in New York to serve as an interpreter for his parents' native country. The audience gathered, but the members of the Japanese mission were all government officials. "What the bureaucrats of foreign countries said failed to impress the Americans, as you know. I tried to do my best, but the gathering utterly failed. Why did Japan not send private citizens to appeal to the American common people, so that the Americans understood the matter better?" He could not forget the day, regretting that "the Japanese do not much understand the Americans' hearts."

In the Postwar Period

Even in the postwar period, Japan faced many difficulties when it hoped to join GATT after the economy recovered to its prewar peak level of 1936–37, finally escaping from the chronic deficits in international trade that had always hampered its potential for growth. Japan's entry into GATT was finally accepted in 1955; the awful delay should be compared with the easier case of West Germany in 1950. On its accession day, major European GATT members instantly applied GATT Article XXXV to Japan. In effect, they declared that they had just let Japan join GATT but they were not treating it as a recognized member.

Nevertheless, the pendulum of history gradually shifted, and support for Japan finally increased after John Fitzgerald Kennedy's declaration for general tax reductions in world trade. Major European GATT countries one by one withdrew the application of Article XXXV by concluding bilateral (not multilateral) treaties with Japan. In the meantime, many colonial nations, after declaring their independence, chose to inherit this formidable right under Article XXXV and applied it to Japan. We can well imagine why Japan proposed in 1973 to GATT to hold the Tokyo Round, with a deep aspiration to utterly overcome the inequalities still existing in international trade.

Deep Insight into World Change

Certain people did see the truth of historical changes in trade conflicts. While Japan was widely condemned for "dumping" in the world around 1933, the British Embassy in Tokyo sent a report to London strongly rejecting the previous reports from Jakarta, which charged the Japanese with unfairness in trade. The British Embassy's Tokyo report said, "If Japanese companies were dumping or subsidized by the Japanese government as mentioned in the Jakarta reports, we need not worry and can forget about the Japanese competition. However, we are concerned that they really acquired international competitiveness." By 1931, the Japanese had acquired competitive strength in the cotton spinning industry by lowering costs stemming from economies of scale and the use of the most modern technologies. In calm observation, the British Embassy in Tokyo recognized the truth not reflected in local reports in Asia. Nevertheless, such reports were unknown to the world until the 1980s, when I asked them to be declassified at the Library of Congress in Washington, D.C.

Another person possessed a similar insight into upcoming world change. An American diplomat's reports sent from Santiago to Washington pointed out that the Japanese were trying to satisfy local doctors' requests for medical forceps and delivered them to the spot exactly on time. It continued that they also fulfilled customers' hopes and requirements, even colorings for money registers, and those Japanese merchants' behavior looked beyond just making profits. They appeared to make a greater effort to cater to the desires and whims of Latin American buyers than the Americans did. "The Japanese regarded profits from a long-term viewpoint. In Mexico, what they offered was to make medical instruments in any size, shape, or type the Mexican doctor desired." He continued that their offer undoubtedly intended to not only get business—since this practice adversely affects profits by increasing production costs—but also to obtain new ideas worldwide to attain a supremacy in design and manufacture. "This policy . . . beyond doubt played an important part in helping the Japanese reach such an outstanding position in the industrial and commercial world in a short time," he concluded.

ECONOMIC DEVELOPMENT AND TRADE FRICTION

Trade conflicts will occur as the economic development of the world witnesses developing countries catching up with the advanced countries. When a backward country once succeeds in industrialization, its growth rate, in general, tends to exceed those of the advanced ones. It will grow even when the world economy is in recession.

Besides the agriculture sector, developing countries can catch up with advanced countries primarily in sectors in which technological progress is slow. When a developing country starts exporting, vested interests in the importing country appeal to politicians for protection by either tightening import restrictions or giving more subsidies. Conflicts occur more often when such related vested interests feel that the market is growing no further and hence is a zero sum game; they condemn foreigners for depriving them of their market share. The markets, however, can be expanded by the use of new technology, new combinations of products, changes in taste, or drastic price-cum-cost reductions for basic products, which people in low-income brackets previously could not afford. Furthermore, quickened technological progress tends to leave behind industries that had just depended on retarded technology. The more developing countries catch up in connection with technologically retarded sectors, the more trade frictions arise.

The economies of emerging countries, in general, tend to be more difficult to grow due to either poor or clustered natural resources, and due to the small scale of domestic markets. Those problems enlarge the gap between the advanced and developing countries.

Thinking about trade friction, we tend to focus our attention on exports and imports of goods and services. But when we consider a country, there exist some ubiquitous, often indigenous, and characteristic phenomena of the society, such as, attitudes in looking at things, ways of thinking, of spending energy and time, culture, habits, and ways of living. We can call those phenomena, conceptually, a social value system unique to the country. When imported goods reach consumers, they reflect portions of the foreign social value system. In the importing country, there is also a specific, autonomous social value system. Imports therefore mean that the importing country is importing not only goods but also a foreign social value system, which results in a surprise or even a shock. It is not easy to understand foreign social value systems since they will be significantly different from the indigenous value system of the importing country. Such differences in social value systems underlie trade frictions and arouse resistance in the importing country. It is, however, unfair and unfortunate only to justify one's own social value system. On the other hand, many people are pleased to encounter a foreign social value system if it is fresh and interesting for them. In addition, the social value system unique to each country changes over time. Furthermore, the social value system is reflected in costs of production via the quality of labor. Thus, a social value system plus governmental policy can encourage or retard economic development.

Exports from a developing country are often accompanied with young, naïve, and internationally inexperienced attitudes. Early in the 1930s, Japanese cotton spinning output already exceeded that of Great Britain. A few years later, some Japanese leaders might have falsely concluded that Japan had caught up with the world powers in all other aspects, and as a result jumped to withdraw from the League of Nations. This type of misunderstanding may cause additional trade conflict.

NEW TRADE RULES

The U.S. Trade Agreements Act of 1934 provided for the retention of unconditional Most Favored Nation status (except for 15 countries) and exemption of certain products, the subject of trade agreement concessions, from the cost-equalization provisions of the 1930 U.S. trade act. The United States proceeded to reduce tariffs sizably through bilateral and multilateral negotiations. Such agreements transmitted tariff reductions to third countries. However, the extension of tariff reductions was only possible if the third country had an unconditional MFN clause with the United States. Japan's MFN clause with the United States was conditional. Thus, the tariff concessions were not extended to Japan in the tariff reduction stream promoted by Secretary Hull, such as in the U.S.-Colombia Commercial Agreement. Such conditional MFN was against GATT principle and discarded. When WTO discussed the acceptance of China, MFN already had become unconditional for any country.

Strong protectionist measures for imports now constitute violations under GATT/WTO rules; such measures include highly forbidding tariffs, quotas, and the custom valuation system (estimating prices or exchange rates for revenue purposes at border tariff offices) that Japan suffered from particularly in the Canadian market, as described in chapter four of this book. All such Japanese suffering during the prewar period now became against GATT regulations under ordinary conditions. GATT also restricted the application of anti-dumping tariffs; for example, the importing country has the burden to prove the practical damages of domestic industries incurred by the import.

Did Japan's Experience End in Vain?

We could interpret, from a historical perspective, Japan's struggles and suffering in the interwar period as a pioneer's fee that it had to pay. That happened at a time when the British hegemony was declining and the world was heading to the Great Depression.

1. A certain level of modern technology attained in the prewar period, supported by the vitality and diligence of the people, contributed, from ashes, to the miraculously fast recovery of the Japanese economy in the early postwar period. With such a flexible technological capability, inherited from previous generations, at hand, the country could seize an opportunity that was a blessing but fleeting in an instant of historical time among changing circumstances. Some scholars still write that Japan then was just lucky.

2. The country kept its old traditional artisanship for adapting original or imported technology to the modern environment, both social and physical, within a country undergoing dynamic change. This flexibility in both mind and technology helped shorten the necessary time for catching up and for industrializing Japan.

3. An American friend was amazed at the vitality of the Japanese making incessant efforts in China to avoid the boycotts and searching out markets in other regions. Finally rejected in trade by Chinese anti-Japanese boycotts, the Japanese went to open markets on other continents.

4. The reports of foreign diplomats inspired me to think about the Japanese: how did those who encountered trade conflicts encourage themselves to continue their efforts? The following could be one possibility.

i. To seek satisfaction only in achievement and not in business success is a source of self-belief and pride for the Japanese. One seeks to achieve regardless of reward and is satisfied with one's accomplishments. This we see even today in some workers and artisans, in innovators who find purpose in work whatever they may be doing, in small- and middle-scale manufacturers and in technological fields. This achievement-oriented spirit is often ubiquitous in ordinary people, not just educated ones.

ii. Many Japanese have a delicate sense to listen to the sound of the wind, as in the traditional Tea Ceremony. They feel that they are a part of nature, and attend to the sound of the wind or any other natural phenomenon. This creates a tranquility of mind since you yourself are an object in nature. This character, when backed with a positive frame of mind, results in naturally listening to customers' requests and understanding well what they want.

iii. One spring morning, a young worker tenderly touched his attending electrical furnace as part of his routine habits. Perceiving a strange sensation in both palms, he took a close look at the machine. The detailed measurements of all sensors in the factory indicated no problem. Only his palms felt a slight and unusual warmth. His superintendent, on receiving his report, believed in this young worker and ordered a check of every part of all machinery from top to bottom since the system in the factory once started can never be stopped. They finally discovered that the furnace had started, little by little, to overheat. If the boss had believed in the automatic sensors instead of in this high school graduate and had ordered the system to be started, it could have resulted in the furnace exploding and, through a series of chain reactions, an incredible mechanical disaster. The prudent actions of the worker saved the furnace and the company, which thankfully announced the details to the public. This was due neither to his expertise nor his school education: His intuition arising from his love of work prevented the unprecedented industrial accident. It is not the high literacy level but also people like him that has supported the level of Japan's technology to the present. I believe that such people exist in other countries too.

Most people, foreign as well as Japanese, engaged in trade in the period covered by this book, may no longer be alive now, but their ideas to move the world a step forward and the results of their efforts are still very much alive. Their suffering in the interwar period was not in vain if you look at the great improvements in the trade system embodied in GATT. Its original spirit to treat every nation fairly on an egalitarian basis without discrimination lives on in the WTO. Albeit imperfectly, this hope is being realized despite a negative view asserting that the twentieth century was one spent in war.

Human development in a sense has been achieved by forgetting what one owes to predecessors. To write this short economic history of Japan was a process of seeing a step forward that the world witnessed in its development: it showed an upward progress in human living. I hope that my research services to witness how we have progressed and will continue to progress in the future.

November 2008

Musasino-shi,
Tokyo

Appendix I

Statistical Tables

Statistical Table S-1: Japan's bilateral trade with selected countries

(millions of U.S. dollars)

	World			U.S.A			U.K.		
	X	M	B	X	M	B	X	M	B
1926	960.6	1116.9	−156.3	404.4	319.5	84.9	27.9	79.9	−52.0
1927	943.9	1032.4	−88.5	395.0	319.1	75.9	30.7	72.1	−41.4
1928	918.3	1022.8	−104.5	384.7	291.3	93.4	27.4	76.7	−49.3
1929	992.4	1023.6	−31.2	422.1	302.2	120.1	29.1	70.6	−41.5
1930	727.4	765.1	−37.7	250.5	219.1	31.5	30.5	45.7	−15.2
1931	560.5	603.8	−43.3	207.8	167.2	40.5	25.9	30.9	−4.9
1932	396.6	402.6	−6.0	125.2	143.4	18.2	17.0	22.1	−5.1
1933	469.5	483.7	−14.1	124.1	156.5	−32.4	22.1	20.8	1.3
1934	640.9	673.9	−32.6	117.7	227.0	−109.3	32.2	20.6	11.5
1935	713.9	706.3	7.6	153.0	231.3	−78.3	34.1	23.4	10.6
1936	779.6	799.9	−20.5	172.0	245.3	−73.3	42.6	21.1	21.5
1937	914.1	1089.1	−174.9	184.0	365.4	−181.4	48.4	30.4	18.0
1938	765.2	757.7	7.4	161.8	352.9	−191.1	38.3	11.9	20.4

(Continued)

Sources: Ministry of Finance (Department of Finance), *Zaisei Keizai Tokei Nenpo* (Financial and Economic Annual of Japan), Tokyo, 1925–28, and 1935–38; Ministry of Finance, *Nihon Gaikoku Boeki Geppo* (Monthly Returns of Foreign Trade of Japan) (Tokyo: Ministry of Finance).

Toyo Keizai Shinposha, *Nihon Boeki Seiran* (Foreign Trade of Japan: A Statistical Survey) (Tokyo: Toyo Keizai Shinposha, 1975 revised ed.) *The Supplement*; Statistical Bureau of the Prime Minister's Office, *Nihon Tokei Nenkan* (Japan Statistical Year Book) (Tokyo: Prime Minister's Office, 1950), 214.

Ippey Yamazawa and Yuzo Yamamoto, *Boeki to Kokusaishushi* (Foreign Trade and Balance of Payments) in Ohkawa Kazushi et al., eds., *Choki Keizai Tokei* (Estimates of Long-term Economic Statistics of Japan since 1868), vol. 14 (Tokyo: Toyo Keizai Shinposha, 1979).

Notes: X = exports

M = imports

B = trade balance

Statistical Table S-1—Continued

(millions of U.S. dollars)

	Canada			Australia			British India		
	X	M	B	X	M	B	X	M	B
1926	11.6	30.3	−18.4	24.2	60.3	−36.1	72.6	18.3	54.8
1927	13.0	26.3	−13.3	23.9	58.2	−34.3	79.3	128.1	−48.8
1928	12.5	30.9	−18.3	20.0	60.7	−40.7	67.9	132.6	−64.7
1929	12.4	31.7	−19.2	20.3	61.2	−40.9	91.4	133.0	−41.5
1930	8.9	22.8	−13.9	12.5	46.6	−34.0	63.8	89.1	−25.3
1931	6.3	17.4	−11.0	9.0	55.4	−46.4	53.8	65.0	−11.3
1932	2.4	11.1	−8.6	10.3	37.7	−27.4	54.1	32.7	21.3
1933	1.6	11.8	−10.1	12.9	51.6	−38.6	70.2	52.5	17.7
1934	2.5	15.9	−13.4	19.0	58.2	−39.2	70.3	85.4	−15.1
1935	2.2	15.0	−12.7	21.3	67.1	−45.8	78.7	87.3	−8.6
1936	4.2	21.1	−16.9	19.9	52.6	−32.7	75.0	107.6	−32.6
1937	5.7	30.1	−24.3	20.7	47.5	−26.8	86.1	129.3	−43.2
1938	4.3	25.9	−21.6	19.7	23.5	−3.8	53.4	57.7	−4.3

	China proper			Hong Kong			Manchukuo[1]		
	X	M	B	X	M	B	X	M	B
1927	158.3	107.0	51.1	31.5	0.7	30.8			
1928	173.7	109.2	64.2	26.1	0.5	25.6			
1929	160.0	96.9	63.1	28.1	0.2	27.9			
1930	129.0	80.0	49.0	27.4	0.2	27.2			
1931	70.2	50.6	19.5	17.9	0.1	19.8	5.7	20.4	−14.7
1932	36.3	21.6	14.5	5.0	0.2	4.8	7.3	14.4	−7.1
1933	27.3	28.5	1.2	6.0	0.5	5.5	20.6	37.3	16.6
1934	34.5	35.2	−0.6	9.8	0.4	9.5	31.6	48.4	16.8
1935	42.4	38.2	4.2	14.2	0.7	13.5	36.0	54.5	18.5
1936	46.2	44.8	1.4	16.9	0.9	16.0	43.7	59.5	15.8
1937	51.6	41.3	10.3	14.1	1.5	12.6	62.1	71.6	−9.5
1938	89.0	46.8	42.2	4.7	3.6	1.1	89.9	96.5	−6.6

(Continued)

[1] Before 1930, figures for Manchukuo (Japanese Manchuria) were included under China in Japanese statistics.

Statistical Table S-1

(millions of U.S. dollars)

	Kwantung			South Sea			Philippines		
	X	M	B	X	M	B	X	M	B
1926	4.3	6.7	2.4	19.4	18.6	0.7	13.0	8.7	4.3
1927	5.2	10.5	-5.3	17.3	16.9	0.4	15.5	8.4	7.1
1928	2.6	8.8	-0.1	9.5	17.0	-7.5	13.5	7.5	6.0
1929	4.8	9.6	-4.7	12.4	19.2	-6.8	14.0	8.3	5.7
1930	4.6	9.3	-4.7	9.4	14.3	-4.8	13.9	5.2	8.7
1931	2.3	3.3	-1.0	12.4	10.6	1.8	9.9	4.3	5.6
1932	2.4	3.1	0.7	12.9	7.1	5.8	6.2	2.7	3.5
1933	4.5	3.0	1.5	15.9	9.7	6.2	6.1	3.6	2.5
1934	8.2	0.4	7.8	14.3	18.6	4.3	10.7	5.5	5.2
1935	11.4	1.5	9.9	16.7	11.6	5.1	13.7	6.8	6.9
1936	12.4	2.5	9.9	19.5	11.9	7.6	15.0	10.4	4.6
1937	14.1	3.8	10.3	5.9	19.5	-13.5	17.3	13.0	4.3
1938	11.1	13.9	-2.8	5.8	15.5	-9.5	9.2	10.1	-0.9

	Dutch East Indies			Other Asia		
	X	M	B	X	M	B
1926	35.1	48.3	-13.2	46.8	73.7	-26.9
1927	39.0	49.1	-10.1	43.1	62.5	-19.4
1928	34.1	32.5	-18.4	51.9	69.8	-18.6
1929	40.2	35.7	4.5	57.2	76.6	-19.4
1930	32.6	29.6	3.0	42.9	59.8	-16.9
1931	30.9	22.4	8.5	32.0	4.4	11.9
1932	28.1	11.3	16.8	33.9	21.5	12.3
1933	40.3	14.3	26.0	55.8	5.0	50.8
1934	46.7	18.7	28.0	87.3	8.0	79.2
1935	40.8	22.3	18.5	85.7	7.3	78.4
1936	37.5	32.8	4.7	100.4	9.8	90.6
1937	57.5	44.1	13.3	113.9	13.3	100.9
1938	29.5	28.1	4.4	152.4	171.5	-19.1

(Continued)

Statistical Table S-1

(millions of U.S. dollars)

	Egypt			Anglo-Egyptian Sudan			French Morocco		
	X	M	B	X	M	B	X	M	B
1926									
1927									
1928									
1929									
1930									
1931									
1932									
1933									
1934	21.5	13.6	7.9	2.7	0.3	2.4	5.6	0.2	5.4
1935	15.3	14.6	0.7	3.7	0.5	3.2	5.3	0.1	5.2
1936	11.8	13.2	−1.4	3.4	0.4	3.0	5.9	0.2	5.7
1937	9.4	21.3	−11.9	4.5	1.6	2.8	5.2	0.4	4.8
1938	3.9	10.3	−6.4	3.3	0.1	3.2	5.3	0.1	5.2

	Kenya, Uganda and Tanganica			Mozambique			Union of South Africa		
	X	M	B	X	M	B	X	M	B
1926									
1927									
1928									
1929									
1930									
1931									
1932									
1933									
1934	6.5	4.4	2.1	2.6	0.3	2.3	8.7	2.4	6.3
1935	7.1	0.8	6.3	3.0	0	3.0	9.3	1.3	8.0
1936	8.8	8.6	0.2	3.1	0.1	3.0	12.0	6.5	5.5
1937	11.5	6.9	4.6	4.6	0.2	4.4	15.4	25.5	−10.0
1938	6.4	1.7	4.7	2.7	0	2.7	10.0	2.2	7.8

(Continued)

Note: No figures were registered in the early years of Japanese statistics for several of these countries.

Statistical Table S-1

(millions of U.S. dollars)

	Iran			Iraq			Syria		
	X	M	B	X	M	B	X	M	B
1926									
1927									
1928									
1929									
1930									
1931									
1932									
1933									
1934				5.0	0	5.0	3.4	0	3.4
1935	2.7	0.2	0.5	6.3	0.3	6.0	3.6	2.4	1.2
1936	1.3	0.4	0.9	5.5	0.8	4.7	3.7	0	3.7
1937	0.4	0.2	0.2	4.0	1.5	2.5	3.2	0.2	3.0
1938	1.3	0.1	1.2	4.8	1.7	3.1	3.5	0.3	3.2

	Palestine			Arabia		
	X	M	B	X	M	B
1926						
1927						
1928						
1929						
1930						
1931						
1932						
1933						
1934	1.9	0	1.9			
1935	2.4	0	2.4	1.3	0.1	1.2
1936	1.5	0	1.5	0.7	0.1	0.6
1937	0.9	0	0.9	0.8	0.1	0.7
1938	0.8	0.1	0.7	1.3	0	1.3

(Continued)

Statistical Table S-1

(millions of U.S. dollars)

	Mexico			Peru			Chile		
	X	M	B	X	M	B	X	M	B
1926	0.5	0	0.5	0.8	0	0.8	0.8	4.0	−3.2
1927	0.5	0	0.5	0.5	0	0.5	0.9	3.7	−2.7
1928	0.6	0	0.6	0.7	0	0.7	0.8	3.6	−2.8
1929	0.6	0.3	0.3	1.2	0	1.2	1.2	4.8	−3.6
1930	0.4	0.1	0.3	1.0	0	1.0	1.1	1.5	−0.4
1931	0.2	0	0.2	0.3	0	0.3	0.3	1.4	−1.1
1932	0.1	0	0.1	0.2	0	0.2	0	0.1	−0.1
1933	0.3	0	0.3	1.0	0.3	0.7	0.3	0.7	−0.4
1934	1.1	0.03	1.1	2.0	0.5	1.5	2.1	1.0	1.1
1935	1.5	1.8	0.3	1.9	3.2	1.3	1.9	1.3	0.6
1936	2.0	5.3	−3.3	1.7	3.7	−2.0	2.1	2.8	−0.7
1937	2.3	2.4	−0.1	1.0	1.0	0	1.8	2.5	−0.7
1938	1.5	1.3	0.2	1.6	0.5	1.1	1.7	3.1	−1.4

	Argentina			Brazil		
	X	M	B	X	M	B
1926	2.9	1.1	1.8	0.7	0	0.7
1927	4.5	1.0	3.5	0.5	0	0.5
1928	3.2	2.1	1.1	0.8	0.1	0.7
1929	3.9			0.6	0.1	0.5
1930	2.1	1.3	0.8	0.4	0.1	0.3
1931	2.2	1.4	0.8	1.4	0.1	1.3
1932	2.1	0.7	1.4	0.3	0.1	0.2
1933	3.1	1.7	1.4	0.6	0.2	0.4
1934	5.9	3.5	2.3	0.9	0.94	−0.04
1935	8.1	4.6	3.5	1.6	1.1	0.5
1936	6.5	8.6	−2.1	2.6	13.7	−11.1
1937	6.0	7.2	−1.1	3.0	10.7	−7.7
1938	5.5	6.9	−1.4	2.9	13.1	−10.2

Statistical Table S-2: Japan's principal exports in various regions in China

(millions of U.S. dollars)

		1926	1929	1932	1935	1937
Cotton:						
Yarn	Total	25.7	6.6	0.2	0.2	6.9
	Manchuria	4.1	2.4			
	North China	7.5	0.9	0.2	-	3.1
	Central China	13.4	3.3	-	0.1	3.5
	South China	0.6	-	-	0.1	-
Material for yarn & thread	Total	25.7	1.3	3.8	4.2	11.7
	Manchuria	4.1	1.2			
	North China	7.5	0.4	2.7	1.0	0.4
	Central China	1.3	0.7	1.1	3.1	11.2
Shirting	Total	33.7	21.1	6.0	1.4	0.9
	Manchuria	13.5	8.0			
	North China	3.7	4.0	5.0	1.3	-
	Central China	15.0	9.0	1.0	-	0.9
	South China	1.0	-	0	0	0
Flannel	Total	9.1	10.8	2.0	-	-
	Manchuria	0.7	1.4			
	North China	0.7	1.1			
	Central China	7.0	8.2	1.2	-	-
	South China	0.5	-	-	-	-
Shirting & sheeting, gray	Total	29.0	13.7	0.9	0.3	0.1
	Manchuria	11.2	6.4			
	North China	6.1	4.0	0.7	0.2	0.1
	Central China	11.1	3.3	0.3	0.1	-
	South China	0.5	-	-	-	-
T-cloth	Total	4.6	2.8	0.4	-	-
	Manchuria	0.8	0.5			
	North China	2.1	1.4	0.3	-	-
	Central China	1.3	0.6	-	-	-
Other textiles	Total	82.2	89.1	27.3	9.7	10.1
	Manchuria	14.7	18.7			
	North China	12.8	15.3	21.1	5.0	1.1
	Central China	52.1	54.8	6.2	4.6	8.8
	South China	12.7	-	-	-	-

(Continued)

Statistical Table S-2

(millions of U.S. dollars)

		1926	1929	1932	1935	1937
Knitted underwear	Total	1.3	5.1	3.9	0.1	-
	Manchuria	0.2	1.3			
	North China	0.3	2.5	0.3	-	-
	Central China	0.4	1.2	0.3	-	-
	South China	0.3	-	-	-	-
Piece goods	Total	n.a.	5.1	3.9	7.7	8.4
	Manchuria	n.a.	1.4			
	North China	n.a.	2.5	3.6	4.0	3.0
	Central China	n.a.	1.3	0.3	3.7	5.3
Sugar	Total	30.9	22.3	2.6	9.7	8.3
	Manchuria	0.8	1.5			
	North China	5.0	6.4	1.9	3.7	2.8
	Central China	24.9	13.3	0.7	6.0	5.5
Flour	Total	0	15.6	6.1	0.2	15.2
	Manchuria	0	6.3			
	North China	0	9.2	6.1	0.2	15.2
Marine products:						
Seaweed	Total	3.4	3.2	1.4	2.8	1.1
	North China	1.0	1.0	1.1	0.4	0.3
	Central China	2.3	2.2	0.3	2.4	0.8
Salted or dried fish	Total	8.4	5.4	1.1	3.1	2.2
	North China	0.6	0.5	0.4	0.5	0.3
	Central China	4.9	4.3	0.6	2.5	1.8
	South China	2.6	0.5	-	0.1	-
Coal	Total	20.0	12.5	3.7	1.1	0
	Central China	18.3	12.3	3.7	1.1	0
	South China	1.3	0	0	0	0
Paper:						
Printed paper	Total	6.1	9.8	3.5	3.5	2.6
	North China	1.6	2.8	3.0	2.4	1.2
	Central China	3.2	6.7	0.4	1.0	1.3
	South China	1.1	0.1	-	-	0.1
Others	Total	4.7	6.5	1.6	3.0	4.3
	Manchuria	0.3	0.2			
	North China	1.7	1.6	1.2	1.6	1.9
	Central China	2.2	4.5	0.3	1.3	2.2
	South China	0.3	0.2	-	0.1	0.1

(Continued)

Statistical Table S-2

(millions of U.S. dollars)

		1926	1929	1932	1935	1937
Accessories for	Total	0	9.1	1.1	2.1	6.9
clothing	Manchuria	0	0.7			
	North China	0	1.0	0.9	1.5	3.1
	Central China	0	7.3	0.2	0.4	3.5
Hats	Total	2.4	1.4	0.2	0.7	1.8
	Manchuria	0.1	0.1			
	North China	0.2	0.1	0.1	0.5	0.6
	Central China	1.8	1.2	0.1	0.2	1.2
	South China	0.2	-	0	0	0
Umbrellas and						
parasols	Total	1.6	-	-	-	-
	Central China	1.6	-	-	-	-
Pottery	Total	2.3	2.3	0.5	1.2	1.1
	Manchuria	0.1	0.2			
	North China	0.5	0.5	0.3	0.5	0.6
	Central China	1.3	1.5	0.2	0.6	0.5
	South China	0.7	-	0	0	0
Glass bottles	Total	1.6	1.3	0.4	0.4	0.4
	North China	0.2	0.2	0.3	0.3	0.2
	Central China	1.1	1.1	0.1	0.1	0.1
	South China	0.2	0	0	0	0
Lamps & parts	Total	1.7	0.6	0.5	0.6	0.5
	North China	0.3	0.1	0.2	0.2	0.1
	Central China	1.2	0.4	0.3	0.3	0.3
	South China	0.2	0	0	0	0
Wood:						
Match wood	Total	1.8	1.1	0.4	0.2	0.1
	North China	0.6	0.4	0.4	0.2	0.1
	Central China	0.7	0.7	-	-	-
	South China	0.5	-	0	0	0
Other	Total	2.3	2.8	1.8	2.7	2.6
	North China	0.7	1.5	1.3	1.9	2.1
	Central China	1.6	1.3	0.5	0.7	0.5
Drugs & Chemicals	Total	0	3.3	2.4	7.2	6.6
(including	Manchuria	0	0.3			
explosives)	North China	0	1.0	1.3	2.6	2.9
	Central China	0	1.9	1.1	3.9	3.6

(Continued)

Statistical Table S-2—Continued

(millions of U.S. dollars)

		1926	1929	1932	1935	1937
Iron	Total	0.8	1.5	1.6	7.4	0
	Manchuria	0.2	0.3			
	North China	0.5	1.0	1.3	4.3	0
	Central China	-	0.2	0.2	3.9	0
Iron manufac-tureds	Total	3.0	2.4	1.4	2.2	2.6
	Manchuria	0.1	0.1			
	North China	0.8	0.8	0.8	1.0	1.5
	Central China	1.7	1.5	0.5	1.1	1.0

Source: Ministry of Finance, *Nihon Gaikoku Boeki Geppyo 1927–1938* (Monthly Returns of Foreign Trade of Japan) (Tokyo: Ministry of Finance, 1928–1939).

Note: A hyphen is used for negligible figures while a blank is left when figures were not registered in Japanese statistics (Manchuria was not listed in 1932, 1935, and 1937 after it became Manchukuo).

Statistical Table S-3:   Japanese silk exports to the United States, 1925–39

	MPT	USIC	USRP	WSP	PR	PS	EX	USC
1925	317752	804	23542	47210	14.35	72.74	40.58	n.a.
1926	328903	826	28870	50380	10.88	69.89	46.98	n.a.
1927	334160	797	34271	53675	11.30	64.50	47.38	n.a.
1928	318127	805	44407	58395	8.29	59.82	46.57	n.a.
1929	356122	847	55067	61410	7.52	53.82	46.19	4662
1930	221468	734	57759	59570	7.37	35.61	49.40	4100
1931	163069	611	68439	58040	7.09	25.54	48.87	3528
1932	106188	465	61086	52620	4.92	18.66	28.13	2446
1933	91659	442	96843	54056	5.10	15.67	25.23	2254
1934	69814	514	94494	56707	5.16	10.85	29.51	2801
1935	90038	567	116827	54792	4.95	15.22	28.57	3080
1936	94967	643	125937	53895	4.36	17.22	28.95	3226
1937	99572	701	145941	54500	3.39	20.66	27.97	3277
1938	83644	651	116859	49500	3.45	18.92	28.45	3337
1939	106959	691	149064	61300	3.45	30.14	25.96	3607

Sources: **For MPT:** Toyo Keizai Shinposha, *Nihon Boeki Seiran* (Foreign Trade of Japan: A Statistical Survey) (Tokyo: Toyo Keizai Shinposha, 1975 revised ed.), *The Supplement*, 24–28. Mitsuhaya Kajinishi et al., eds., *Nihon Sen'i Sangyoshi Soronhen* (History of Japanese Textile Industries) (Tokyo, Toyo Keizai Shinposha,1958), 941.

Bank of Japan, *Meiji Iko Honpo Shuyo Keizai Tokei* (Hundred-Year Statistics of the Japanese Economy) (Tokyo: Bank of Japan, 1966), 131–32.

For EX: Ippey Yamazawa and Yuzo Yamamoto, *Boeki to Kokusaishushi* (Foreign Trade and Balance of Payments), in Kazushi Ohkawa et al., eds., *Choki Keizai Tokei* (Estimate of Long-term Economic Statistics of Japan since 1868), Vol. 14 (Tokyo: Toyo Keizai Shinposha, 1965), 257.

Statistical Bureau of the Prime Minister's Office, *Nihon Tokei Nenkan* (Japan Statistical Year-Book) (Tokyo: Prime Minister Office, 1950).

For PS and WSP: Ministry of International Trade and Industry, *Monthly Report of Textile Statistics,* Tokyo.

For USI, USRP, PR, and USC: U.S. Dept. of Commerce, *Statistical Abstract of the United States* (Washington: U.S. Dept. of Commerce, 1932,1940), 314.

Note: **Dependent variable:**
MPT: value of raw silk exports to the United States in dollar terms. The volume of raw silk exports did not decline, but increased, during the period when the value of raw silk exports had sharply fallen.
Independent variables:
USIC: capita income of the United States.
USRP: volume of rayon output in the United States.
WSP: index of world silk production with a one-year time lag.
PR: unit price of rayon in the United States.
PS: unit price of silk in New York.
EX: foreign exchange rates.
USC: level of consumption in the United States, an alternative variable for the USIC, the U.S. per capita income.

Appendix II

Original Materials: Unpublished Official Documents

The original materials are in the following archives.

I. *Archives of the Ministry of Foreign Affairs, Tokyo*

Ministry of Commerce and Industry, Department of Foreign Trade, *The Influence of the Chinese Boycott on Trade, The Manchurian Incident, II*

Ministry of Foreign Affairs, *Diplomatic Documents* (abbreviated as *The Documents*)

List of *The Documents*

Call number	Title	Volume No.	Year
A 110, 2-14, XV	*The Tsuinan Incident*	I-IV	1928–29
	The Western Countries,		
	San Francisco, New York	XV	1928
A 110, 20-2-1	*Reports of the Kwantung*		
	Government	I-VI	1931
A 110, 20-2	*The Wanpaoshan Incident*	I-V	
A 110, 21-5, I	*China, except Shanghai*	I-V	1931
A 110, 21-5	*China*		
	South China	V-VI	
	Central China	VII-XI	1932–33
A 110, 21-5	*Nanking*		1926–36
A 110, 21-5	*Shanghai*	XI	1931
		XII	1926–32
		XIV	1933

(Continued)

Call number	Title	Volume No.	Year
	After the Shanghai Incident	XVI	1932
		XXVII	1933
	Central China	XXVIII	
	North China	XII-XIV	
	South Asia	XV	
	Europe and North America	XVI	
A 110, 21-5, II, XI	The Manchurian Incident		1931–38
	General	I-IV	
	The Cotton-Spinning Industry	III	
	South China	V-XI	
	Central China	XII-XXI	
	North China	XXII-XXV	
	Manchuria	XXVI	
	Seattle	XXVII	1932
	The Reports of the Kwantung Government	XXVIII	1931–38
	South Asia (Siam, Bangkok, Hanoi, Saigon, Batavia)	XXIX	1932–33
	The Western Countries	XXX	
E 3, 30 J/X1	Anti-Japanese Boycotts, Miscellaneous (U.S., U.K., Taiwan)		1929–39
E 3, 30 J/X1 2	Singapore, Rangoon		1928–39
E 3, 30 J/X1-B1, 1	British Empire		1928–37
E 3, 30 J/X1-B1, 2	Singapore, Hong Kong		1928–37
E 3, 30 J/X1-B	Canada	I-II	
E 3, 30 J/X1-B2-2	Fishery Law		
E 3, 30 J/X1-B3	Australia		
E 3, 30 J/X1-B6	South Asian Countries		
E 3, 30 J/X1-BR	Belgium		
E 3, 30 J/X1-C1	China (incl. Batavia)	I-VII	1927–38
E 3, 30 J/X1-C1-3	China, Hankow	I-II	1927–31

(Continued)

Call number	Title	Volume No.	Year
E 3, 30 J/X1-E1	*Egypt*		
E 330 J/X1-N1	*Netherlands and its Colonies* (Batavia)		1929–37
E 330 J/X1-P1	*Peru*		1935
E 330 J/X1-U1 1–3	*United States, Vancouver* (Canada)		1932
E 330 J/X1-U1, 11	*United States*		1938
A 110, J/X1	*Foreign Countries, except China, Miscellaneous*	I-II	1931
J 110, J/X1-M1	*Mexico*		
J 110, J/X1-N	*Netherlands* (includes colonies)		
J 110, J/X1-R1	*USSR*	I-II	1936
J 110, J/X1-R1-1	*USSR, Boycotts* (Riots)		
J 110, J/X1-U1	*United States*	I-IX	1932
J 110, J/X1-U2	*Philippines*	I-II	
E 340, 3-6	*Tariffs, Tariff Autonomy*		1932

II. The Public Record Office, Richmond, United Kingdom

These materials are confidential and contain details of telegrams, dispatches, letters, and reports sent to London from the Embassies and General Consulates of the United Kingdom in relevant regions for this research.

BT	59.	Department of Overseas Trade
BT	61.	Department of Overseas Trade
BT	64.	Industries and Manufactures Department
FO	262/1839.	Netherlands East Indies
FO	262/1870.	Netherlands East Indies, Japanese Activity
FO	262/1896.	British Dominions
FO	262/1877.	Japan-Canada: Trade Relations
FO	262/1895.	North China Autonomy: Effects on Japan
FO	262/1896.	British Empire

III. The National Archives, Washington, D.C., U.S.A.
The Diplomatic Section

635.4131, 635.9415, 635.9417, 635.9431, 635.946	Argentina
635.9417, 625.9431	Chile
621.9417, 621.9421, 621.9424, 621.9431	Colombia
683.9431	Egypt
612.9417, 612.943, 6129431, 612.948	Mexico
623.9415, 623.9417, 623.9431, 623.949	Peru
633.9417, 633.9431	Uruguay

IV. Supplement: Documents concerning anti-Japanese boycotts in the Archives of the Ministry of Foreign Affairs, Tokyo

Call number	Title	Volume No.	Year
E C1-3	*China, Hankow*	1–2	1927–31
A 11. 02-4	*The Tsinan Incident*	1–4	1928–29
	South China	5–6	
	Central China	7–11	
	North China	12–14	
	South Asia	15	
	Europe and North America	16	
E 3, 30 J/X1-C1	*China*		1927–30
E 3, 30 J/X1-B1, 1-2	*Great Britain*		1928–37
A 110, 20-2	*The Wanpaoshan Incident*	1–5	1931
A 110, 21-5	*China except Shanghai, the Wanpaoshan Incident*	1–5	1931
A 110, 20-2-1	*Reports to the Kwantung Government*	1–6	1931
A 110, 21-5	*The Manchurian Incident*		1931–34
	General	1–4	
	South China	5–11	
	Central China	12–21	
	North China	22–25	
	Manchuria	26–27	

(Continued)

Call number	Title	Volume No.	Year
	Reports of the Kwantung Government	28	
	South Asia	29	
	The Western Countries	30	
A 110, J/X1	*Foreign Countries except China, Miscellaneous*	1–2	1931
-B	*Canada*	1–2	
-B2-2	*Fishery Law*	1	
-B-3	*Australia*	1	
-B6	*South Asian Countries*	1	
-BR 1	*Belgium*	1	
J 110, J/X1-M1	*Mexico*	1	
-N	*Netherlands* (includes colonies)	1	
-P1	*USSR*	1–2	
-P1-1	*USSR, Boycotts (Riots)*	1	
-U1	*United States*	1–9	
-U2	*Philippines*	1–2	

Notes

Chapter 1: Research Objectives

1. Introduction

1. Jan Tumlir et al., *Trade Liberalization and Interdependence* (Geneva: General Agreement on Tariffs and Trade, 1977).

   GATT, *Press Release*, Geneva: March 4, 1983: 16.

2. The inferred idea seems exemplified also today by the emergence of the NIEs with speedy growth rates and strong competitiveness.

3. Alexander Gerschenkron claims, in *Economic Backwardness in Historical Perspective* (Cambridge: Belknap Press of Harvard University Press, 1962), that the latecomers in economic development enjoy faster growth because of advantages of borrowed technology and because of learning from development paths experienced by the advanced countries.

4. Some exceptional research has been done on U.S.-Japan trade by William W. Lockwood: *Trade and Trade Rivalry between the United States and Japan* (New York: American Council, Institute of Pacific Relations, 1936); and *The Foreign Trade Policy of the United States* (New York: American Council, Institute of Pacific Relations, l936); *The State and Economic Enterprise in Japan* (Princeton, N.J.: Princeton University Press, 1965).

2. Definitions of Protectionism and Discrimination

1. Useful discussions on marginal cost, average cost, and pricing in increasing returns to scale in international competition are found in W. Max Corden, *Protection, Growth, and Trade: Essays in International Economics* (Oxford: Basil Blackwell, 1985), in ch. 3 "Monopoly, Tariffs and Subsidies," 47–57, and ch. 4 "Economics of Scale and Customs Union Theory," 59–68.

2. Today, an appreciation of the currency of an exporting country sometimes causes antidumping actions by the importing country because the cost of production in the exporting country calculated in terms of the currency of the importing country automatically increases in comparison with the imported sales price of the commodity. The importing country argues that even if the imported good's sales price is raised by an increase of its export price, the raise is usually insufficient in the long run to cover the margin caused by the appreciated cost of production in the exporting country. For example, a

Japanese copying machine previously sold at US$1,000 (¥260,000). Now it should be sold at US$2,000 (¥260,000) because of the yen's recent appreciation ($1=¥130). If it is sold at US$1,600 instead of US$2,000, the importing country could argue for an antidumping duty.

3. See ch. 4, sec. 2 of this work concerning Canadian dumping duties.

4. Kazushi Ohkawa and Henry Rosovsky, *Japanese Economic Growth: Trend Acceleration in the Twentieth Century* (Stanford, Calif.: Stanford University Press, 1973), 174. For an excellent survey relevant to our research, see ch. 7 "Foreign Trade."

5. Ohkawa and Rosovsky, *Japanese Economic Growth*, 180.

3. Export Trends of Japan's Main Overseas Markets

1. The proportional shares in total world trade of countries whose currencies depreciated from January 1929 to March 1935, and their rates of depreciation, are shown below.

Table N-1. Rates of depreciation of currencies, January 1929–March 1935

	Percentage of depreciation of currency in relation to gold	Share in world trade
Canada	41	3.27
Spain	44	1.21
Sweden	45	1.72
Norway	46	0.84
Finland	50	0.62
Denmark	52	1.41
Uruguay	52	0.26
Iran	53	0.38
Australia	54	1.87
New Zealand	54	0.79
Greece	57	0.34
Bolivia	59	0.08
Argentina	65	2.18
Japan	66	3.32
Colombia	67	0.30
Mexico	67	0.68
Brazil	67	1.27
Ecuador	73	0.04
Chile	75	0.37

Sources: League of Nations, *Remarks on the Present Phase of International Economic Relations* (Geneva, September 14, 1936): 17, table 36. Original figures were taken from the *Fifth Annual Report of the Bank for International Settlement.*

2. Kwantung leased territory is the south tip of Liaotung Peninsula in northeast China, in southern Manchuria, lying between the Gulf of Liaotung and Korea Bay. The territory came under Japanese control as a result of the Russo-Japanese War (1904–05). The chief city is Dairen. In 1945, Kwantung was returned to the Chinese.

3. League of Nations, *Industrialization and Foreign Trade* (Geneva: League of Nations, 1945), 13. These data reveal that the USSR's share in world industrial output increased remarkably, to 18.5 percent (1936–38), from 4.3 percent (1926–29).

4. THE JAPANESE ECONOMY IN THE SURVEY PERIOD

1. Mitsuhaya Kajinishi et al., eds., *Zoku, Nihon Shihonshugi Hattatsushi* (The History of the Development of Japanese Capitalism) (Tokyo: Kawade Shobo, 1954) II: 131. (Hereafter referred to as *Nihon Shihonshugi Hattatsushi*).

2. Table N-2 shows Japanese price indices.

Table N-2. Japanese price indexes

Year	Retail price		Wholesale price	
1925	1.44	100	1.305	100
1929	1.185	83.3	1.057	80.9
1930	0.885	61.3	0.855	65.1

Bank of Japan, *Meiji Iko Honpo Shuyo Keizai Tokei* (Hundred-Year Statistics of the Japanese Economy) (Tokyo: Bank of Japan, 1966), 76, 80. (Hereafter referred to as *Honpo Shuyo Keizai Tokei*).

3. Ippei Yamazawa and Yuzo Yamamoto, eds., *Boeki to Kokusaishushi* (Foreign Trade and Balance of Payments), in Kazushi Ohkawa et al., eds., *Choki Keizai Tokei* (Estimates of Long-Term Economic Statistics of Japan since 1868), Vol. 14, (Tokyo: Toyo Keizai Shinposha, 1965), 257. (Hereafter referred to as *Boeki to Kokusaishushi*). Also, M. Kajinishi, *Nihon Shihonshugi Hattatsushi,* II: 128–31.

4. Bank of Japan, *Honpo Shuyo Keizai Tokei,* 132.

5. Finance Minister Korekiyo Takahashi bravely exercised Keynesian fiscal monetary policies in Japan in 1932 without knowing the Keynesian model. Acting on intuition, he significantly limited his expansionary policy so that inflation would not overheat the Japanese economy. Takahashi, who had served as the finance minister on five different occasions, was denounced for limiting expansion, and at age 83 he was assassinated by members of a radical young military officers' group on February 26, 1936.

6. Japan had experienced an industrial upsurge three times before the period of our research: The first occurred in the cotton-spinning industry after the Sino-Japanese War (1894–95); the second was centered on the establishment of the iron-steel industry after the Russo-Japanese War (1904–05); and the third occurred during World War I.

7. Bank of Japan, *Honpo Shuyo Keizai Tokei,* 320, Foreign exchange rates. For a cross-country comparison of the fall in foreign exchange rates, see note 1 in sec. 3 of this chapter.

5. FOREIGN TRADE AS A SUBSTITUTE FOR "PREREQUISITES"

1. At the initial stage of Japanese industrialization before 1878, the government sponsored five small cotton-spinning factories that failed because of their size and the standard of technology. Electric lights instead of gas lamps, for example, which easily started fires in cotton dust, had to be installed in the factories.

2. The success of the first large-scale modern spinning factory, Osaka Boseki Kabushikigaisha, established in 1883, encouraged investments and led to the establishment in 1887 of the cotton-spinning industry in Japan. The volume of domestic machine-made cotton yarn exceeded imported yarn in 1890. The Japanese cotton industry first drove Indian cotton products out of Japan, a country without tariff autonomy, then British products in the next year. A unitary tariff of 5 percent was levied on all imports and exports until 1911, when the unequal treaties expired. Exports of cotton cloth exceeded those of imports for the first time in 1897.

3. Although cotton had been grown in Japan, it was the short staple variety, which is unsuitable for industrial purposes, and the quantity was limited. These two elements led to the failure of the five cotton-spinning mills set up by the government when it tried to industrialize the country.

4. William W. Lockwood, *The Economic Development of Japan* (Princeton: Princeton University Press, 1954), chs. 6 and 7. Silk and tea were exceptions. Ninety percent of the silk produced was exported in the prewar period.

5. The swiftness of large export-related companies in adapting themselves to changing world economic conditions was achieved by sacrificing small- and medium-scale factories. The latter were left with low technological levels in the interwar period. Toy makers and match makers were especially found in that category.

   The technological standards of small- and medium-scale factories, however, have changed in recent years. These factories are increasingly purchasing industrial robots because of recent worker shortages, and through the use of high technology they are now quick and flexible in adapting to changing economic circumstances.

6. G. E. Hubbard, *Eastern Industrialization and Its Effect on the West* (London: Oxford University Press, 1935), 361–62.

7. Joseph A. Schumpeter, *The Theory of Economic Development,* trans. by Redvers Opie (Cambridge, Mass.: Harvard University Press, 1934), pages on the entrepreneur.

8. Anthony Y. C. Koo, ed., *Selected Essays of Gottfried Haberler* (Cambridge: MIT Press, 1985), chs. 16 and 17.

Chapter 2: ANTI-JAPANESE BOYCOTTS AS TRADE BARRIERS IN CHINA

1. THREE FACTORS IN THE DETERIORATION OF JAPAN'S TRADE WITH CHINA

1. League of Nations, *Report of the Commission of Enquiry,* Official No. C. 663. M 320, 1932, Vol. VII, 9: 119. This document is known as the Lytton Report.

2. Lytton Report, 120.

3. League of Nations, "Observations of the Japanese Government in the Report of the Commission of Enquiry and Communication from the Chinese Delegation." Official No. C. 663. M. 320, 1932, Vol. VII, and No. A (Extr.) A. 155, 1932, Vol. VII. For information on the anti-Japanese boycotts in this period, please refer to Charles F. Remer, *A Study of Chinese Boycotts with Special Reference to Their Economic Effectiveness* (Baltimore: Johns Hopkins University Press, 1933), 128 ff., especially chapters XIV–XVI. (Hereafter referred to as *A Study of Chinese Boycotts.*)

4. See statistical table 1 in appendix I.

5. Although China's share of Japan's total exports in the same period remained very low, less than 6 percent, the difference was attributable to the larger size of Japan's trade.

6. Yu-Kwei Cheng, *Foreign Trade and Industrial Development of China* (Washington, D.C.: University Press of Washington, 1956), 67–70, table 25.

7. Hsiao Liang-lin, *China's Foreign Trade Statistics 1864–1949* (Cambridge, Mass.: East Asian Research Center, Harvard University Press, 1974), 154. (Hereafter referred to as *China's Foreign Trade Statistics.*) Cheng, *Foreign Trade and Industrial Development of China,* 58, table 20.

8. Before 1926, Britain was the biggest loser in the China market. China, Inspector General of Customs, *The Trade of China* (Shanghai, 1932–).

9. Remer, *A Study of Chinese Boycotts.* See his appendix for trade figures.

10. Cheng, *Foreign Trade and Industrial Development of China,* 65–67.

11. Ministry of Finance, *Nihon Gaikoku Boeki Geppyo* (Monthly Reports on Foreign Trade of Japan) (Tokyo: Ministry of Finance, 1927–1939).

12. Naosuke Takamura, *Kindai Nihon Mengyo to Chugoku* (The Modern Japanese Cotton Textile Industry and China) (Tokyo: University of Tokyo Press, 1982), 172.

13. Yen Chung p'ing, *Chung kuo mien fang chih shih kao* (A Draft History of Chinese Cotton Spinning and Weaving) (Peking, 1955), 224.

2. THE ANTI-JAPANESE BOYCOTTS IN CHINA

1. Cheng, *Foreign Trade and Industrial Development of China*, 56. Hou Chi-ming, *Foreign Investment and Economic Development in China 1840–1937*, Harvard East Asian Series 21 (Cambridge: Harvard University Press, 1965), 107–09.

2. See Remer, *A Study of Chinese Boycotts*, 7–36.

3. For anti-Japanese boycotts in China before 1926, see Remer, *A Study of Chinese Boycotts*, 40–96, 111–18, 126–27.

4. Charles F. Remer's book is rich in information on the causes, events, and the process of boycotts against foreign countries, including Japan. He analyzed the effectiveness of the boycotts essentially from a short-term viewpoint; his book only covers up to the beginning of 1932. The purpose of this chapter is to analyze the repercussion of the anti-Japanese boycott on Japan's trade and Japan's economy from a long-term standpoint, as stated in the introduction.

   Remer's statistical tables in appendixes A and B include imports from Hong Kong to China as imports from Japan. This inclusion of Hong Kong trade in Japanese figures made imports from Japan to south China in the 1926–32 period unproportionally high, compared with those in our tables (such as in table 2.10) in the next section.

5. Remer, *A Study of Chinese Boycotts*, 55.

6. Ibid., 103.

7. League of Nations, *Report of the Commission of Enquiry* (Geneva: League of Nations, 1932), 120.

8. See appendix II: Unpublished Official Documents in the Archives of the Ministry of Foreign Affairs, Tokyo.

   Ministry of Commerce and Industry, Department of Foreign Trade, *The Manchurian Incident*, II, "The Influence of the Chinese Boycott on Trade." (Hereafter referred to as *The Manchurian Incident*.)

   Ministry of Foreign Affairs, *Diplomatic Documents*. (Hereafter referred to as *The Documents*.)

   The Tsinan Incident, A 110, 2–4, XV.

   The Manchurian Incident, A 110, 21-5, II; A 110, 21-5, XI.

   Shanghai, A 110, 21-5, XII, XIV, XXVII, XXVIII.

   Anti-Japanese Boycotts in China, J/X1-C1, I–VII.

   Hankow, J/X1-C1-3, I, II.

9. This anti-British boycott was modified by the expulsion of communist members from the Nationalist party at the end of the year.

10. Kiyoshi Oshima, *Nihon Kyoko-shi Ron* (The History of Crisis in Japan), vol. II, (Tokyo: University of Tokyo Press, 1961), 278.

11. The number of spindles increased by 351 in 1927, amounting to a total of 6,467,000 bales in the Cotton Spinning Association (a cartel organization with

257 member companies in 1927). The output was reduced by 79,000 bales, resulting in a total of 2,452,000 bales. Oshima, *Nihon Kyoko-shi Ron,* 278.

12. Ministry of Finance, *Nihon Gaikoku Boeki Nenpyo* (Annual Returns of Foreign Trade of Japan) (Tokyo: Ministry of Finance, 1926, 1929).

13. Research in this subsection heavily depends on *Hankow,* J/X1-C1-3, I–II. In *Anti-Japanese Boycotts* (Unpublished Official Documents). Ministry of Foreign Affairs, *The Documents,* in the Archives of the Ministry of Foreign Affairs, Tokyo.

14. *The Documents,* E3, 30, J/X1-C1-3, *China, Hankow,* vol. I, Telegram 195, Secrecy, Hankow, July 30, 1928, from Deputy Consul General Harada in Hankow to the Minister of Foreign Affairs, Giichi Tanaka, in Tokyo.

15. Ibid., E3, 30, J/X1-C1-3, Code 15301, Nov. 15, 1928.

16. Ibid., E3, 30, J/X1-C1-3, Code 792, Jan. 19, 1929.

17. Ibid., E3, 30, J/X1-C1-3, Code 2143, Feb. 15, 1929.

18. Ibid., E3, 30, J/X1-C1-3, *China, Hankow,* Pamphlet, 7, Jan. 25, 1929. Products of foreign factories in China were treated as foreign imports and could be shipped to the interior without any *likin* or other transit tax being paid after the payment of tariff duties. Cheng, *Foreign Trade and Industrial Development of China,* 37, 41, 54. Hou Chi-ming, *Foreign Investment and Economic Development in China,* 108.

19. *The Documents,* E3, 30, J/X1-C1-3, *China, Hankow,* Code 5142, April 9, 1929.

20. Ibid., E3, 30, J/X1-C1-3, Telegram 14, Jan. 25, 1929.

21. Ibid., E3, 30, J/X1-C1-3, Code 5142, April 9, 1929

22. Ibid., A 110, 20-2, *The Wanpaoshan Incident.*

23. Ibid., A 110, 21-5, XI, *Division Middle China,* Shanghai, *The Manchurian Incident,* Code 16428, Oct. 18, 1931, from Consul General Kuramatsu Murai to Kiichiro Hidehara, Minister of Foreign Affairs in Tokyo.

24. Ibid., A 110, 21-5, XI, Secrecy 1223, Oct. 12, 1931.

25. Thirty volumes are relevant to the boycott concerning the Manchurian incident. See the Archives of the Ministry of Foreign Affairs, Tokyo, Japan.

26. *The Documents,* A 110, 21-5, XI, *Central China,* Secrecy 1223, Oct. 12, 1931.

27. Ibid., 282–83.

28. Ibid., Code 17508, Oct. 27, 1931, 286–87. The employment figures include the workers in Japanese-owned factories that were inside and outside the Japanese concession in Shanghai.

29. Ibid., A 110, 21-5, XII, *Shanghai,* Code 19043, Nov. 11, 1931. 1 picul = 63.55 kg. The Japanese companies had unpaid credit sales and were unable to purchase local cotton for input.

30. Ibid., A 110, 21-5, XI, Telegram 1297, Oct. 26, 1931.

31. Ibid., A 110, 21-5, XVI, Code 15848 and 16530, 200–207.

32. Richard A. Kraus, *Cotton and Cotton Goods in China, 1918–1936* (Ph.D. diss., Harvard Univ., 1968), 49

33. Ibid., 208–15.

34. *The Documents,* A 110, 21-5, I, 201, 208.

35. Ibid., A 110, 21-5, II, 1428–29.

36. Ibid., 680.

37. $141/503.7 \times 100 = 28.15$ (percent)

38. $0.75/3.3 \times 100 = 22.72$

39. $95.3/358 \times 100 = 26.89$

40. For the exchange rate, see Bank of Japan, *Honpo Shuyo Keizai Tokei,* 320. One hundred yen = 49.375 U.S. dollars. Of the total, *fu* comprised 6.9 percent, rape seed 6.3 percent, and cotton seed 5.7 percent.

41. *The Documents,* A 110, 21-5, XI, (Oct. 27, 1931): 284, 286–87.

42. See the latter part of this section.

43. Yen Chung-p'ing, *Chung-kuo mien fang chih shih kao* (A Draft History of Chinese Cotton Spinning and Weaving) (Peking: 1955), 300–301. Most of his passages refer to the boycott of July 1931, though some mention the one after September.

44. Among many Japanese writings, see, for example, Takehisa Hayashi, et al., eds., *Koza Teikoku Shugi no Kenkyu VI, Nihon Shihon Shugi* (A Study of Imperialism, VI, Japanese Capitalism) (Tokyo: Aoki Shoten, 1973), 265.

    Another possible change relevant to the decline was that Chinese consumption of cotton cloth drastically dropped in that period.

45. An estimate of losses in principal exports from Japan to Shanghai (Sept. 18–Oct. 18, 1931) is shown below.

    Table N-3. Losses in exports to Shanghai

    (millions of dollars)

	Cotton cloth	Paper	Sea products	Metal products	Chemicals
Value of 1930 imports	200.27	44.1	28.69	16.84	16.79
Coverage of the items	44.4%	9.8%	6.3%	3.7%	3.7%
Substituted by	China	U.S.A.	China	Britain	Britain
	Britain	Switzerland	U.S.A.	U.S.A.	Germany
		Norway	USSR	Germany	
		Canada	South Seas countries		

    Source: *The Documents,The Manchurian Incident,* A 110, 21-5, XI. *Shanghai,* Commercial Secrecy No. 327: 254–83.

46. *The Manchurian Incident,* A 110: 21-5, II, 1853.

47. Hsiao Liang-lin, *China's Foreign Trade Statistics,* 68.

48. Ibid., 33.

49. Takamura, *Kindai Nihon Mengyo to Chugoku*, 196–97.

50. *The Documents*, A 110, 21-5, XIV, 269. League of Nations, *Supplementary Documents to the Report of the Commission of Enquiry*, 218.

51. See Katsumi Shirai, *The Japan-China War* (Tokyo: Chuo Koronsha, 1967).

3. Japan's Export Distortion: Japanese Exports to Six Regions of China

1. Statistical table 1 in appendix I.

2. The term "immiserizing growth" is used here in a broader sense than originally defined. It was originally explained as it mainly occurs: When exports grow, the terms of trade decline more, offsetting the gain in export growth. Charles P. Kindleberger and Peter H. Lindert, *International Economics*, 6th ed. (Homewood, Ill.: R. D. Irwin, 1978), 65, 68, 81. The conditions of immiserizing growth are noted on page 69.

3. Other considerations for the Japanese government, such as the Soviet threat, are outside the realm of this work.

4. Ministry of Finance, *Nihon Gaikoku Boeki Nenpyo*.

    Toyo Keizai Shinposha, *Nihon Boeki Seiran* (Foreign Trade of Japan: A Statistical Survey) (Tokyo: Toyo Keizai Shinposha, 1975 rev.), *Supplement*, 24–28. (Hereafter referred to as *Boeki Seiran, Supplement*)

    * The figures of cotton cloth exports in value terms are not available for 1926–27; therefore the increases are calculated as 1937 over 1928.

5. Sugar was brought from Taiwan to Japan. The imports of sugar and rice brought on an annual deficit of the balance of payments of Japan proper with Taiwan over the period of this survey. Toyo Keizai Shinposha, *Boeki Seiran, Supplement*, 663.

6. See tables 2.4 and 2.5. Total sugar imports declined after 1932. Hsiao Lianglin, *China's Foreign Trade Statistics*, 68.

7. *The Documents*, A 110, 21-5, XI, *The Manchurian Incident, Central China, 1931–34*, 107–08.

8. Ministry of Finance, *Nihon Gaikoku Boeki Nenpo*.

    Toyo Keizai Shinposha, *Boeki Seiran, Supplement*, 32–36.

9. Ministry of Finance, *Nihon Gaikoku Boeki Nenpo*.

10. See, for example, *Dainihon Boseki Kabushikigaisha Gojunen Kiyo* (Memory of 50 Years at the Dainihon Boseki Co. Ltd.) (Osaka, 1941). This company was one of the five largest cotton-spinning companies in Japan. In 1934 it started to build a factory to produce rayon; production started in 1936 and expanded within three months (56–57). It built another factory in Korea in 1937 (59–60). The company then became the largest stockholder of Kishiwada Jinken (Kishiwada Rayon), which also was established in 1934, and the two companies merged in 1937 to become one of the largest rayon producers in Japan (100–02).

11. More detailed original figures of this table are presented as statistical table 2 in appendix I.
12. For the vigorous activity of Japanese-owned cotton textile factories in this region, see Takamura, *Kindai Nihon Mengyo to Chugoku,* 200–24. The average rate of profit of these seven Japanese cotton-spinning companies was very low in 1932–33. It recovered to 22 percent in the second half of 1936, approaching the average rate of profit of total cotton-spinning companies in Japan. Ibid., 125, table 8.

4. Distortion in Japan's Imports from China

1. Ministry of Finance, *Nihon Gaikoku Boeki Nenpyo 1927* (1928), 33–37. Tin, salt, and hides and skins constituted only 0.17, 0.1, and 3.2 percent, respectively, of the total imports from China in 1926; because of their small relative shares they are excluded from table 2.14.
2. Toyo Keizai Shinposha, *Boeki Seiran, Supplement,* 32, 34, 36.
3. Ministry of Finance, *Nihon Gaikoku Boeki Nenpyo 1937* (1938), 83–85. Yamazawa and Yamamoto, *Boeki to Kokusaishushi,* 114.
4. Alexander Eckstein, *China's Economic Development* (Ann Arbor: University of Michigan Press, 1976), 166.
5. Toyo Keizai Shinposha, *Boeki Seiran, Supplement,* 33, 35, 37.
6. Imports of ginned cotton replaced shipments of raw cotton from China after 1895 as thousands of gins were exported from Japan to China. Takamura, *Kindai Nihon Mengyo to Chugoku,* 46–48.
7. Kang Chao, "The Growth of a Modern Cotton Textile Industry and the Competition with Handicrafts," in Dwight H. Perkins, ed., *China's Modern Economy in Historical Perspective* (Stanford, Calif.: Stanford University Press, 1975), 171–72, table 2.
8. Cheng, *Foreign Trade and Industrial Development of China,* 32–33. Eckstein, *China's Economic Development,* 166–67.
9. Kraus, *Cotton and Cotton Goods in China,* 48, 51.
10. Ministry of Foreign Affairs, *History of Encouragement of Cotton Cultivation in China Investigation,* No. 29 (Tokyo: Ministry of Foreign Affairs, 1935), 163.
11. Akira Hara, "The Balance of Payments in the Period of the Sino-Japanese War," *Shakai Keizai-shi Gaku,* XXXIV: 6, 47–74. For statistics see Yamazawa and Yamamoto, *Boeki to Kokusaishushi,* 41.

Chapter 3: THE DRASTIC DECLINE OF JAPANESE EXPORTS TO THE UNITED STATES

1. Introduction to Japan-U.S. Trade Relations

1. See statistical table 1, appendix I, for figures of Japan's trade with the United States. Quoted percentage points are also based on the figures in this table.

2. See ch. 1, sec. 4, endnote 6, for the previous three stages of Japan's industrial upsurge.

3. Lockwood, *Trade and Trade Rivalry between the United States and Japan*, 41.

2. U.S. INTELLECTUALS SUPPORT THE BOYCOTT

1. *The Documents, The Tsinan Incident*, A 110, 2-14, XVI, 54–59, 62–66, 69–72, 77, 84, 103.

   Ibid., *The Manchurian Incident*, A 110, 2-14, XVI, 106–107

   Ibid., *The United States*, J 110, J/X1-U1, I and III.

   These documents are especially filled with information on the boycott of Japan in the United States. This section heavily depends on information from them.

2. Ibid., *The United States*, J 110, J/XI, U1, I, 33, Feb. 20, 1932.

3. *The United States*, J 110, J/XI, U1, I, 52–53, Mar. 3, 1932.

   In Japanese government data, the number of Japanese farm families engaged in the sericultural industry in this period was 2,210,000, not 3,000,000.

4. Ibid., *The United States*, J 110, J/X1, U1, I, Telegrams 144, 168, 191.

5. Ibid., *The Manchurian Incident*, A 110, 21-5, XXVIII, Telegram 15793.

6. Ibid., *The Manchurian Incident*, E 3, 30, J/X1-U1, II, Telegram 32, New York

7. Ibid., *The United States*, E 3, 30 J/X1 U1, code 9, Feb. 11, 1932.

8. Ibid., *The United States, New York Times*, Oct. 24, 1931, Telegram 17938.

9. Ibid., *The Manchurian Incident*, A 110, 21-5, XXVII, Seattle Telegram 270.

10. American Council, Institute of Pacific Relations, "Memorandum on Embargo or Boycott of Japan" (New York: American Council Institute of Pacific Relations, March 9, 1932), 3–4. Article 16 of the League Covenant calls for the severance of all trade, financial relations, and other relations between the nationals of the covenant-breaking state and all other nationals, regardless of their membership in the League of Nations.

11. Ibid., 4.

12. Chicago Council on Foreign Relations, *Foreign Notes*, April 2, 1932, IX, 7, 6.

13. Associated Press, *Washington Post*, March 29, 1932.

3. ANALYSIS OF THE CATASTROPHIC COLLAPSE OF SILK EXPORTS

1. Of a Japanese farmer's total output in those days, about 33 percent was for taxes and another 33 percent for rent in kind. Therefore what remained was only a third of the total harvest to sustain a minimum level of subsistence.

2. Dept. of General Statistics in the Imperial Cabinet, *The Statistical Survey of Imperial Japan* (Tokyo: Dept. of General Statistics in the Imperial Cabinet, 1935), 28–29.

3. Tomoichi Mizunuma, "Showa Kyoko"(Showa crisis) in Mikio Sumiya, ed., *Showa Kyoko* (Showa Crisis) (Tokyo: Yuhikaku, 1975, second ed., 184–85. (Hereafter referred to as *Showa Kyoko.*) The figures are based on ones from the Sericultural Section, Dept. of Agriculture and Forestry, *Yosan Keiei Chosa Seiseki* (Report on Sericultural Farming) (Tokyo: Dept. of Agriculture and Forestry, 1934).

4. Seiichiro Ono, "Showa Kyoko to Noson Kyusai Seisaku" (Relief Policies for Farmers in the Showa Crisis). In *Nihon Keizai Seisaku-shi Ron* (History of Japan's Economic Policies), Yoshio Ando, ed. (Tokyo: University of Tokyo Press, 1976), 32.

5. For example, it was reported that 200,000 elementary school pupils carried no lunch to school in Nagano Prefecture in the fall of 1932. *Asahi Shimbun ni Miru Nihon no Ayumi* (The History of Modern Japan Reported in the *Asahi Shimbun*) (Tokyo: Asahi Shimbunsha, 1974), 150 ff. Mizunuma, *Showa Kyoko,* 81–191.

6. Keizo Nagahara, Masanori Nakamura, et al., *Nihon Jinushisei no Kosei to Dankai* (The Structure and Stages in the Japanese Landowner System) (Tokyo: University of Tokyo Press, 1972), 542–46.

7. Kan'ichi Ishii, *Nihon Sanshigyo-shi Bunseki* (An Analysis of the History of the Japanese Sericultural Industry) (Tokyo: University of Tokyo Press, 1978), 265–70.

8. U.S. Dept. of Commerce, *Foreign Commerce and Navigation of the United States* (Washington: U.S. Dept. of Commerce, 1925–39). The statements on U.S. tariffs in this section are based on data from this source.

9. Ibid. The rates are as of ad valorem incidence. In this period, U.S. tariff rates were regarded as the highest nominal level for manufacturers among advanced countries.

Ian Little, Tibor Scitovsky, and Maurice Scott, *Industry and Trade in Some Developing Countries* (London: Oxford University Press, 1970), 162. Ratios of raw silk exports to total silk exports are calculated in value terms.

10. U.S. Dept. of Commerce, *Foreign Commerce and Navigation of the United States.*

11. See note 4 above.

12. Ministry of Finance, *Nihon Gaikoku Boeki Nenpyo* (1927–39). The trade figures and descriptions in this passage are based on various issues of this compilation of Japanese government statistics.

13. Jesse W. Markhan, *Competition in the Rayon Industry* (Cambridge: Harvard University Press, 1952), 172. The Tariff Act of 1930 in the United States called for a 45 percent ad valorem (a minimum duty of $0.45/pound) even on standard rayon yarns if they were of foreign origin.

14. Markhan, *Competition in the Rayon Industry,* 33: chart 1.

15. Ibid., 33: appendix. The quality improvement of rayon products and an acceleration in the substitution for silk were coincident with the appearance of the delustered viscose yarns and expansion in acetate yarn products.

16. Ibid., 66. Rayon prices are quoted from Textile Organan.

17. Toyo Keizai Shinposha, *Boeki Seiran.*

Kinyu Tokei Nenkan (Annual Statistics of Financial Affairs) (Tokyo: Ministry of Finance, 1934–40).

4. U.S. TARIFFS ON MANUFACTURED JAPANESE PRODUCTS

1. A conditional MFN customs agreement discriminated against third countries because reductions in tariffs and other benefits stemming from an accord between two countries were extended to third countries only if they made "equivalent reciprocal concessions" by later agreements. William B. Kelly, Jr., ed., *Studies in United States Commercial Policy* (Chapel Hill: University of North Carolina Press, [1963]), chs. I and II. Most European countries had adopted unconditional MFN tariff policies following the Cobden-Chevalier Treaty of 1860. The U.S. tariff system adhered to a conditional MFN clause because U.S. tariffs were originally founded on navigational laws and colonial trade policies.

2. Exceptions to the nondiscriminatory principle at that time were legislated as threats to get nondiscriminatory treatment from European countries for U.S. products.

3. The presidential power increased to change duty rates by 50 percent to equalize differences between foreign and domestic costs of production after an investigation was made by the Tariff Commission. An application of tariffs to equalize costs of production between two countries entails the elimination of all comparative cost advantages stemming from superiority and dissimilarity in some economic and social features, such as natural resource endowments and a high level of human skills, natural climate, social climate, heritage, and tradition. Under the cost of a production-equalizing scheme, domestic producers can sell products at monopolistic home market prices. If a tariff is high enough, it could also cut off all product imports to the home market. The concept of equalizing production costs is meaningful when it is known whose costs they are and at what specific period the equalization took place. But it is difficult and almost impossible to measure them when applied in general terms. The meaninglessness of cost equalization as a basis for tariffs is discussed in Charles P. Kindleberger, *International Economics* (Homewood, Ill.: Irwin, 1953), 187–188.

4. *New York Times*, Sept. 13, 1925, from Kelly, ed., *Studies in United States Commercial Policy*, 10.

5. Kelly, ed., *Studies in United States Commercial Policy*, 66.

6. The Hawley-Smoot Act of 1930 was said to be more a consequence of logrolling than its predecessor, the 1922 tariff act. (Kelly, ed., *Studies in United States Commercial Policy*, 11 ff.)

The high rates of the tariff acts of 1922 and of 1930 could be modified to equalize foreign and domestic production costs, but the tariff reduction was not considered a subject for negotiation under Sec. 315 of the 1922 act during the 1920s and early 1930s.

President Herbert Hoover objected to the negotiation of agreements for the mutual lowering of tariff barriers because he assumed that these agreements must intrinsically be preferential. Kelly, ed., *Studies in United States Commercial Policy*, 28–29.

7. Lockwood, *Trade and Trade Rivalry between the United States and Japan*, 33.

8. Kelly, ed., *Studies in United States Commercial Policy*, 76–77.

9. Ibid., 66.

10. Lockwood, *Trade and Trade Rivalry between the United States and Japan*, 34–35.

11. USITC (U.S. International Trade Commission), *Conversion of Specific and Compound Rates of Duty to Ad Valorem Rates—Report to the President on Investigation No. 332-99 Under Section 332 of the Tariff Act of 1930, as Amended*, 896 (Washington: USITC, July 1978), 20436.

12. U.S. Dept. of Commerce, *Foreign Commerce and Navigation of the United States* (Washington: U.S. Dept. of Commerce, 1937), 286.

13. Ibid. Ministry of International Trade and Industry, "Monthly Report of Trade Statistics."

14. U.S. Dept. of Commerce, *Foreign Commerce and Navigation of the United States*.

15. The Dainippon Boseki Kyokai "voluntarily" restricted cotton textile exports to the Philippines. (Thomas A. Bisson, *American Policy in the Far East 1931–1940* [New York: International Secretariat, Institute of Pacific Relations, 1939], 40–41).

16. Gardner Patterson, *Discrimination in International Trade* (Princeton, N.J.: Princeton University Press, 1966), 296.

17. The data are from U.S. Dept. of Commerce, *Foreign Commerce and Navigation of the United States*, 5.

18. Ibid., 99.

19. Ibid.

20. Ibid., 100. Calculated by the author in the same way as table 3.6.

21. The Japanese government also intervened in the free flow of commodities by the control of imports of raw cotton and by the link system (with India) in July 1938. As an inessential commodity for war materials, raw cotton had no import priority. Compared with the purchase of raw cotton, Japan was able to sell a small amount of cotton products to the United States. The Japanese cotton textile industry could import fine U.S. raw cotton only up to the value of its U.S.-bound exports of cotton products.

22. Thomas A. Bisson, *American Policy in the Far East 1931–1940*, 41. See also Lockwood, *Trade and Trade Rivalry between the United States and Japan*, 16–17, 56–57.

Chapter 4: BRITISH COMMONWEALTH DISCRIMINATION AGAINST JAPANESE
TRADE

1. HISTORICAL BACKGROUND

1. Koo, ed., *Selected Essays of Gottfried Haberler,* chapters 16 and 17. "The World Economy, Money and the Great Depression," "The Great Depression of the 1930's—Can It Happen Again?"

2. Trade figures in this chapter are from *Survey of the World Economy* (Geneva: League of Nations, 1933 and 1938). Figures for Japanese trade in textiles are based on the data in *Nihon Sen'i Sangyo-shi, Kakuron Hen* (The History of the Japanese Textile Industry, edition for details) (Tokyo: Sen'i Nenkan Kankokai, 1958), 53, and Toyo Keizai Shinposha, *Boeki Seiran, Supplement,* 25.

2. THE JAPAN-CANADA TARIFF WAR

1. The figures for 1913 are taken from Toyo Keizai Shinposha, *Boeki Seiran, The Supplement,* 695. The exchange rates are from the Bank of Japan, *Honpo Shuyo Keizai Tokei,* 320. ¥100 = $49.375 in 1912.

2. *Survey of International Trade* (Geneva: League of Nations, 1938), 2, statistical table 1, appendix 1.

3. See table 2.1 in ch. 2.

4. Japan Academy of Science, *Tsusho Joyaku to Tsusho Seisaku no Hensen* (The Evolution of Commercial Treaties and Foreign Trade Policies), *A Supplement to Diplomatic Documents Relating Reforms of Commercial Treaties* (Tokyo: Research Institute for the World Economy, 1951), 943. (Hereafter cited as *Tsusho Joyaku.*)

5. Ibid., 943, 959.

6. Bank of Japan, *Honpo Shuyo Keizai Tokei,* table 139, 395.

7. Ibid., 320.

8. Japan Academy of Science, *Tsusho Joyaku,* 960.

9. Table N-4 shows the names, and proportional shares in total world trade, of 18 countries whose currencies depreciated 5 percent more than the fall in the Canadian dollar vis-à-vis gold from 1929 to March 1935.

Table N-4 Rates of depreciation of currencies, 1929–March 1935

	Percentage of depreciation of currency in relation to gold	Share of world trade
Canada	41	3.27
Spain	44	1.21
Sweden	45	1.72
Norway	46	0.84
Finland	50	0.62
Denmark	52	1.41
Uruguay	52	0.26

(Continued)

Iran	53	0.38
Australia	54	1.87
New Zealand	54	0.79
Greece	57	0.34
Bolivia	59	0.08
Argentina	65	2.18
Japan	66	3.32
Colombia	67	0.30
Mexico	67	0.68
Brazil	67	1.27
Ecuador	73	0.04
Chile	75	0.37

Sources: League of Nations, *Remarks on the Present Phase of International Economic Relations* (Geneva: League of Nations Economic Committee, 1936), table 36: 17. The original figures were taken from the *Fifth Annual Report of the Bank for International Settlement.*

10. Japan Academy of Science, *Tsusho Joyaku,* 961.

11. An ad valorem tax rate of 35 percent was common for a product "identical" to one of a nonprotected industry. Japan Academy of Science, *Tsusho Joyaku,* 948.

12. Ministry of Commerce and Industry, *Index of Wholesale Prices in Thirteen Cities* (Tokyo: Ministry of Commerce and Industry, 1934).

Wholesale price index	
November 1932	100
1934	145

Japan Academy of Science, *Tsusho Joyaku,* 961.

13. Japan Academy of Science, *Tsusho Joyaku,* 961.

14. Ibid., 961.

15. Ibid., 961.

16. All quotations in this paragraph are from official letters and telegrams of the British Embassy in Tokyo. Confidential minutes, No. 260, Dec. 21, 1934, and Confidential No. 261, May 10, 1935, FO 262/1896, Public Record Office (Richmond, U.K.).

17. Business section, *Vancouver Sun,* April 27, 1936, quoted in Japan Academy of Science, *Tsusho Joyaku,* 962.

18. Ibid., 963 ff.

19. Ibid., 965.

20. This occurred even though the Canadian government had exempted these new additional duties for imports of Japanese goods that had been contracted for before July 20 and had arrived at Canada by Nov. 5, 1936.

21. *Vancouver Sun,* in Japan Academy of Science, *Tsusho Joyaku,* 955.

22. *Ottawa Journal,* July 13, 1935, in Japan Academy of Science, *Tsusho Joyaku,* 965.

23. Japan Academy of Science, *Tsusho Joyaku,* 969.

24. Ibid., 973–74.

25. Ibid., 954.

26. William Arthur Seavey, *Dumping Since the War: The GATT and National Laws*, Thesis 205 (Oakland, Calif.: Office Service Corp., 1970).

27. *Ottawa Journal*, in Japan Academy of Science, *Tsusho Joyaku*, 959.

28. Jacob Viner, *The Customs Union Issue* (New York: Carnegie Endowment for International Peace, 1950), 15.

29. GATT, Article VIII, states the following:

Article 1. The customs value of imported goods shall be the transaction value, that is, the actual amount paid or payable for the goods when they are sold for exporters, adjusted with provision (1) of Article 8.

Article 8. The provisions include the following: (1) (a) commission and costs for containers; (b) materials and tools; (c) royalties; (d) resale rewards. (2) Freight and loading and insurance.

Protocol to the GATT. Code: Agreements of Implementation of Article VIII of GATT. Rules on Customs Valuation (Geneva: GATT, 1979).

Even in 1986, a few instances of customs valuations were well known, in Korea, for example.

30. For situations of serious injury to a domestic industry, see GATT Tokyo Round, Article 14, Committee on Anti-dumping Practices; Article 6, Determination of Injuries and Imposition of Countervailing Duties; and GATT Article XIX (escape clause).

3. Japanese Trade Conflict with British India

1. The source of the figures: Japan Academy of Science, *Tsusho Joyaku*, 869–70.

The original figures were in million rupees and were converted to U.S. dollars at the annual average exchange rate. U.S. Dept. of Commerce, *Statistical Abstract of the United States* (Washington: U.S. Dept. of Commerce, 1932, 1938), 1932: 275; 1938: 279.

2. Toyo Keizai Shinposha, *Boeki Seiran, Supplement*, 20.

3. Ibid., 26–27.

4. Yu Yanagisawa, "Dai Ichiji Nichi-In Kaisho (1933–34) o Meguru Ei–In Kankei" (The First Japan-India Commercial Conference and Commercial Relations Between Britain and India) in Yokohama City University, *Keizai to Boeki* (Industry and Trade) 129: 31, table 1. The figures are originally based on *Report of the Indian Tariff Board for Regarding the Grant of Protection to the Cotton Textile Industry* (Calcutta: Government of India Central Publication Branch, 1932), 28.

5. Japan Academy of Science, *Tsusho Joyaku*, 895. This source further states that the output of cotton cloth in India increased to 4.363 billion square yards in 1931–32, from 2.959 billion in 1928–29, and rose to 6.130 billion in 1936–37.

6. Japan Academy of Science, *Tsusho Joyaku*, 865.

7. Yanagisawa, 34; *Indian Tariff Board*, XI.

8. Arthur Redford, *Manchester Merchant and Foreign Trade* (Manchester: Manchester University Press, 1956), Vol. II, 1850–1939, 253.

9. Yanagisawa, 37.

10. The new rate was 50 percent in ad valorem, or 5.25 annas per pound. One anna is 1/16 of 1 rupee. In 1934, 1 rupee = U.S.$0.3788. See note 1 above for the source of the exchange rate.

11. For details of the negotiation process, see Yanagisawa; *Indian Tariff Board XI*, 39–43. Changes in the distribution of quotas of different kinds of cloths were allowed depending on kind, but the difference was limited to 10 to 20 percent of the original allotment amount.

12. Yanagisawa, 44, footnote 46; Secretary of State for India, "Trade Negotiations between India and Japan," July 20, 1933 (Calcutta, 1932). The British cotton industry was inclined to ally with the Bombay cotton industry to defeat Japan.

13. The figures are based on Toyo Keizai Shinposha, *Boeki Seiran* (Foreign Trade of Japan: A Statistical Survey), 34–36. See Japan Academy of Science, *Tsusho Joyaku*, 936–37.

14. Toyo Keizai Shinposha, *Boeki Seiran, Supplement,* 45.

15. Ibid., 32–36.

4. THE AUSTRALIAN QUOTA SYSTEM

1. Japan Academy of Science, *Tsusho Joyaku,* 937–86.

   Australia's per capita trade value was relatively large at US$202.5 in 1929, nearly seven times Japan's US$29.8. This value declined to US$81.6 (40 percent of the 1929 level) by 1937, with the severe fall in world trade, but it was still much higher compared with Japan's US$16.4. Ibid., 976–77.

2. Japan Academy of Science, *Tsusho Joyaku,* 987–89. The figures are converted: one pound equals 4.8665 mint par. U.S. Dept. of Commerce, *Statistical Abstract of the United States* (Washington: U.S. Dept. of Commerce, 1932), 276.

3. Japan Academy of Science, *Tsusho Joyaku,* 990.

4. Ibid., 992.

5. Ibid., 980.

6. League of Nations, *Statistical Year-Book 1939* (Geneva: League of Nations, 1940), 70.

7. League of Nations, *World Economic Survey, 1937/38* (Geneva: League of Nations, 1939), 167.

8. The act stated that if the fall in the value of the Australian currency was higher than 16-2/3 percent vis-à-vis the value of the British pound, the tariff reduction for British products would be a quarter of the original. If the fall was lower than 16-2/3 percent, the reduction would be an eighth of the original tariff rates.

9. Hubbard, *Eastern Industrialization and Its Effect on the West,* 314–29, 334 ff.

10. Earlier, in April 1934, the Japanese government passed the Trade Defense Act. Defense in Japanese connotes "to protect, foster, and defend." The purpose of the act was to alleviate the heavy commodity trade deficit by countervailing measures. The Japanese thus hoped to mitigate protective trade barriers exercised by its trade partners. This act was applied for the first time to Canadian products in July 1935.

11. Japan Academy of Science, *Tsusho Joyaku,* 1001.

12. Ibid., 1010–11.

13. The conclusion of the new Japanese–Australian Trade Agreement was made possible by Japan's compromise for an Australian triumph. League of Nations, *World Economic Survey, 1937/38,* 167.

14. One *hyo*: a Japanese unit of volume. One *hyo* is roughly equivalent to 60 kg.

15. League of Nations, *International Trade Statistics 1930* (Geneva: League of Nations, (1930), 284; *1937* (1938), 284; *1938* (1939), 284.

16. Japan Academy of Science, *Tsusho Joyaku,* 991–92.

5. EGYPT AND MIDDLE EASTERN COUNTRIES

1. Japan Academy of Science, *Tsusho Joyaku,* 571.

2. Gordon P. Merrium, Changé d'Affairs ad interim, Embassy of the United States of America, 683.9431/9, 1 (Cairo, Aug. 19, 1935), 2.

3. Warrington Dawson, U.S. Embassy, 683.9431/8 (Paris, Aug. 19, 1935), 2.

4. Ibid., 3.

5. Merriam, 3.

6. J. Rives Childs, chargé d'affaires ad interim, Legation of the U.S., 683/9841/19 (Cairo, Nov. 2, 1936), 3.

7. Legation of the United States of America, 583.9431/15 (Cairo, March 17, 1936), 2.

8. Warrington Dawson, U.S. Embassy, 683.9431/8 (Paris, Aug. 19, 1935), 4.

9. Ibid., 6.

10. Ibid., 4.

CHAPTER 5: JAPAN-NETHERLANDS TRADE SQUABBLES

1. The percentage of manufactured products here is calculated based only on cotton textiles, yarn, clothing, silk and synthetic textiles, sugar, and paper. Japanese manufactured exports then also included cement, china and porcelain, glassware, bicycles and parts, and toys, but the contribution of these exports was either small or did not expand until the later years of the period in our survey. They are treated in the subsection of manufactured exports. *Source:* Ministry of Finance, *Nihon Gaikoku Boeki Geppyo* (Monthly Returns of Foreign Trade of Japan) (Tokyo: Ministry of Finance, 1928–38). See appendix I, statistical table 2.

2. The Netherlands levied low, unitary tariffs for every commodity imported from all countries, including regions with no commercial treaties. Japan's main exports to the Netherlands were timber, materials for soybean oil and fish oil, china, and miscellaneous goods. The Netherlands controlled imports of Japanese cotton textiles: Their value did not even reach 0.3 percent of Japan's total exports to the Netherlands in 1933. Japan's trade with the Netherlands took the pattern of exports from a backward country to an advanced one, namely, exports in primary goods, while its trade with the Dutch East Indies took the pattern of exports from an advanced to a backward one of the exporting of manufactured goods.

3. Japan Academy of Science, *Tsusho Joyaku*, 1046.

4. Ministry of Finance, *Nihon Gaikoku Boeki Geppyo*.

5. Japan Academy of Science, *Tsusho Joyaku*, 1048.

6. Ibid., 2030.

7. Ibid., 1046.

8. U.S. Dept. of Commerce, *Statistical Abstract of the United States* (Washington: U.S. Dept. of Commerce, 1938).

9. Japan Academy of Science, *Tsusho Joyaku*, 1047.

10. Ibid., 1051.

11. Ibid., 1028. Committee members consisted of representatives of three nations: a Dutch minister, a French minister, and the Japanese minister of the Foreign Office.

12. *The Manchurian Incident, XXVII, Boycotts, in South Seas Areas, Secrecy,* No. 56, March 1933.

13. Toyo Keizai Shinposha, *Boeki Seiran, Supplement,* 29–34.

14. Japan Academy of Science, *Tsusho Joyaku*, 1051–52.

15. Ibid., 1054.

16. Ibid., 1055.

17. Ibid., 1055.

18. According to reports of the Association of the Japanese Cotton Spinning Industry.

19. From a dispatch of the British Embassy, Tokyo, April 11, 1934, FO 262/1839, Public Record Office, Kew, Richmond, U.K.

20. British Embassy, June 21, 1934, FO 262 1875, Public Record Office, Richmond, U.K. The Embassy had been looking into this matter for a long time.

21. British Embassy, July 13, 1934, FO 262 1875.

22. Japan Academy of Science, *Tsusho Joyaku*, 1034.

23. Ministry of Finance, *Nihon Gaikoku Boeki Geppyo* (Monthly Reports on Foreign Trade of Japan) (Tokyo: Ministry of Finance, Dec. 1928, 1931, 1934, 1936, 1939).

24. Ibid.

CHAPTER 6: LATIN AMERICA: THE NEW TRADE FRONTIER

1. TTHE LATIN AMERICAN MARKET

1. *Chugai Shogyo*, May 16, 1935.

2. FO 625. 9417/6, Edward A. Dow, American Consul General, Santiago, Chile, July 23, 1937 (Washington: National Archives), 4.

3. *Japan Times*, April 16, 1934.

4. FO 625. 9417/6, Dow, 7.

5. FO 625. 9417/6, Dow, 7.

6. *Chugai Shogyo*, May 16, 1935.

2. CHILE AND COLOMBIA

1. National Archives, Washington, Diplomatic Section, 625.9417/1, Edward A. Dow, American Consul General, Santiago, Chile, Oct. 10, 1934.

2. 625.9417/1, Dow, 2.

3. 625.9417/3, Dow, Dec. 18, 1934.

4. 625.9417/3, Dow, 3.

5. 625.9417/3, Dow, 3.

6. 625.9417/3, Dow, 7.

7. 625.9417/3, Dow, 11.

8. 625.9417/3, Dow, 12.

9. 625.9417/3, Dow, 4.

10. 625.9417/3, Dow, 6.

11. 625.9417/3, Dow, 5.

12. Ministry of Finance, *Nihon Gaikoku Boeki Nenpyo*.

13. 625.9417/3, Dow, 15.

14. 625.9417/6, Dow, American Consul General, Santiago, Chile, July 23, 1937, 1–3.

15. League of Nations, *International Trade Statistics 1930* (Geneva: League of Nations, 1932), 321, and *1938* (1939), 294.

16. 625.9417/6, Dow, July 23, 1937, 11.

17. 625.9417/6, Dow, 10.

18. 621.9431/10, S. Walter Washington, U.S. chargé d'affaires ad interim, Colombia, April 13, 1935, 1.

19. League of Nations, *International Trade Statistics 1930* (Geneva: League of Nations, 1932), 322, and *1938* (Geneva: League of Nations, 1939), 294.
   621.9431/8, State Dept. Secretary Hull, memo Feb. 19, 1935.

20. 621.9431/10, U.S. chargé d'affaires ad interim, Colombia, April 13, 1935, 2–3.

21. 621.9431/11, William Dawson, Legation of the United States of America, Bogota, Colombia, May 16, 1935, 1–3.

22. 621.9431/14, Legation of the United States of America, Colombia, June 22, 1935, 3.

23. 621.9431/15, U.S. chargé d'affaires, July 11, 1935.

24. 621.9431/15, U.S. chargé d'affaires, 2.

25. 621.9431/15, U.S. chargé d'affaires, 2.

26. 621.9431/15, U.S. chargé d'affaires, Strictly Confidential, Article IV, 2.

27. 621.9431/19, U.S. chargé d'affaires, 1.

28. Quotations from 621.9431/18, *Annual Report of the Minister of Foreign Relations*, 1935, Bogota, Colombia, Jan. 13, 1936, 385.

29. League of Nations, *International Trade Statistics 1938* (Geneva: League of Nations, 1939), 294.

3. PERU AND MEXICO

1. 623.9417/8, Encl. Dispatch 5317, August 28, 1937, Lima, Peru (Washington: Diplomatic Section, National Archives).

2. Ministry of Finance, *Nihon Gaikoku Boeki Nenpyo* (Annual Returns of Foreign Trade of Japan) (Tokyo: Ministry of Finance, 1927–1940).

3. 623.9417/7, James Barclay Young, American Consul General, Callao-Lima, Peru, April 5, 1935, 1.

4. 623.9417/7, Young, 1 (Washington: Diplomatic Section, National Archives).

5. 623.9417/4, Dec. 1934, 1.

6. 623.946/1, May 11, 1935, Lima, Peru, to Secretary of State (Washington: Diplomatic Section, National Archives).

7. 623.946/4, Jan. 25, 1936, Encl. No. 2, 1. The decree further exempted 47 of the 167 items in the cotton schedule from any quota limitation.

8. 623.9417/8, Encl. Dispatch 5317, Lima, Peru, August 28, 1937, 4.

9. 623.646/6, Lima, Peru, June 17, 1937, 2.

10. 635.946/8, Lima, Peru, Jan. 18, 1938, 2 (Washington: Diplomatic Section, National Archives.)

11. 624/9415/4, Lima, Peru, Nov. 8, 1934, 3 (Washington: Diplomatic Section, National Archives).

12. Ministry of Finance, *Nihon Gaikoku Boeki Nenpyo* (Annual Returns of Foreign Trade of Japan) (Tokyo: Ministry of Finance, 1925–1940).

13. 635.946/8, Jan. 18, 1938, Lima, Peru, 7.

14. 612.9417/6, Guy W. Ray, American Vice Consul, Guaymas, Mexico, April 25, 1935 (Washington: Diplomatic Section, National Archives), 20. Figures are converted according to exchange values in U.S. Dept. of Commerce Statistical Abstract of the United States, 1932, 275, and 1938, 279.

15. 612.9417/5, Ray, Guaymas, Feb. 4, 1935, 2.

16. 612.9417/5, Ray, 2.

17. 612.9417/4, Henry Norweb, chargé d'affaires ad interim, Guaymas, Mexico, May 11, 1934, 1.
18. 612.9417/4, Norweb, 1.
19. 612.9417/5, Guaymas, Feb. 4, 1935, 2.
20. 612.9417/5, Ray, 2.
21. 612.9417/5, Ray, 4.
22. 612.9417/8, A. F. Yepis, American Vice Consul, Guaymas, Mexico, June 20, 1935, 2.
23. 612.9417/8, Yepis, 2.
24. 612.9417/8, Yepis, 3.
25. 612.9417/8, Yepis, Encl.
26. Confidential mimeographed instruction of June 18, 1937. 621.9417/13, American Consul General, Oct. 26, 1937.
27. 612.943/2, Aug. 1, 1936 (Washington: Diplomatic Section, National Archives), 4.

4. ARGENTINA AND BRAZIL

1. 635.9415, Argentina No. 1972, Feb. 19, 1933 (Washington: National Archives).
2. 635.9417/24, American Consulate General, Buenos Aires, Jan. 25, 1935, 39.
3. 635.9417/26, American Consulate General, Buenos Aires, May 1, 1935.
4. 635.9417/26, 5.
5. 635.9417/26, 2-3.
6. 635.9417/26, 6.
7. 635.9417/26, 6.
8. 635.9417/13, American Consul General, Buenos Aires, May 24, 1934.
9. 635.9417/13, May 24.
10. 635.9431/18, American Consul General, Buenos Aires, July 7, 1937, 3.
11. 635.9431/18, 15.
12. 635.9431/18, 16.
13. 635.9431/6, American Consul General, Buenos Aires, Jan. 15, 1935.
14. 635.9431/18, American Consul General, Buenos Aires, 6.
15. 635.9431/13, American Consul General, Buenos Aires, Jan. 25, 1935, 2.
16. See chapter four, section two, Canada for the customs valuations.
17. For the customs valuation system, please refer to chapter four, section two: The Japan-Canada Tariff War.
18. 635.9416/29, American Consul General, Buenos Aires, 1938.
19. 635.9416/29, 15.
20. 635.9416/29, 15.
21. 635.9417/29, 1938. 4.

22. League of Nations, *International Trade Statistics. 1930* (Geneva: League of Nations, 1932), 320; *1936* (1938), 292; *1937* (1939), 292.

23. Calculated on figures in appendix I, statistical table 1.

24. 635.9416/29, American Consul General, Buenos Aires, 1938, 5–6.

25. 632.9431/1, American Consul General, Buenos Aires, May 11, 1935.

26. 632.9431/1, American Consul General, Buenos Aires, May 11, 1935, 7.

27. League of Nations, *International Trade Statistics 1930* (Geneva: League of Nations, 1932); *1936* (1938), 321; *1937* (1939), 293.

28. 632.9431/1, American Consul General, Buenos Aires, May 11, 1935, 7, 6.

29. See appendix I, statistical table 1.

CHAPTER 7: JAPAN'S ACCESSION TO GATT

1. Gardner Patterson, *Discrimination in International Trade: The Policy Issues, 1945–1965* (Princeton, New Jersey: Princeton University Press, 1966). The author is a former professor at Princeton University and served a long time as the Deputy General Director of GATT, until the beginning of the 1980s.

2. The preface of the General Agreement on Tariffs and Trade includes all these countries and is dated Oct. 30, 1947.

3. Ibid. The years of entrance and the member countries are based on this GATT material.

4. The following descriptions are based on GATT internal documents, *Accession of Japan, 1952–1955.*

5. GATT internal documents, GATT/CP. 2/SR. 12. Summary Record of the Twelfth Meeting, August 25, 1948, 6.

6. GATT/CP. 2/SR. 12. Summary Record, 3.

7. GATT/CP. 2/SR. 12. Summary Record, 4.

8. GATT/CP. 2/SR. 12. Summary Record, 5–6.

9. See discrimination toward Japan in Patterson, *Discrimination in International Trade.* New Jersey: 1966.

10. Chapters. 4 (British Commonwealth discrimination), 5, and 6.

11. GATT internal documents, *Accession of Japan 1952–1955*, GATT/CP. 2/SR. 12., Summary Record of the Twelfth Meeting. GATT internal documents L/29/Add., L/76, Feb. 13, 1953.

12. GATT Secretariat, L/107, 3 (f).

13. GATT Secretariat, G/55/Rev. 1, Oct. 23, 1953.

14. GATT Secretariat, G/55/Rev. 1, Oct. 24, 1953.

15. GATT Secretariat internal documents.

16. It was reported in the GATT balance sheet at the end of 1954 that Japan, as a nonmember of GATT, had contributed $12,000 to the organization.

17. GATT Secretariat, L/225/Add. [Addendum] 1.

18. GATT Secretariat, L/225/Add. 2.

CHAPTER 8: GATT ARTICLE XXXV

1. GATT internal document L/405, March 13, 1955. This chapter heavily depends on the original materials of the GATT secretariat's internal documents, especially from 1955 to 1992. Other original GATT documents that are not quoted as a separate note, but that are relevant to this chapter, are mainly L/1446 and L/1482. See also Patterson, *Discrimination in International Trade*, 268 ff.

2. L/1466, May 11, 1961.

3. Telegram No. 116, March 1, 1960, E'0072, 1603. Telegrams No. 22 and 25 (quoted, refer also to telegram No. 142), March 19, 1960, E'0072, 1604. Archives of the Foreign Ministry, Tokyo.

4. L/1545, Dec. 7, 1961.

5. Ibid.

6. Daniel I. Okimoto and Gary R. Saxonhouse, "Technology and Future of the Economy," in Kozo Yamamura and Yasukichi Yasuba, eds. *The Political Economy of Japan*, vol. 1 (Stanford University Press: 1987, 386).

Table N-5. Comparison of the growth rate at total factor productivity size

(percent)

	1959–63 / 1964–68	1969–68 / 1969–73
U.S.	2.25	0.92
Japan	1.66	2.59

7. GATT memorandum to the directors of the secretariat, August 1, 1962.

8. GATT secretariat L/1531, August 22, 1962.

9. Telegram No. 142, March 19, 1960, E'0072, 1604. Archives of the Foreign Ministry, Tokyo.

10. Telegrams No. 22, 25, and 116, March 1, 1960, E'0072, 1603. Archives of the Foreign Ministry, Tokyo.

11. L/2208, April 2, 1964.

12. L/3396, May 25, 1970.

13. L/2896, Nov. 9, 1967.

14. L/1744.

15. May 13, 1970. Telex 22956 by Adnan Buxlon, U.K. Mission in Geneva to GATT Secretariat.

16. L/4234, Dec. 18, 1974.

17. L/6998, April 27, 1992.

Bibliography

Books

Allen, G. C. *Japan: the Hungry Guest*. London: G. Allen & Unwin, Ltd., 1938.

Anderson, Kym and Robert E. Baldwin. *The Political Market for Protection in Industrial Countries: Empirical Evidence*. World Bank Staff Working Paper No. 492, Washington: World Bank, October 1981.

Ando Yoshio, ed., *Nihon Keizai Seisaku-shi Ron* (History of Japan's economic policies). Tokyo: University of Tokyo Press, 1976.

———, ed. *Ryo Taisen Kan no Nihon Shihon Shugi* (Japanese capitalism in the interwar period). Tokyo:, 1978.

Asahi Shimbunsha, *Asahi Shimbun ni Miru Nihon no Ayumi* (The History of Modern Japan reported in the *Asashi Shimbun*). Tokyo: Asahi Shimbunsha, 1974.

Bank for International Settlement (BIS), *Fifth Annual Report of the Bank for International Settlement*.

Bisson, Thomas. A. *American Policy in the Far East 1931–1940*. New York: International Secretariat, Institute of Pacific Relations, 1939.

Blackhurst, Richard, Nicolas Marian, and Jan Tumlir. *Adjustment, Trade and Growth in Developed and Developing Countries*. GATT Studies in International Trade No. 6. Geneva: General Agreement on Tariffs and Trade, 1978.

Cheng, Yu-Kwei. *Foreign Trade and Industrial Development of China*. Washington, D.C.: University Press of Washington, 1956.

Clements, Kenneth W. and Larry A. Sjaastad. *How Protection Taxes Exports*, Thomas Essay No. 39. London: Trade Policy Research Center, 1984.

Corden, W. Max. *Protection, Growth and Trade: Essays in International Economics*. Oxford: Basil Blackwell, 1985.

———. *Protection and Liberalization: A Review of Analytical Issues*. Occasional Papers of the International Monetary Fund, No. 54. Washington, D.C.: International Monetary Fund, 1987.

Dainihon Boseki Kabushkigaisha Gojunen kiyo (Memory of Fifty Years in the Dainihon Boseki Co. Ltd.). Osaka: Dainihon Boseki Kabushikigaisha, 1941.

Dobson, John M. *Two Centuries of Tariffs: The Background and Emergence of the U.S. International Trade Commission*. Washington, D.C.: U.S. Government Printing Office, 1976.

Donges, Juergen B. *Whither International Trade Policies? Worries about Continuing Protectionism*. Kieler Diskussionbeitrage 125. Kiel: Institut fur Weltwirtschaft, October 1986.

Eichengreen, Barry J. *International Policy Coordination in Historical Perspective: A View from the Interwar Years*. National Bureau of Economic Research Working Paper Series No.1440. Cambridge, Mass.: National Bureau of Economic Research, September 1984.

———. *The Political Economy of the Smooth-Hawley Tariff*. National Bureau of Economic Research Working Paper Series No. 2001. Cambridge, Mass.: National Bureau of Economic Research, August 1986.

———. *Starling and the Tariff, 1929–32*. Princeton Studies in International Finance No. 48. Princeton, N.J.: International Finance Secton, Dept. of Economics, Princeton University, 1981.

Eichengreen, Barry J. and Jeffrey Sachs. *Exchange Rates and Economic Recovery in the 1930s*. National Bureau of Economic Research Working Paper Series No.1498. Cambridge, Mass.: National Bureau of Economic Research, November 1984.

Fairbank, John K. *The United States and China*, 4th ed. Cambridge, Mass: Harvard University Press, 1979.

Freemen, Christopher, ed. *Long Wave in the World Economy*. London/ Boston: Butterworths, 1983.

Friedman, Milton, and Anna Jacobson Schwartz. *The Great Depression 1929– 1933*. Princeton, N.J.: Princeton University Press, 1973.

General Agreement on Tariffs and Trade (GATT). *Press Release*. Geneva, 4 March, 1983.

———. *Protocol to the GATT*. Geneva, 1979.

———. *Review of Development in the Trading System*. Geneva, April– September 1987.

————. *Textiles and Clothing in the World Economy and Appendices I–IV*. Geneva, 1984.

————. *Trade Policies for a Better Future: Proposal for Action*. Geneva, 1985.

————. *The Use of Quantitative Import Restrictions for Protective and Other Commercial Purposes*. Geneva, 1950.

————. *The Use of Quantitative Import Restrictions to Safeguard Balances of Payments*. Geneva, 1951.

Gerschenkron, Alexander. *Economic Backwardness in Historical Perspective, A Book of Essays*. Cambridge: Harvard University Press, Belknap Press, 1962.

Giersch, Herbert, ed. *Free Trade in the World Economy*: (Toward an Opening of Markets: Symposium 1986) Tubingen: J.C.B. Mohr (P. Siebeck), c1987.

Greenaway, David, and Brian Hindley. *What Britain Pays for Voluntary Export Restraints*. Thomas Essay No. 43. London: 1985.

Hayashi Takehisa, et al. *Koza Teikoku Shugi no Kenkyu VI, Nihon Shihon Shugi* (A study of imperialism VI, Japanese capitalism). Tokyo: Aoki Shoten, 1973.

Hou Chi-ming. *Foreign Investment and Economic Development in China*. Harvard East Asian Series 21. Cambridge, Mass.: Harvard University Press, 1965.

Hubbard, Gilbert E. *Eastern Industrialization and Its Effect on the West, With Special Reference to Great Britain and Japan*. London: Oxford University Press, 1935.

Ishii Kan'ichi. *Nihon Sanshigyo-shi Bunseki* (An Analysis of the History of the Japanese Sericultural Industry). Tokyo: University of Tokyo Press, 1972.

Kajinishi Mitsuhaya et al, eds. Nihon Sen'i Sangyo-shi Soronhen (History of Japanese Textile Industries). Tokyo: Sen'i Nenkan Kankokai, 1958.

Kelly, William B. Jr., ed. *Studies in United States Commercial Policy*. Chapel Hill: University of North Carolina Press, 1963.

Kierzkowsky, Henryk, ed. *Protection and Competition in International Trade*. Oxford: Basil Blackwell, 1987.

Kindleberger, Charles P., and Peter H. Lindert. *International Economics*. 6th ed. Homewood, Ill.: R. D. Irwin, 1978.

Koo, Anthony Y. C., ed. *Selected Essays of Gottfried Haberler*. Cambridge, Mass.: MIT Press, 1985.

Kraus, Richard A. *Cotton and Cotton Goods in China, 1918–1936.* New York: Garland Pub., 1980. Originally presented as a Ph.D. thesis, Harvard University, 1968.

Krugman, Paul R., ed. *Strategic Trade Policy and the New International Economics.* Cambridge, Mass.: MIT Press, 1987.

Kuznets, Simon. *Growth, Population, and Income Distribution.* New York: Norton, 1979.

———. *Six Lectures on Economic Growth.* Baltimore: Johns Hopkins University Press, 1959.

League of Nations. *Article 16 of the League Covenant.* Geneva: League of Nations

———. *Industrialization and Foreign Trade.* League of Nations publications. II, Economic and financial; 1945, II.A.10. Geneva, 1945.

———. *Memorandum on International Trade and Balance of Payments.* Vol. I, Review of World Trade. Geneva, 1927/1929–1932/1939.

———. *Remarks on the Present Phase of International Economic Relations.* Geneva, September 14, 1936.

———. *Report of the Commission of Enquiry.* Official No. C. 663. M. 320, Geneva, 1932. Vol. VII. (Also known as the Lytton Report.)

———. *Supplementary Documents to the Report of the Commission of Enquiry.* Geneva, 1932.

———. *Survey of International Trade.* Geneva, 1938.

———. *World Economic Survey.* 1930/31–1937/38.

———. *World Production and Prices.* 1925/32–1938/39.

League of Nations Economic Committee. *Remarks on the Present Phase of International Economic Relations.* Geneva, 1935.

League of Nations, Economic, Financial and Transit Department. *Industrialization and Foreign Trade.* [Geneva]: League of nations, 1945.

Little, Ian, Tibor Scitovsky, and Maurice Scott. *Industry and Trade in Some Developing Countries.* London: Oxford University Press, 1970.

Lockwood, William W. *The Economic Development of Japan.* Princeton, N.J.: Princeton University Press, 1954.

———. *The Foreign Trade Policy of the United States.* New York: American Council, Institute of Pacific Relations, 1936.

———. *The State and Economic Enterprise in Japan.* Princeton, N.J.: Princeton University Press, 1965.

————. *Trade and Trade Rivalry between the United States and Japan.* New York: American Council, Institute of Pacific Relations, 1936.

Markhan, Jesse W. *Competition in the Rayon Industry.* Cambridge, Mass.: Harvard University Press, 1952.

Ministry of Agriculture and Forestry, Sericultural Section. *Yosan Keiei Seiseki Chosa* (Report on Sericultural Farming). Tokyo: Ministry of Agriculture and Forestry, 1934.

Ministry of Finance, Customs Division. *Kanzei Hyaknen Shi* (A One Hundred-Year History of Japanese Customs). Vol. I. Tokyo: Ministry of Finance, 1972.

Ministry of Foreign Affairs, ed. Compiled by the Japan Academy of Science, *Tsusho Joyaku to Tsusho Seisaku no Hensen* (The Evolution of Commercial Treaties and Foreign Trade Policies), *A Supplement to Diplomatic Documents relating Reforms of Commercial Treaties.* Tokyo: The Research Institute for the World Economy, 1951.

Mizunuma Tomoichi. "Showa Kyoko" (Showa Crisis) in Sumiya Mikio, ed. *Showa Kyoko* (Showa Crisis). 2nd ed. Tokyo; Yuhikaku, 1975.

Nagahara Keizo, Nakamura Masanori, and others. *Nihon Jinushisei no Kosei to Dankai* (The Structure and Stages in the Japanese landowner System). Tokyo: University of Tokyo Press, 1972.

Nihon Sen'i Kyogikai (The Japan Textile Conference), ed. *Nihon Sen'i Sangyo-shi, Kakuron Hen* (The History of the Japanese Textile Industry, Edition for Details). Tokyo: Sen'i Nenkan Kankokai, 1958.

Ohkawa Kazushi, and Henry Rosovsky. *Japanese Economic Growth: Trend Acceleration in the Twentieth Century.* Stanford, Calif.: Stanford University Press, 1973.

Ono Seiichiro. "Showa Kyoko to Noson Kyusai Seisaku" (Relief Policies for Farmers in the Showa Crisis). In *Nihon Keizai Seisaku-shi Ron* (History of Japan's Economic Policies). Edited by Ando Yoshio. Tokyo: University of Tokyo Press, 1976.

Orchard, John E. *Japan's Economic Position.* New York: Whittlesey House, 1930.

Oshima Kiyoshi. *Nihon Kyoko-shi Ron* (The History of Crisis in Japan). Tokyo: University of Tokyo Press, 1961.

Patterson, Gardner. *Discrimination in International Trade: The Policy Issues,1945–1965.* Princeton, N.J.: Princeton University Press, 1966.

Redford, A. *Manchester Merchant and Foreign Trade.* Vol. II. [Manchester, Eng.]: Manchester University Press, 1956.

Remer, C. F. *A Study of Chinese Boycotts with Special Reference to Their Economic Effectiveness*. Baltimore: Johns Hopkins University Press, 1933; reprint, New York: Arno Press, 1979.

Rieger, Hans Christoph. "Game Theory and the Analysis of Protectionist Trends." *The World Economy*, Vol. 9, No. 2. London: Basil Blackwell.

Sampson, Gary P. "Protection in Agriculture and Manufacturing— Meeting the Objectives of the Uruguay Round." *Proceedings of the Seventh World Congress of the International Economics Association*. New Delhi, 1986.

Sampson, Gary P., and Wendy Takacs. *Return Textile Trade to the Normal Workings of GATT: A Practical Proposal for Reform*. Institute for International Economic Studies Seminar Paper No. 404. Stockholm 1988.

Schumpeter, Joseph A. *The Theory of Economic Development*. Translated from German by Redvers Opie. New Brunswick, N.J.: Transaction Books, 1983. First published by Dept. of Economics of Harvard University, 1934.

————, et al. *The Industrialization of Japan and Manchukou*, New York: Macmillan Company, 1940. For Manchukou trade, see esp. pp. 789–864.

Seavey, William Arthur. *Dumping Since the War: The GATT and National Laws*. Oakland, Calif.: Office Service Corp., 1970.

Strange, Susan. "Protectionism and World Politics," *International Organization* 39, no. 2, (spring 1985).

Takamura Naosuke. *Kindai Nihon Mengyo to Chugoku* (The modern Japanese cotton textile industry and China). Tokyo: University of Tokyo Press, 1982.

Toyo Keizai Shinposha, *Showa Sangyo-shi*. Vol. II, *Se'ni* (The History of Industries in the Showa Era, Vol. II, Textiles). Tokyo: Toyo Keizai Shinposha, 1950.

Tumlir, Jan. "The New Protectionism, Cartels, and the International Order" in *Challenges to a Liberal International Economic Order*. Edited by Ryan C. Amacher, Gottfried Haberler, and Thomas D. Willett. Washington, D.C.: American Enterprise Institute for Public Policy Research, 1979

————. *Protectionism: Trade Policy in Democratic Societies*. Washington, D.C.: American Enterprise Institute for Public Policy Research, 1985.

————, et al. *Trade Liberalization, Protectionism, and Interdependence*. Geneva: General Agreement on Tariffs and Trade, 1977.

Usui Katsumi. *Nitchu senso: wahei ka sensen kakudai ka* (The Japan-China War). Tokyo: Chuo Koron Sha, 1967.

Utley, Freda. *Japan's Feet of Clay*. New York: Norton, [1937]. First edition printed in Great Britain.

Vernon, Raymond. "International Investment and International Trade in the Product Cycle." *Quarterly Journal of Economics* 80, no. 2, (May, 1966).

Viner, Jacob. *The Customs Union Issue*. New York: Carnegie Endowment for International Peace, 1950.

Yen Chung-p'ing. *Chung-kuo mien fang chih shih kao* (A Draft History of Chinese Cotton Spinning and Weaving). Peking, 1955

ARTICLES

American Council Institute of Pacific Relations. "Memorandum on Embargo or Boycott of Japan" (New York, March 9, 1932).

Capie, Forest. "The British Tariff and Industrial Protection in the 1930s." *Economic History Review*. October 1978.

Chicago Council on Foreign Relations. *Foreign Notes*. IX, no. 7.

China, Inspector General of Customs, *The Trade of China. The Maritime Customs, I. Statistical series; 1* (Shanghai, 1932–) published by Order of the Inspector General of Customs.

Curzon, Gerard, "Neo-Protectionism, the MFA and the European Community," *The World Economy*, September 1981. (London: Basil Blackwell).

Indian Tariff Board. *Report of the Indian Tariff Board for Regarding the Grant of Protection to the Cotton Textile Industry*, Calcutta: Government of India Central Publication Branch, 1934.

New York Times, 13 September 1925.

Ottawa Journal, 13 July 1935.

Pertersmann, Ernst-Ulrich, "Economic, Legal and Political Functions of the Principle of Non-discrimination," *The World Economy* (London) 9, no. 1.

Sampson, Gary P., "Pseudo-economics of the MFA—A Proposal for Reform," *The World Economy* (London) 10, no. 4.

Secretary of the States for India. "Trade Negotiations between India and Japan," 20 July 1934.

Textile Organan.

USITC (U.S. International Trade Commission). *Conversion of Specific and Compound Rates of Duty to Ad Valorem Rates—Report to the President on Investigation No. 332-99 Under Section 332 of the Tariff Act of 1930, as Amended,* USITC publication 896 (July 1978).

Vancouver Sun.

A. P., *Washington Post,* 29 March 1932.

Yanagisawa Haruka, "Dai Ichiji Nichi-In Kaisho (1933–34) o Meguru Ei-In Kankei" (The First Japan-India Commercial Conference and Commercial Relations between Britain and India) in Yokohama City University, *Keizai to Boeki* (Industry and Trade), no. 129.

STATISTICAL SOURCES

Bank of Japan, *Meiji Iko Honpo Shuyo Keizai Tokei* (Hundred-Year Statistics of the Japanese Economy). Tokyo: Bank of Japan, 1966.

Department of General Statistics in the Imperial Cabinet, *Teikoku Tokei Chosa* (Statistical Survey of Imperial Japan), Tokyo, 1935.

Hsiao Liang-lin. *China's Foreign Trade Statistics, 1864–1949*. Cambridge, Mass.: East Asian Research Center, Harvard University Press, 1974.

League of Nations. *International Trade Statistics 1930,* Geneva, 1932, and 1938, 1939.

———. *Memorandum on International Trade and Balance of Payments,* Vol. 1, *Review of World Trade and World Economic Survey,* 1926–28, 1927–29, 1931–33, 1934–36, and 1935–37.

———. *Statistical Survey,* 1939.

———, Economic and Financial Section, *International Statistical Year Book,* Geneva, 1926–1938.

Ministry of Commerce and Industry, *Jusan Toshi Oroshiuri Bukka Shisu* (Index of Wholesale Prices in Thirteen Cities). Tokyo, 1934.

Ministry of Finance, *Nihon Gaikoku Boeki Nenpyo* (Annual Return of Foreign Trade of Japan). Tokyo: Ministry of Finance, 1929–1961.

Ministry of Finance, *Kinyu Tokei Nenkan* (Annual Statistics of Financial Affairs). Tokyo: Ministry of Finance, 1934–1940.

Ministry of Finance, Department of Finance, *Financial and Economic Annual of Japan,* 1925–28, and 1935–38.

Ministry of Finance, *Gaikoku Boeli Geppyo* (Monthly Returns of Foreign Trade of Japan). Tokyo: Ministry of Finance, 1928–1940.

Ministry of International Trade and Industry, *Sen'i Tokei Geppo* (Monthly Report of Textile Statistics).

Ministry of International Trade and Industry, *Sen'i Tokei Nenpo* (Year Book of Textiles Statistics). Tokyo: Sen'inenkan Kankokai, 1954–2002.

Prime Minister's Office, Statistical Bureau, *Nihon Tokei Nenkan* (Japan Statistical Year-Book). Tokyo: Nihon Tokei Kyokai, 1949–.

Toyo Keizai Shimposhia, *Nihon Boeki Seiran* (Foreign Trade of Japan: A Statistical Survey). Tokyo: Toyo Keizai Shinposhia, 1935, 1975 revised ed., *Supplement.*

U.S. Department of Commerce, *Statistical Abstract of the United States,* 1932, 1935, 1938, and 1940.

U.S. Department of Commerce, *Foreign Commerce and Navigation of the United States,* Washington, D.C., various issues 1925 to 1939.

Yamazawa, Ippey and Yuzo Yamamoto, *Boeki to Kokusaishushi* (Foreign Trade and Balance of Payments). Kazushi Ohkawa et al., eds, *Choki Keizai Tokei* (Estimates of Long-Term Economic Statistics of Japan since 1868), vol. 14. Tokyo: Toyo Keizai Shinposha, 1979.

INDEX